Blade Runner 2049
and Philosophy

Popular Culture and Philosophy® Series Editor: George A. Reisch

Popular Culture and Philosophy®

Blade Runner 2049 and Philosophy

This Breaks the World

Edited by

ROBIN BUNCE AND
TRIP MCCROSSIN

OPEN COURT
Chicago

Volume 127 in the series, Popular Culture and Philosophy ®, edited by George A. Reisch

To find out more about Open Court books, visit our website at www.opencourtbooks.com.

Open Court Publishing Company is a division of Carus Publishing Company, dba Cricket Media.

Copyright © 2019 by Carus Publishing Company, dba Cricket Media

First printing 2019

Printed and bound in the United States of America.

Blade Runner 2049 and Philosophy: This Breaks the World

ISBN: 978-0-8126-9471-0

Library of Congress Control Number: 2019934549

This book is also available as an e-book (ISBN 978-0-8126-9475-8).

Contents

Thanks

Life is short, and art long, opportunity fleeting, experimentations perilous, and judgment difficult.

—HIPPOCRATES

Life is short, and editing—an art all of its own—is long. Putting together this book has been a labor of love, love for *Blade Runner 2049*, and love for philosophy—the love of wisdom. Thank you to all of those who have helped with the production of the book.

Robin's Thanks

Thank you to India Bunce, Ellie Low, Marc Perrier, Niamh McNabb and Richard Kwei, who accompanied me to see *Blade Runner 2049* in the autumn of 2016. However uncomfortable the seats, however disappointing the snacks, the experience was always sublime. Thank you to my Mum and Dad who nurtured my love of science fiction, buying a copy of *Blade Runner* on VHS in the late 1980s, and in so doing introducing me to a beautiful new world. Thank you also to Keith MacKenzie-Ingle, my English teacher, who encouraged me to write an essay on *Blade Runner* and Philip K. Dick's *Do Androids Dream of Electric Sheep?* back in 1989.

I must also acknowledge my gratitude to the Fellows and the Principal of Homerton College, University of Cambridge for their support with this project, particularly Melanie Keene, Catherine MacKenzie, Alison Wood, David Belin, Julie Blake and Geoff Ward. The editors at the *New Statesman* were particularly generous in publishing my initial thoughts on *Blade Runner 2049* in an essay entitled 'Blade Runner 2049's Politics Resonate because They Are So Perilously Close to Our Own' on 16th October 2017.

I would also like to offer my thanks to J.M. Prater, Patrick Greene, Dan Ferlito, and Micah Greene the hosts of *Shoulder of Orion: The Blade Runner Podcast* for supporting this project, and for engaging me in the intelligent discussion of all things *Blade Runner*. And thank you to Eftychia Papanikolaou, for sharing her essay 'Eclectic Soundscapes in Blade Runner 2049', a paper presented at the annual conference, Music and the Moving Image, New York University, May 2018, and allowing it to inform my thoughts on Niender Wallace. Thank you to Iain Souter, a gentleman and a scholar, for sharing his ideas, and for the good work he does moderating the *Blade Runner 2049—Worldwide Fans Facebook Group*. I'm also indebted to Vangelis, Hans Zimmer, and Benjamin Wallfisch whose music has been the soundtrack to this project. Sincere thanks to Trip McCrossin, my partner in crime. His wisdom and grace under pressure has been brilliant throughout this project.

Thank you to David Ramsay Steele, Richard Greene, Rachel Robison-Greene, Courtland Lewis, Paula Smithka and everyone who I have worked with through Open Court for your help, encouragement and for your commitment to promoting great philosophy.

I owe heartfelt thanks to Lucy, my wife, without whose love and support this book would never have been conceived, started, let alone finished.

Finally, I am no less obliged to John Shade for his thoughts on the first draft, and to Charles Kinbote, who shared his extensive and invaluable editorial experience throughout the project. Enjoying sunset rambles with both writers in New Wye, Appalachia, was one of the real highlights of this project.

Trip's Thanks

Thanks, deep and abiding, to . . .

My son, Sean, of course, first and foremost . . .

His mom, Jayne, just as naturally . . .

My mom and dad, one gone, the other fading, in need of implants . . . if only . . .

Spectacular friends, lovers, spouses, teachers, students, partners in mischief generally, over the years, who it's been the privilege of my life to know, to learn from . . . Darrell Burrow, Cait Callahan, Erin Carlston, Azeem Chaudry, Rachel Devlin,

Greg Downing, Kit Fine, Deborah Greenwood, Cara Hood, Tamara Joseph, Michalene Morelli, Stephen Neale, Susan Neiman, Kathy Newman, Gina Pearson, John Perry, Marvin Roberson, Carol Rovane, Marina Sitrin, and Sue Zemka . . . for getting me here from there . . . and for putting up with me.

The Rutgers Philosophy Department . . . for taking me in, giving me a home . . . and, again, for putting up with me . . .

Mercedes Diaz, without whom we'd have to shutter . . . and, yet again, for putting up with me . . .

The volume editors I've been so fortunate to work with . . . Nick Michaud, who first took a chance on me, goodness knows why, and later Rob Arp, Adam Barkman, Christian Cotton, Kevin Decker, Jason Eberl, Richard Greene, Jacob Held, Josh Heter, Alex Hooke, Court Lewis, Jacob May, Kevin McCain, Eric and Holly Mohr, Janelle Pötzsch, Heather Rivera, Rachel Robison-Greene, Jessica Watkins, Antonio Sanna, and Joseph Westfall . . . for helping me learn how to write again . . . and for this opportunity in particular, the Open Court series editor, George Reisch and editorial director David Ramsay Steele, and of course Robin . . . and, once more, for putting up with me . . .

The union . . . without which, where would we be . . .

And, of course, the love of my life . . . always . . .

All of you, for making me . . . t.

Philosophy and Reality in *Blade Runner 2049*

ROBIN BUNCE

Blade Runner was simple enough. A bounty hunter sought four replicants and "retired" them one by one, falling in love along the way. But underneath the simplicity of the plot lay mind-bending philosophical complexity. What does it mean to be human? Can we trust our memories? How can we truly know what we are? Rather than answering these questions *Blade Runner 2049* complicated them, throwing up questions of its own.

2049 poses the most fundamental philosophical question of all: what is real? In a world of replicants, AI, and synthetic farming what does it mean to say something is real? Hampton Fancher and Michael Green clearly had fun with this question. In fact the word "real" appears more than fifty times in the shooting script. But crucially, the word "real" rarely means the same thing twice. When Joshi says "We're all just looking out for something *real,*" she means authentic, as opposed to inauthentic.

However, when K says that his memories are "not *real,*" he means that they are counterfeits, "real" here meaning genuine. Nonetheless, when Joi calls K "A *real* boy now" she means he is a natural human, rather than synthetic. Dr. Ana Stelline, by contrast, uses "real" to mean naturalistic when she opines that authentic memories allow replicants to display "real human responses." Mariette's question, "Don't like *real* girls?" implicitly equates "real" with physical, as opposed to virtual. Joi uses the word "real" in much the same way, in a similar context, when during the famous love scene she tells K, "I want to be *real* for you." But K means something altogether different when he responds "You are *real* for me," perhaps implying that Joi is real in the sense that she is meaningful.

When Dr. Badger offers to get K a *"real* horse," he means an actual horse, rather than a representation of a horse. Finally, when Deckard says "I know what's real" he means he knows what's true, that he doesn't believe Wallace's fictional account of his relationship with Rachael. Physical, authentic, true, natural, meaningful, actual—"real" means different things throughout *2049*. As Ana Stelline says, "Anything real should be a mess."

2049 is a world where reality itself is up for grabs. This is reflected in the different chapters that make up this book, and different authors, like the characters in *2049*, have used the word differently in their discussions of *Blade Runner 2049* and philosophy. Following Jean Baudrillard, Bonnie McLean's chapter on women, birth, and patriarchy in *2049*, contrasts reality with fiction, and with simulacra. Ali Riza Taşkale and Reşat Volkan Günel's chapter on *2049* as a capitalist dystopia uses "real" to describe the oppressive nature of power in modern society. Leah D. Schade and Emily Askew take a different approach, using "real" to mean actual, in their chapter about *2049* and the construction of "illegality." M.J. Ryder's essay on Joi equates "real" with natural, while Beth Singler's chapter on AI and reproduction questions the link between being born and being real. Patrick Greene, J.M. Prater, and Iain Souter do something new, and link "real" to socialist realism, in their chapter on the meaning of Niander Wallace. Aron Ericson's chapter equates being real with being special. We, the editors, have done nothing to persuade, cajole, chivvy, or force our authors to use the word "real" in the same way. Reality is an essentially contested concept in the movie, and it's an essentially contested concept in this book.

The chapters in this book, reflecting diverse interests and points of view, grapple with the questions and themes thrown up by *Blade Runner 2049* and the *Blade Runner* universe, in a variety of ways, reaching various and often conflicting conclusions. *Blade Runner 2049* was a revelation, a *real* revelation. This is our homage.

I

What Makes Us Human?

1
Do You Long for Having Your Heart Interlinked?

Timothy Shanahan

Could you have a romantic relationship with a *computer*? What if you knew (or even merely suspected) that it was *programmed* to show a romantic interest in you? Would that suspicion undermine any feeling you might have of being desired *as you*?

What if your soulmate died and you were offered an *indistinguishable copy* to replace them—would you be delighted, or would that just creep you out?

Suppose that you're having sex with someone while fantasizing about having sex with someone *else*, while at the same time that someone else is fantasizing about having sex with *you*. (Never mind explaining *that* to the someone you'll soon be spooning with). With whom are you, *in fact*, having sex?

What are we really, deep down, searching for when we seek and enter into intimate relationships? And why am I asking you such strange questions?

The Best Movies Begin after You've Left the Theater

Watching *Blade Runner 2049*, especially on the big screen, it's easy to become totally immersed in the spectacle of it all. From the visually stunning panoramic opening shot of a world denuded of the natural, to its haunting soundtrack, to its rust-orange-saturated depiction of a Las Vegas in ruins, it's quite a banquet for the eyes and ears.

The movie is also filled with striking characters, memorable dialogue, and some very cool technology. But at its core, it's really a film about the *heart* that invites us to reflect on the nature of intimate relations—especially romance, sex, and love. What unites these distinct but often confusingly intertwined experiences?

Happy Anniversary!

Let's take "romance" here to refer to any freely-chosen *relationship* involving mutual attraction to, and a desire to experience physical and emotional intimacy with, another person, along with efforts to please the other person, enhance their attraction to oneself, and thereby (we hope) bring about such intimacy.

Ironically, the most "fleshed out" (so to speak) romance in *2049* is between K and Joi—the latter being an advanced AI (artificial intelligence) system marketed by the Wallace Corporation as a customizable digital companion. Enhanced with a holographic avatar, her every action seems intended to please K—for instance, by asking him about his day, making him "dinner," changing her appearance to suit his mood, or encouraging his growing belief that he is "special."

K and Joi use pet names for each other ("honey" and "baby-sweet"), as sweethearts might. K is obviously quite smitten with Joi; we never see him alone at home when he doesn't choose to make her present as well. It also seems obvious that he wants to please her. He spends the hard-earned bonus money he garnered by retiring Sapper Morton on a special "anniversary" (even though he admits it isn't!) present—an "emanator" device that permits Joi to go anywhere, including the rooftop terrace of his apartment building where they share a tender moment—until, that is, he receives an incoming call that, um, rains on their special time together.

Whether Joi experiences, or even *could* experience, a romantic attraction to K is obviously a more difficult question. In fact, there are at least a couple of reasons to doubt that she does, both stemming from her basic nature an artificial intelligence.

To begin with, entering into a romantic relationship seems to require, at a minimum, that you be a *person*. The seventeenth-century English philosopher (and lover of commas) John Locke famously defined a "person" as "a thinking intelligent being, that has reason and reflection, and can consider itself as itself, the same thinking thing, in different times and places."

But is Joi *really* a "thinking intelligent being"? Granted, she behaves *as if* she is one; and maybe if an AI system behaves *as if* it is thinking, then it really *is* thinking. What else could we reasonably want or demand? Heck, how could I know that *you're* really a "thinking intelligent being" except by observing your behavior? On the other hand, perhaps Joi's designers are just really good at fooling their customers, and us. Perhaps the best that a mere computer can do is *mimic* the sorts of behavior that we normally associate with a first-person, subjective experience like feeling romantic interest. Whether a being like Joi could possess the characteristics required for being a person, and for feeling romantic attraction, is at present simply impossible to say.

Second, because entering into a romantic relationship is a *choice*, we might suppose that possessing *free will* is a requirement for both partners. Yet there are reasons to wonder whether Joi is truly free. In towering advertisements, "joi" is marketed as providing "everything you want to see, everything you want to hear." K's "joi" has been customized by him to approximate his ideal of feminine beauty, to provide a sense of domestic quasi-normalcy, perhaps even to bolster his self-esteem (which, frankly, needs a lot of help).

She certainly *seems* attracted to him; but it's hard not to wonder whether that's just a basic feature of her programming. But that's not all. In a bona fide romantic relationship you have to *believe* that the other person is sincerely expressing their feelings, not just parroting words they've been programmed to repeat. If my computer has been programmed to flash the message, "Well, hello there, handsome!" whenever it boots up, I'm not likely to feel flattered and desired (despite knowing that it speaks the truth). Now, if Joi's expressions of romantic interest in K are simply a function of her programming, she hasn't freely chosen K at all; and to the extent that K knows or even suspects that this is the case, it may be difficult for him to rise to the occasion with authentic feelings. Talk about an *anti-aphrodisiac*!

From another perspective, though, this might be setting the bar too high. After all, *we* enter into romantic relationships, yet it is not self-evident that *we* possess the sort of robust free will we might suppose is required. No one knows for sure whether "determinism" (roughly, the thesis that all events, including all human actions, are causally necessitated) is true. Perhaps determinism *is* true, as many philosophers believe. Well, if *they* can still get weak-kneed at the sight of their beloveds, why can't Joi? (Ignore the fact that her knees are merely holographic.) Then again, perhaps determinism is false. Perhaps, thanks to our large, wrinkled brains we are (somehow) able to escape from the chains of necessity. Maybe Joi manages a similar feat. *2049* screenwriter Hampton Fancher says that although Joi's responses *are* programmed, nevertheless through her attachment to K she "escapes her own . . . digital limitations." Now *there's* a thought. Love wins!

The Joi of Sex

Let's think about sex. (Perhaps you already were.) Here's a seemingly straightforward claim: Joi hires Mariette, a replicant prostitute to whom she thinks K is sexually attracted, so that he can have sex with her. Right. But *which* "her" does he have sex with?

It depends. Look up "sex" in the dictionary (maybe you already did this once to try to figure out what all the fuss was about) and you'll find a hodge-podge of different definitions (complicated by the fact that living things from microbes to magistrates do it) that are not easy to reconcile.

Fortunately, we don't need to. For our purposes, let "sex" be any physical activity aimed at achieving *union* with someone else. A notion akin to this idea has an ancient pedigree. In his *Symposium* (a dramatic account of a drinking party in which the guests, in various states of inebriation, vie with one another to praise *Eros*—erotic love), Plato recounts the ancient Greek mythic explanation of sexual desire. According to the myth, each human being originally had four arms and four legs, one head with two faces looking in opposite directions, and two sets of sexual organs. Such primordial people could walk upright as we do, or (when they were late for work) could use all eight arms and legs to propel themselves along at great speed—like an octopus on amphetamines doing cartwheels.

Fearing that such powerful creatures might one day challenge his supremacy, Zeus divided each one down the middle, in the process creating a race of beings who would forever long to be physically reunited with their other half. Now, while I wouldn't want to vouch for the truth of this wonderful story in *all* respects, it does nicely convey the poignant human longing for *physical union* with that part of ourselves that feels missing.

In a physical sense, it seems obvious that K has sex with Mariette. After all, K physically interacts (and unites, in a sense) with *her* body. But that's not the only way we could look at it. Mackenzie Davis, the actor who plays Mariette, says that "Mariette has this strange out-of-body experience when Joi hires her as a sex surrogate. As a hologram, she [that is, Joi] can superimpose herself upon Mariette to have an actual sexual relationship with K." According to this view, it is *Joi* who has sex with K despite the fact that she lacks a physical body, human or otherwise.

This is certainly odd, but nonetheless is close to the view that some philosophers take—whether they realize it or not. *Substance dualists* maintain that human beings consist of two parts: a body and a mind (or maybe a soul). In this view, the mind or soul is (somehow) *in* the body. The *former* is the *person*; the latter is merely a "vehicle" of sorts that the person uses while in an embodied state. Consequently, if two people have sex, their bodies are merely the instruments by which those persons (minds or souls) have sex. Mariette's body would then be merely a proxy by which the person who is Joi can have sex with the person who is K.

Alternatively, we could adopt a view inspired by recent developments in cognitive neuroscience (but harkening back to an idea of the German philosopher Immanuel Kant) and note that all of our conscious experiences of the external world are like a form of "controlled hallucination" arising from the brain's attempt to gain a predictive toehold over incoming sensory information. We may *perceive* our bodies as part of the external world, but if this "predictive processing" view is right, it is more accurate to say that (as experienced) our bodies exist solely in our minds.

Regardless of what you think of these ideas (and you could be forgiven if you feel the need to lie down for a while), they would tend to diminish any difference between K and Joi's rather unusual sexual encounter and more run-of-the-mill human sex. All sex, in these two views, is fundamentally a person-to-person conscious connection using physical bodies, or mental representations of physical bodies, as mere (albeit perhaps necessary) intermediaries. The same would be true for K and Mariette, who also meet the conditions for personhood, in which case there would be *three* persons having sex together. You have to admit, two replicants and an AI certainly makes one of the more memorable *ménages à trois* in the history of cinema!

What Happens if I Finish This?

Then there's Lt. Joshi. The shooting script for *2049* describes her as "a 50ish woman. Ambitious, officious, impatient. K's backtalk gives fuel to her irritation so she tolerates it. Or maybe she just likes the look of him. More than she should." We see subtle evidence of this when she pays an unexpected visit to his apartment, and pours herself a drink. "I've known a lot of your kind. All useful but . . . No wonder with you I sometimes forget." A half-finished bottle later, she is "whatever comes past tipsy," gazes at him, "a little too long" (as the script says), then at the bottle, then back at him: "What happens if I finish this?"

She knows that she can order him to have sex with her, and that he'll have to comply. But she doesn't. That would be to have a more intimate connection with him, but not one based on reciprocity. As she confided to him moments before in a rare, unguarded moment, "We're all just looking out for something real." She leaves. This scene is revealing. Lt. Joshi is normally all business. Focused. Professional. Tough as nails. But deep down she, too, longs for an *authentic* human connection, "for something real."

Don't You Love Me?

An old movie title proclaims that "love is a many-splendored thing." Indeed it is. So it might seem foolhardy to try to offer a concise definition that captures love's many meanings. But we need *some* characterization to guide our discussion. Science fiction writer Robert Heinlein's definition expresses, I think, a key insight: "Love is that condition in which the happiness of another person is essential to your own."

That seems right. But we can narrow it down further by noting that *romantic love* is also an *emotion* marked by special affection for a specific person because of what are perceived to be their uniquely-realized romantically-desirable attributes.

Deckard loves Rachael in this sense. Although in *Blade Runner* we never witness him verbally expressing his love for her, it becomes evident in *2049* that he did love her and continued to cherish her memory for almost thirty years after her death. He keeps a framed photo of her. He's visibly shaken when Wallace tempts him with an ersatz "Rachael," and is deeply moved by seeing Rachael's skull. Although we're given few details of their brief time together, every indication is that Deckard's love for Rachael was both genuine and enduring.

Her Eyes Were Green

Which brings us back to that scene just mentioned. Why does Deckard reject Wallace's striking offer of "An angel. Made again. For you"? The reason he gives—"Her eyes were green"— seems to imply that he rejects the offer because this new "Rachael" is not an exact enough copy of the original. But that can't be right, because as everyone who has seen *Blade Runner* knows, Rachael's eyes were *brown*. Suppose, however, purely for the sake of argument, that Rachael's eyes *were* green, and that Wallace had responded: "Dang. Got that part wrong. Wait right here while we manufacture another one with green eyes." Would Deckard have changed his mind? It seems unlikely. So, we need to consider other explanations.

We know that Wallace was dangling this ersatz "Rachael" in front of Deckard to entice him to divulge information concerning the whereabouts of his daughter, whom Wallace wants to dissect so that he can discover the secret of replicant procreation. No doubt Deckard was unwilling to barter his daughter's life in exchange for a carrot, and was throwing Wallace's attempted bribe back in his face, telling him, in effect: "I can't be bought." Perhaps it was his way of saying, "You may be a genius, but you're not as powerful or as skilled as you think you are."

All that might be true. But there is another possibility as well. I can imagine Deckard rejecting Wallace's offer even if it didn't require him to divulge any information about his daughter's location, and even if the replacement "Rachael" was physically indistinguishable from the original, and even (for good measure) had implanted memories of their previous time together. I think that Deckard realized that no matter how physically and even psychologically *indistinguishable* from the original this new "Rachael" might be, it could never *be* the original, and therefore would always, necessarily, lack something essential, something crucial. But we're supposing that this new "Rachael" is physically and psychologically indistinguishable from the original. What, then, could she be missing?

Did You Miss Me?

A criminal mastermind creates a forgery of the *Mona Lisa*— one so accurate down to the last detail that even the world's foremost art experts cannot identify it as a fake. Then, in the dead of night, he breaks into the Louvre in Paris, manages to circumvent the museum's elaborate security systems, removes the *Mona Lisa*, and replaces it with the copy. Visitors to the museum the next day have no idea that they're looking at a clever forgery. The pleasure they experience in viewing the forgery is no different than it would be if they were viewing the original. Why would it be?

Now, suppose that you were among those visitors, and that you *knew* what had transpired the night before. You would know that something important—indeed, something essential—was missing from the Louvre. But it wouldn't be anything you could see or detect with your senses because, after all, the painting on the wall is supposed to be completely indistinguishable from the original. What would be missing is, of course, the *Mona Lisa itself*—the particular object that once rested on an easel in Leonardo da Vinci's studio, felt the impress of his brush, and is hundreds of years old. Those properties contribute to it being the unique work of art that it is— one that can be *replicated*, but never *recreated*.

Deckard may have understood that, in this regard at least, Rachael was like the *Mona Lisa*. Wallace didn't grasp that it wasn't a replicable cluster of abstract "Rachael properties" that was the object of Deckard's enduring love. It was the singular, special, irreplaceable person, *Rachael*. Sadly, once that was person was gone, she was never again—forever. Eldon Tyrell was more right than he knew when he told Deckard, "Rachael is special." She was. We all are.

Do You Long for Having Your Heart Interlinked?

The baseline test in *2049* is intended to detect any developing emotional reactions blade runners might have to the violent work they have been created to do. Seemingly random questions are aggressively hurled at K from an ominous, unseen interrogator. "Have you ever been in an institution?" "Do they keep you in a cell?" Each time K stoically responds: "Cells." Gradually, however, the nature of the questions shifts: "What is it like to hold the hand of someone you love?" "Did they teach you how to feel, finger to finger?" "Do you long for having your heart interlinked?" "Do you dream about being interlinked?" Now K responds to each question: "Interlinked."

"Constant K" has passed another baseline test, but at a price. Cells are by their very nature distinct, bounded, separate things. To be "interlinked," however, is to be connected to others while retaining one's individuality. Evidently, K is still a "cell" at this point in the film. Later, however, he fails the test and is forced to flee. He has found himself, or has chosen to become, intimately interlinked with others, and that profound internal change cannot elude detection.

We're not so different from Lt. Joshi, K, Deckard, and even Joi. Romance, sex, and love are all expressions of a fundamental human desire to overcome our sense of isolation as distinct, lonely, conscious cells of awareness and feelings. They speak to something deep, and precious, within us. At the end of the day, and at the end of the movie, we *all* long for having our hearts interlinked.[1]

---

[1] Many thanks to the editors of this volume for helpful comments on earlier drafts.

2

Is Joi a Person?

Chris Lay

We first meet Joi—the replicant K's holographic companion—dressed to please as a 1950s-era American housewife, grumbling about how the elaborate "dinner" she prepared hasn't turned out quite right. She greets K with enthusiasm, encourages him to put his feet up, and lights a cigarette for him to settle his nerves after a long day of work.

This is all telling, of course, since Jois are a luxury product in the universe of *Blade Runner 2049*. It's in the name, really: she exists solely to bring *joy* to the lonely and troubled lives of her purchasers. However, she's just a digital entity, so Joi's "joy" is artificial! K's Joi can't give him a meaningful relationship any more than an Amazon Alexa or an iPhone running Siri could. This is probably obvious to most of us. And I'm going to spend the rest of this chapter telling you why nearly everything I just said is wrong.

Blade Runner pushed us originally to sympathize with its fugitive replicants and their all-too-human goals. They hope to meet their creators, discover their identities, and—as Roy Batty proclaims to Tyrell—they emphatically "want more life!" By the time Batty gives his rooftop soliloquy and spares Rick Deckard, at a time he so easily could have killed the injured blade runner, it becomes difficult to argue that replicants aren't moral subjects like you and me—*persons*, in other words.

Whether replicants are as worthy of moral concern as the humans who developed and built them is still a live question in *2049*. But the sequel carries considerations of personhood to a much more radical place than its predecessor, mostly because of Joi. In fact, I think *2049* shows us that Joi is a person (and probably so are other digital entities like her).

Do You Like Being Separated from Other People?

That Joi—something like a computer program—might be a person is likely hard to accept. We often ask questions about personhood because *we're* persons, and so when things act sufficiently like *us*, we wonder if *they* might be persons, too. Hence, the most immediate case against the thought that Joi, or even replicants like K or Sapper Morton, are persons is that they're actually not as much like you or me as they seem. Rather, Jois and replicants have a lot more in common with your laptop, coffee maker, or thermostat because they're really just programs *designed to follow formal instructions*. In all likelihood, this is what the tenants in K's apartment block and his "fellow" officers in the LAPD precinct hall are thinking when they shout disparaging slurs like "tinplate soldier" and "skin-job."

What does it mean to "follow formal instructions?" Consider the thermostat I mentioned. When the thermostat detects the "input" of a rise in temperature to a certain level, it returns the appropriate "output": the air conditioning clicks on. The idea is that a Joi's or a replicant's evidently human-like behavior is just a more sophisticated version of an input-output chain. So, it may *appear* that Joi is delighted to see K when he arrives home or is terrified at the thought of him coming to harm when their spinner crashes in the wastes outside LA's walls. But these are just outputs elicited by corresponding, pre-programmed inputs.

Let's bring in a contemporary philosopher to help illustrate the point. Although John Searle might not hurl verbal abuse at replicants, he probably also wouldn't be too worried about hurting K's feelings. Like many of the humans in *2049*, Searle believes that artificial things wouldn't count as persons because they're not the right *kind of thing*.

According to Searle, programs just *simulate* this or that process without *understanding* it. Sapper Morton may *seem* to have a preference for garlic—he grows it "just for me"—Luv may *seem* to have an obsessive desire for Wallace's approval, and K may *seem* to have the belief that "he doesn't have a soul," as he tells Lieutenant Joshi. But these aren't genuine preferences, desires, and beliefs. They're just behaviors that follow the right rules to *look* like the real thing. No, anything that *actually* thinks, feels, or whatever else we might say bona fide persons do has to be more than a program: it would have to be *instantiated* in the right "stuff," too.

According to Searle, only the biological states of certain organisms are the 'right' kind of material that could give meaning to rule-following behaviors. Put differently, only certain organisms can *understand* what they're doing, and only then is authentic thinking and feeling going on. The bottom line is that only organisms could be persons, and artificial things like Joi and K are merely pretending at personhood.

Now, we might think *2049* sides with Searle on this point, especially in Joi's case. Shortly after Joi's 'death,' K encounters an enormous Joi hologram that behaves in many of the characteristic ways as *his* Joi—even calling him Joe, the nickname she gave K to set him apart from other replicants. We're drawn in this scene to see Joi as a commodity: a manufactured product that can be exactly reproduced and bought at any suitable Joi retailer. Similarly, we should remember Mariette's caustic insult after their shared tryst with K: "I've been inside you. Not so much there as you think." What this gives us is a picture from *2049* that Joi is no more a person than K's survey drone, because she just follows the same set of empty rules programmed into *every* Joi.

But this is a false signal. For one, we can see that Joi actually violates her programming. The tagline on the various Joi advertisements we see interspersed throughout the film is "Everything you want her to be." This means that if Joi *only* follows her programming, she ought to do exactly what K—her "owner"—says. But this isn't what happens. When Joi first experiences the "freedom" the emanator provides while shuddering in the rain, she gushes to K, "I'm so happy when I'm with you." K replies, "You don't have to say that."

From this interaction, we can tease apart K's instructions to Joi. By telling Joi that she doesn't *have* to dote on him, he says to her that if she's going to care for him, she should do it because she wants to and not because she's programmed to cling to his every word. So, if Joi truly were "whatever K wants her to be," she would either care for him independently of her programming, or, barring that, not at all. Since Joi continues to care deeply for K, it seems that she has either defied her programming and chosen to care for K on her own, or *followed* her programming and done what K asked—to reject her programming and, again, freely chosen to care for K. Either way, Joi's affection for K seems authentic.

Equipped with this knowledge, we can reinterpret K's experience with the giant Joi ad not as a penetrating realization that his 'relationship' with Joi was just a hollow imitation, but instead as reinforcement that *his* Joi was sincere in her love and a painful reminder of what K has lost in her "death." Like Wallace revealingly tells an imprisoned Deckard, "Pain reminds you that the *joy* you felt was *real*."

Do You Feel Like There Is a Part of You that Is Missing?

Even if *2049* allows that Joi is more than a simple input-output machine, that doesn't mean that she's a person. So, what exactly constitutes a person? First, we can admit that 'person' apparently doesn't mean the same thing as "human being." As early modern philosopher John Locke observes, "human" is a way of designating an animal with a specific kind of functional organization to its parts. It's a biological term that picks out one species among many, and so "human" should be distinguished from "person"—whatever that word means.

Yet, characters in *2049* often talk *as if* a human and a person are one and the same thing. Mariette calls replicants "more human than humans," and Luv entices a prospective buyer with the promise that Wallace's replicants will be "as human as you want them to be." Although these characters *say* "human," I think it's obvious they don't mean "biologically human." It would be silly to think that Mariette *really* means, "Even though replicants are engineered in labs as human surrogates, they are more biologically human than natural-born human beings." Rather, what I think *2049*'s characters have in mind when they say "human" is something like "the qualities that are part of human-like experiences." It's from these qualities that we assign moral status, and so, whatever's the source of these qualities is what's going to be the mark of whether something counts as a person.

What would be a good candidate for the source of these person-making qualities? It's tempting to look for a clue in K's line that replicants are different from living things because living things have *souls*. Another early modern philosopher, René Descartes, thinks that souls are a unique and essential human feature. Like the characters in *2049*, Descartes prefers "human" to "person."

Descartes thinks that the soul is something entirely distinct from the body it animates, even if the two enjoy an important bond. Ultimately, we can understand Descartes as saying that humans are fundamentally souls: the soul can still exist without the body, and it's where all of the essential human qualities—like thought—are found. This means that souls are purely *non-physical* substances and made of wholly different "stuff" than physical bodies. By contrast, Descartes famously argues that non-human animals are soulless automata that don't do anything even approximating thought or feeling. So, Descartes's language about the soul and human nature gives us an analog for "person," even if personhood isn't something he discusses directly.

Whatever else can be said about replicants like K and whether they have souls, Joi actually seems to fit the Cartesian model pretty well. As she ponders aloud in the precinct records room, "Mere data makes a man . . . All from four symbols. I am only two: one and zero." The point is not lost in this moment that little separates Joi from humans—both are at their core abstract information.

Between the two, though, only Joi is *purely* information, as human 'data' actually refers to the DNA composition of a given *physical* body. On the other hand, Joi's binary data make her almost exclusively a *non-physical* entity. We can see this when we recall that Joi is transferred from her primary system in K's apartment to the emanator he buys her, which lets her travel everywhere from his rainy apartment roof to the bombed-out ruins of Las Vegas. If we then think of the apartment system and the emanator as something akin to bodies, then Joi actually *swaps* bodies several times. So, what at first blush might appear to distance Joi from humans and even replicants—the fact that Joi doesn't *have* a proper physical body—really brings her closer to the Cartesian idea of what is most essentially human: Joi is pure, disembodied "soul."

Did They Teach You How to Feel, Finger to Finger?

Perhaps we want to reject the Cartesian claim, though. Not least of all, the comparison between an immaterial soul and a pattern of binary data is surely imperfect, and it would probably be better to deal with a thinker who more explicitly engages with "personhood." In that case, we can return to John Locke. Locke writes in *An Essay concerning Human Understanding* that personhood is rooted in the properties of intelligence, rationality, self-consciousness, and the ability to feel things like happiness and misery. This last property is commonly called *sentience*—being conscious of our felt experiences. To Locke, anything that has all of these properties counts as a person, and anything that lacks even one of them doesn't.

Now, Joi clearly seems capable of rational expression, and she often demonstrates intelligence, like in her ability to have meaningful conversations with K. But Joi also seems to have genuine emotions, desires, and sensations. She exhibits a sense of wonder when she leaves LA for the first time and marvels at the world outside, and she betrays her jealousy when Joshi propositions K in his apartment, snarking, "You don't prefer your Madam?" Likewise, we see a clear desire—to feel "real"— in her insistence that K destroy her antenna and fully transfer her into the emanator. K fears that this will effectively "trap" her, but Joi welcomes the chance to be "like a real girl": perishable and present in only a single place.

Joi's status as a program limits *some* of her possible experiences. For one, she lacks tactile sensations. Joi must simulate the feeling of raindrops on the rooftop, and her hands always hover around but never on K; she can't ever "feel" his touch. Yet, she has access to other sense modalities: she can see and hear, for instance. And anyway, that *some* sensations must be simulated surely doesn't invite the conclusion that *none* of Joi's felt experiences are genuine. Humans lack a bat's ability to echolocate, and we only ever see a limited spectrum of color. We don't for this reason say that humans lack conscious feeling altogether, though.

So, grant with me that Joi is sentient. Is she also self-conscious in Locke's sense of the word? I see two good reasons to think she is. First, Ana proudly tells K that "If you have authentic memories, you have real human responses." This is part of Locke's view, as well. He thinks that memories are how we're conscious of ourselves and the things we've done. Joi *also* has memories of her experiences—of the things *she*, and not someone else, has done.

Before convincing K to permanently install her in the emanator, Joi voices her worry that Wallace's thugs could use her "backup" data in the apartment to find and harm K by accessing her memories. Through these memories, Joi is clearly aware of "herself as herself," to paraphrase Locke. That is, she knows that she's a program that can be instantiated in multiple places at once, and that their pursuers could exploit this fact to locate them. Similarly, Joi remembers certain feelings and endorses them as *hers*. For example, her fear that she is an inadequate lover to K is about *her*, not Joshi or someone else, and this fear is built out of past experiences she considers *her own*.

Beyond her memories, Joi's decision to sacrifice herself for K is another indicator of self-consciousness. When she calls out to stop Luv from beating K, Joi glances down at the emanator, fully aware that Luv could destroy it (and her). To sacrifice herself that she might save K's life implies that she understands her own finitude. Clearly, this is one kind of self-consciousness: that one's existence could end. At the same time, sacrifice additionally demonstrates a high-level understanding of herself in relation to other subjects.

Joi's action is comprehensible as "hers" because of the context of the others involved, and it distinguishes her as one subject among the rest. She recognizes that Luv's intentions are to "kill" her, which in turn leads to Joi's awareness that in calling out, she might "die." But calling out has an additional effect—it could spare K from "death," too. Joi can thus discern how the actions of other subjects affect her *and* how her actions affect others. This is *also* a kind of self-consciousness: where one stands in relation to the world.

All of this lines up nicely with Freysa's assurance to K that "Dying for the right cause is the most human thing we could do." Freysa might be right *because* the act of sacrifice seems to require the person-making property of self-consciousness.

Not Even Close to Baseline

Twice in *2049,* K is subjected to a baseline test to check for "deviancy." His measured responses to the provocative questions on the first test lead the operator to address him as "Constant K." By the time he fails the second test, though, K is emotionally volatile and believes he's the very natural-born replicant that he's been assigned to hunt down and "retire." What's of interest to us is what K's "failure" says about "deviancy." K is deviant when he's feeling powerful emotions and endorsing his memories—like hiding the horse figure in the orphanage boiler room—as events that happened to *him.* (Recall that before this he simply thought these were implanted but *false* memories.)

Put another way, K is considered deviant when he exhibits Lockean person-making qualities like sentience and self-consciousness. This makes sense. If replicants are persons just like human beings, then the "wall that separates kind" comes down, so institutions of power need to curb 'deviant' instances of replicant personhood early on. But I've argued that Joi is *also* sentient and self-conscious; if I'm right, surely Joi would fail the baseline, too. How much worse would things be for those same institutions if there are *digital* persons like Joi?

This is less a collapsing of walls and more hitting the reset button on society altogether. So, perhaps Mariette is wrong: there *is* more substance to Joi than there seems to be. Or maybe we just misinterpreted her. What if the real lesson is that there's not so much to *us*, since it doesn't seem as if we humans have any special claim to being persons. If that's true, then we're going to have to re-evaluate how we treat non-human things that meet the personhood criteria.

Does this mean that Joshi is right and society gets turned on its head? Maybe! At the very least, if a program like Joi can be a person—a moral subject—we should probably start being nicer to Alexa and Siri.

3
Are You for Real?

Aron Ericson

Blade Runner 2049 continues *Blade Runner*'s investigation into selfhood and freedom. This time around, however, the big question is what it means to be *real*.

The main character, K, faces the question whether or not he's a "real boy." At the beginning, this is the question whether he was manufactured or born. K believes he's a replicant, a kind of bioengineered human manufactured for slave labor and other unpleasant business that humans prefer not to do themselves. He works for the LAPD, tasked with tracking down and "retiring" (a nice word for killing) replicants who misbehave.

The story is set in motion as it's discovered that a replicant woman (Rachael from the earlier movie) has given birth, something replicants, or so it was thought, can't do. K is ordered to find the child (who would now be an adult) and kill it, but a series of clues leads him to believe that, in fact, *he* is that very child—and that this is something that would qualify him as a real boy.

K, it turns out, is not the child of Rachael and Deckard. But his investigations lead to the bigger question of what being real really means.

To be real, in the movie, is linked by the dialogue to being *special*. To be real means to be, in some sense, unique. The requirement here boils down simply (or not so simply) to having an existence that is your own, a self that is not just someone else's tool or plaything.

Is Joi Real?

Joi, K's holographic girlfriend, is a tricky character to analyze since it's difficult, if not impossible, to determine to what extent

Joi's personality is her own and how much of it is wish-fulfill-ment for K. She is a piece of AI promised to be whatever the customer wants. Staggeringly intuitive, she caters to K's desires. During the course of the movie, however, she *seems* (again, it's hard to know how much of it is her, and how much is a reflection of K's emerging sense of self) to come in to her own, expressing her own desires.

"The moral" of Joi's story echoes the lessons of the first *Blade Runner* movie in some interesting ways. The interpreta-tion of *Blade Runner* that I'm working with here is shamelessly stolen from the British philosopher Stephen Mulhall. He is someone who has delved deep into the world of movies in order to think about the big philosophical issues, and in his book, entitled *On Film*, one of the films he analyzes is *Blade Runner*. Mulhall does a good job showing how the film is a sophisticated exploration into the meaning of mortality.

For Mulhall, the lesson of *Blade Runner*, the lesson the replicant Roy Batty has to learn, and finally passes on to Deckard, is how life gets its meaning in relation to death. Roy is raging against the four-year lifespan allotted to replicants. What he has to learn is that a longer lifespan would not make his life more human. Rather, Mulhall says, the meaning of mor-tality is "constituted by the fact that every moment of human life is necessarily shadowed by the possibility of its own non-existence."

While death is certain it is also indefinite; we know *that* we will die, but not *when*. That the replicants have a "death date," their four-year limit, does not alter this, as is violently proved when they are killed in the movie. Both the Bible and cell biol-ogists agree that humans too have such a death date; our limit is 120 years.

To be a real boy or girl is accomplished not by avoiding death at all cost, but through adopting a certain attitude to the finite time you do have. This is the moral spelled out to Roy by his creator, Tyrell: "He who burns twice as brightly burns half as long. And you have burned so very, very brightly." The mean-ingfulness of his life is determined by the intensity with which Roy experiences each moment of it, and to engage with these moments as moments, not meant to last, but disappearing, "like tears in the rain."

As Mulhall says, "The transience of the present moment is taken not to show its insignificance but the nature of its signif-icance—the fact that it is a moment in transition, always hav-ing been delivered from the future and always about to be delivered over to the past, and hence that human existence is always endless becoming." This, for Mulhall (and I tend to agree) is the take-home philosophical lesson of *Blade Runner*.

This philosophical lesson is revisited in Joi's storyline in *2049*. We see it when Joi insists that K must delete her from the console, so that her memories backed up there can't be used to track them down as they go on the run from the authorities. She will exist only on the "emanator" K has given her, a gizmo that allows her to go outside their apartment. "My present," Joi tells K, "put me there." And by a happy accident the word "present" means both "gift" and "now." Without a backup, she will now live in the present (in the moment), burning brightly. K protests that it would be dangerous. If something were to happen to the emanator, Joi would be gone forever. "Yes," she answers him, "like a real girl."

For Joi, to become real means embracing mortality, living life without a safety net. To embrace mortality does not mean to be morbid. On the contrary, it is to experience life in its fullness and to let each moment burn brightly, all the while—perhaps precisely *by*—still acknowledging that it will pass.

Is Deckard Real?

If part of the moral of *Blade Runner* is that your realness is determined not by any characteristic that might be ascertained by some objectively valid test, but by an attitude you have toward all such characteristics, then it is fitting that this is the view Deckard seems to hold when K catches up with him in the sequel.

In the deserted Las Vegas that he has made his hideout home, he has for company a wolf-like dog. "Is it real?" asks K (meaning is it artificial or not). "Ask him," Deckard sneers back. This is partly Deckard being a rude host to an uninvited guest, but we might also take the line as an indication that Deckard views being real as something having little to do with your origin and that it is something you can only judge in your own case. The burning question about Deckard's own origin—human or replicant—is for him a non-issue.

That's all very well, but of course things become more complicated. "Anything real should be a mess," says Dr. Ana Stelline (who, it will turn out, is actually the daughter of Deckard and Rachael). She's talking about the creation of authentic-feeling memories that are to be implanted in replicants, but I feel comfortable generalizing her statement.

And things do get messy. Not as stealthy as he thinks, K has been followed to Las Vegas. Joi is killed, and Deckard is captured and brought to Niander Wallace. Wallace, the top name in replicant engineering, is looking for Deckard's child to solve the mystery of replicant procreation so that he can increase the speed of production and get a replicant workforce large enough to conquer space beyond the measly nine new worlds already established. If the replicants could have children, he would soon have enough so that his angels could storm the heavens.

Wallace puts Deckard through the wringer, poking and prodding at all his insecurities. Deckard, of course, is as terse as they come but it's not easy for him. Warding off the demons Wallace is trying to implant in his mind, he responds, "I know what's real." But he doesn't sound all that certain as he says it.

"Help me and very, very good things can come to you," promises Wallace. But Deckard clings tightly to what is most real for him: the love he felt for Rachael, and the child they had. A first requirement of being real is to have an existence that is your own. But, as we can see in this scene, this should not be mistaken as meaning that you should have an existence that is not influenced by the surrounding world. On the contrary, the question of your realness is intimately bound up with the ties you have to the world, your home in it. The love Deckard feels for a child he's never met is at the core of who he; it is this love that orients him as a person. He has an existence of his own, and at its center is the responsibility he feels for his daughter.

In staying true to his responsibility for another he stays true to himself, sneering at Wallace, "You don't have children, do you?" Wallace, staying true to himself by staying true to his ego, bites back, "Oh, I have millions." Such a self-bolstering answer shows that Wallace doesn't share the transference of importance that for Deckard is part and parcel of what it is to be a father. For Wallace, his "children" are proof of how he has mastered nature. For Deckard, having a child means no longer being master in his own house.

Wallace goes further and tempts Deckard with a copy of Rachael. "An angel, made again. For you." Deckard refuses to make this devil's bargain. Deckard also notes that Wallace didn't get the color of Rachael's eyes right, but I don't think that if Rachael 2.0 had had green eyes, that would've made all the difference. Still, it pains him as the new Rachael gets a bullet through the head. That he knows that she is not the Rachael he knew, that she is not "real," does not mean that he doesn't experience phantom pains as she is killed.

Is K Real?

K's boss, Lieutenant Joshi, tells him that everyone is looking for something real, something to hold on to as the going gets rough. But K, in the beginning of the movie, seems to embrace his unreality. Perhaps this is how he endures his situation. As we saw in the case of Deckard, a sense of one's own realness is bound up with a sense of the surrounding world as real, and for K playing down his own realness might help him tolerate the horrors of his world.

Replicant officers are subjected to a baseline test where their emotions are monitored so that potential troublemakers can be caught. When we first see K taking his baseline test it is intercut with him walking through the LAPD corridors receiving abuse from human colleagues ("Fuck off, skinjob"). Still, he passes the test with not a dot out of place—"Constant K," notes the interrogator. Most teflon-like, he doesn't let anything stick to him. Everything slides right off, and he can maintain this protective coating only by avoiding reality.

This also raises more questions about his relationship to Joi, the place where K appears to be most honest. It's always Joi who pushes the idea that K might be special, while K cautiously warns that for someone like him it would be dangerous to feel and think that way. It's Joi that insists that he should have a real boy name: Joe. The question, of course, is whether Joi is saying these things on her own accord or whether she is the mouthpiece for the desires that K feels but knows he mustn't show.

K notes that Joi hates the book *Pale Fire* by Vladimir Nabokov, the book from which the poem K has to recite for his baseline test is taken. If Joi hates the book, and Joi's emotions are the emotions that K has but can't express, does this mean that oh-so-constant K harbors some feelings of hatred and rage over how he is treated, the test he has to take, the shit he has to scrape? Perhaps. Or perhaps Joi just found *Pale Fire* disappointing after loving *Lolita*. Who knows?

It takes a miracle to make a dent in K's armor of unreality, a dent where dirt gets caught and festers. In the opening scene he's sent out to retire Sapper Morton, an older model replicant who has gone off the grid, setting himself up as a protein farmer, supplying people with a diet of worms. Sapper, with his dying words, gives K a piece of his mind: "You new models are happy scraping the shit because you've never seen a miracle." These words echo in K's mind throughout the movie, and as their full meaning is revealed to him they amount to something he can't brush off.

The miracle Sapper has in mind is of course Rachael and Deckard's child. After Joi has been killed and Deckard kidnapped, the injured K is taken care of by the underground movement of the replicant resistance. Its leader, Freysa, spells out the importance of the child she saw born twenty-eight years earlier: "I saw a miracle delivered. A perfect little face crying up at me, mad as thunder. I knew that baby meant we are more than just slaves. If a baby can come from one of us we are our own masters." This miracle gave replicants something to rally around, to organize a resistance movement and be ready to fight, and die, for their cause. And, says Freysa, "Dying for the right cause is the most human thing we can do."

Having left the replicant base, K, like Deckard, has a "blade-runner-meets-his-dead-girlfriend" scene. Walking through a rainy night, depressed and bleeding, K is addressed by a giant advertisement version of Joi. The ad uses the same phrase that his Joi used to say ("What a day"), and even calls him by the name Joi chose: "You look like a good Joe." What are we to make of this? Is it evidence that his relationship with Joi was all unreal? Or is the way ad-Joi shares traits with K's Joi rather a way of highlighting how, while they are objectively similar, there is an abyss separating the two; that even if Joi is a mass-produced appliance, what K and his Joi had was special, unique, *real*, and while it would be a simple matter to buy another Joi copy, it would not be the same? Personally, I'm leaning toward the romantic interpretation, but there's no conclusive evidence, and it's far from clear what K thinks. Viewers will have to make up their own minds.

Whatever K thinks, it's a decisive moment that informs his actions in the final act of the movie. Freysa's words about the honor of dying for the right cause echo in his head, and he sets out to rescue Deckard. Some gritty underwater fighting later, he has succeeded in doing this, but in the process he has become mortally wounded.

What is the cause that K is ready to die for, the piece of reality he holds on to? Again, I'm a romantic. I think he dies thinking about Joi. She taught him what it is to have the courage to risk it all for something you believe in, and her sacrifice is what drives K to follow in her footsteps. He does a good deed, and he does it out of love.

Reality Check

2049 does not give us a once-and-for-all criterion for determining whether someone is real. It does give us some suggestions that I've tried to spell out as best I can, but in the end it leaves more questions than answers. And this may be the answer.

Rather than offering rules for avoiding chaos, *2049* claims that anything real should be a mess. Remembering that the meaning of an experience is bound up with its transience, that our existence is one of endless becoming, what it means to be real is a question that must be continuously grappled with, always posed anew, especially when we ask it about ourselves. If things are running too smoothly that could be a sign that we're being deceived, most often by oneselves. Most of the time reality is grueling and thankless, full of disappointments and compromises.

But in the mess glimmer moments of effulgence. This can happen when fact and fiction conspire to bring something new into being. As K lies dying on the snowy steps outside Ana's memory factory, on the inside the woman whose memories he has is conjuring up an illusion of snowfall by using her imagination.

To love his daughter Deckard has been forced to be a stranger. Now he can, because of the fiction that makes him officially dead, finally walk through the door and into her life, allowed to be a real father to a real daughter.

4

The Aesthetics of Being a Person

S. EVAN KREIDER

Are the replicants of *Blade Runner 2049* people? They certainly aren't treated as such by the humans of that world. This is especially true of K, who is treated as less than human throughout the movie.

One essential human quality is the capacity for aesthetic experience. Humans can judge scenes and sounds as beautiful or ugly. Another human quality is the ability of individuals to relate to other individuals as persons. The replicants do demonstrate a capacity for aesthetic experience and they do sometimes interact as persons with humans and with each other.

The Beautiful and the Sublime

According to Kant, aesthetic beauty is less about beautiful objects themselves and more about the aesthetic reactions that we have to them, through aesthetic sensibilities unique to human beings. Objects that we call "beautiful" are those with formal features that stimulate a special aesthetic emotion, a feeling that only humans can experience, and that we experience only in reaction to these aesthetic objects.

These objects engage with our human faculties through what Kant characterizes as the free play between our understanding and imagination: a kind of higher thinking distinct from more straightforward reasoning, a kind of thinking without clear concepts that results in a special kind of aesthetic pleasure.

One particularly human reaction is to the sublime. Kant says that there are two types of sublime. The mathematically sublime is related to the magnitude of an aesthetic object, such as the massive widths and depths of the sea or the infinite distances of the night sky. These objects make us feel overwhelmed with their sheer size, and unimportant compared to them. At the same time, it gives us pleasure to realize that only we human beings are fully capable of conceiving of such magnitudes, and even conquering them in a way, as we do through sciences such as mathematics, geography, and astronomy.

The other kind of sublime is the dynamically sublime, which is related to the power of an aesthetic object, such as a raging thunderstorm or the churning waves of the ocean. These objects make us feel insignificant and afraid. However, here too we derive a certain sense of pleasure when we realize that we humans can overcome our sense of helplessness by using our powers of reason and free will to choose not to be afraid of such simple natural phenomena. In both cases, the aesthetic pleasure we experience is directly related to our special capacities as human beings.

The overall aesthetic of *2049* is sublime. Early in the movie, as K returns to Los Angeles after a mission, we are treated to a shot of the sprawling city, tucked behind a massive wall, drenched in a seemingly never-ending storm of acid rain, and cloaked in immense dense smog. The soundtrack complements the visuals, with loud industrial atonal music that overwhelms our hearing just as the visuals overwhelm our vision. Inside the city itself, harsh lights and garish colors are everywhere, especially in the form of advertisements, many of them explicitly sexual in nature.

The combined aesthetic effect is one of hopelessness and powerlessness, as evidenced by the complete control that the corporations have over the inhabitants. K himself clearly experiences the aesthetic of the city and is cowed by its size and power (not to mention its abusive human inhabitants), moving as he does through the city like a mouse among predators. This behavior shows his capacity for aesthetic experience of the sublime, but not yet his ability to overcome it.

This is quite different from another scene toward the end of the movie, in which K fights to save Deckard from the psychopathic replicant Luv, right-hand of Niander Wallace, head of the Wallace Corporation. Their transport has crashed into the sea in the middle of a raging storm, and torrential rain and rising waters threatening to overpower them, but K overcomes them in order to defeat Luv and save Deckard. He is able to do this not simply through physical strength or martial prowess, but through strength of will and moral conviction, and his ability to choose to overcome the large and the powerful sublimity of nature.

In short, he wins against the antagonists, both natural and replicant, because he is more than his creators have made him: he is a human being. By this scene, K is a different person than he began; indeed, he is, quite clearly now, a person. But how exactly did he become this person? To address this, we can now look more closely at the connection between the aesthetic, emotions, and interpersonal relationships.

The Aesthetics of Expression

The idea of a connection between aesthetics and emotions is nothing particularly new. Many philosophers have argued that art works by arousing emotional responses in the audience. Plato argued that poetry and music were especially good at this, and that they ought to be censored or even banned in order to ensure that no morally inappropriate emotions were aroused. Aristotle argued similarly but more positively by claiming that tragedies were best designed to arouse emotions such as fear and pity, but also to bring about a catharsis of these emotions.

Tolstoy, apparently taking a cue from the ancients, also claimed that art should be created in order to arouse and to promote emotions advocated by Christian moral values such as the love of God and one's fellow human being. In each of these cases, the focus is on the explicit arousal of emotions, and an evaluation of the corresponding aesthetic object in terms of a moral standard. However, these approaches were generally seen by modern aestheticians as too simple. Newer approaches were taken by Benedetto Croce and R.G. Collingwood.

Croce and Collingwood denied that the purpose of art was to arouse morally appropriate emotions. For one thing, far too many obviously good works of art would fail to qualify as good art, or even art at all, as they either arouse "bad" emotions, or no emotions at all. For another thing, the arousal view fails to distinguish between art and non-art, a great deal of which is also capable of arousing emotions (for example, a slap in the face). Instead, Croce and Collingwood claimed that aesthetic objects are not meant to arouse emotions, but rather to express emotions. Aesthetics serves as a means of communication that allows for a kind of interpersonal relationship between an artist and an audience via an aesthetic medium (such as songs, paintings, movies). In doing so, the artist communicates not just personal feelings, but feelings that she believes will resonate with the audience, perhaps communicating not just something about herself, but something about humanity in general.

For their part, the audience needn't literally feel the emotion, but simply imagine it, contemplate its deeper meaning, and consider the relation in which this content puts the audience to the artist and other human beings through their shared emotional imaginings. This is not unlike Kant's discussion of the free play between the understanding and the imagination, and like Kant, it assumes something unique to human beings, a special capacity for aesthetic imagination and a higher power of reason by which one might contemplate the emotions and their larger significance, rather than merely feel them directly, as any other animal might. In this way, aesthetic reaction is a distinctly, definitively human experience, and allows for distinctly kind of relationship among humans. Croce and Collingwood's expression theory is not without its problems; however, it certainly seems to reflect the function of a great deal of art.

There are several scenes of replicants expressing their humanity through a desire for authentic aesthetic experiences. One example early in the movie involves a rogue replicant, Sapper Morton, whom K has been tasked to bring in or retire. Conversing before the violence breaks out, K discusses Sapper's work, raising grubs for food.

Such a meal couldn't possibly be particularly aesthetically pleasing, but it would presumably provide the survival value required of food, meeting the needs of any simple animal. Sapper, however, desires more than this, as evidenced when K asks him about the aroma emanating from the kitchen. Sapper informs him that it's the smell of garlic, which he grows just for himself. Sapper also demonstrates genuine moral commitment to an interpersonal relationship through the aesthetic gesture of placing a flower on the grave of Rachael, the replicant whom he hid from the authorities and helped give birth. Another example, also dealing with food, is that of K himself, who also eats a very plain meal back at his apartment, but one onto which a virtual plate is holographically superimposed to make it look like a gourmet meal. Though K seems not to take the holograph too seriously, he does accept the gesture from Joi, his virtual companion, who added those aesthetic touches as a means of expressing her fondness for K and her commitment to their relationship. In these otherwise trivial examples, the replicants show themselves more than mere animals, but people with higher order desires for more complex aesthetic experiences and the emotional interaction and interpersonal relationships that they facilitate.

A more striking example, one key to the movie in general and K's personhood, is that of K's baseline tests. We see two such tests play out, the first of which takes place immediately after K retires Sapper Morton. During the test, the interrogator has K recite his baseline, an excerpt from a poem. The interrogator then has K repeat a word from the poem as a response to a number of questions to which he might have an emotional response, if he were a full-fledged human being and not just a mere replicant.

The interrogation continues until the interrogator is satisfied that the replicant is operating normally, without inappropriately human emotional responses. K passes with flying colors this first time, but later, after having evolved emotionally in response to his various interactions with others, K does not do as well. He hesitates in response to certain questions (most notably, "What's it like to hold the hand of someone you love?"), and the machines monitoring his brainwave patterns detect inappropriate and anomalous emotional responses.

The interrogation becomes more confrontational, even sinister, as reflected in the baseline words and phrases chosen for K to respond with ("dreadfully," "dreadfully distinct," "dark"). What alarms K's superiors, and would certainly require his termination under normal circumstances, is that K is demonstrating fully human emotional responses, inappropriate for a replicant. The key to detecting this was not simply through what was said, but how it was said. The content of K's responses was immaterial; rather, the aesthetics (pronunciation, timing, rhythm) of the responses were what counted.

Notice the difference between this and the similar tests in *Blade Runner*, which were based on what was said rather than how it was said, on whether the replicant was able to give the kind of answers that a real person would give in response to the questions asked. In the more sophisticated tests of *2049*, the aesthetics of the interaction were key to determining the personhood of the replicant, interlinked by the emotional responses, especially those stemming from K's interactions with other persons, and related to interpersonal relationships such as love.

Langer on the Virtual

The twentieth-century philosopher Suzanne Langer takes a cue from her predecessors Croce and Collingwood and connects the aesthetic to the expressive, but does so by way of another far more ancient idea in aesthetics, that of *mimesis*, loosely translated as "imitation." Philosophers such as Plato and Aristotle believed that art was an imitation or representation of reality. In Plato's mind, this was a bad thing: art was an imitation in the negative sense of the word, a kind of imperfect forgery or faking of reality. Aristotle was more positive about this, believing that *mimesis* can teach us moral lessons. Langer puts a similarly positive spin on the subject by claiming that art creates something virtual, something more than just the literal reality of the work: painting creates virtual space, music creates virtual time, architecture creates virtual environment, and so forth.

One function of art's virtual nature is to express emotions. Like Aristotle, Langer argues that art does this by creating virtual spaces that give the audience an opportunity to contemplate emotions that they might not have access to in real life. Following Croce and Collingwood, Langer also argues that art serves as a means of communication of its emotional content to the audience, and that it can do so in more direct ways than everyday means of communication such as plain language.

By functioning as an expressive symbol, art allows us to contemplate its emotional content in more sophisticated and disinterested ways than we are able when experiencing emotions directly in real life. Once again, there is something about this kind of aesthetic experience and contemplation that is uniquely human, and allows for a uniquely human kind of interaction, a special interpersonal relationship between the artist and the audience, through the emotional content expressed through aesthetic experiences.

If anyone knows about the virtual, it would be Joi. She is a virtual person, a holographic AI that serves as a companion (essentially a housewife) to K (who, we imagine, is not legally entitled to marry). As an anniversary present, K gifts Joi with an emanator, an upgrade that grants her freedom of movement outside of the hardware built into the apartment. It also gives her additional sensory experience in the form of the most personal, interpersonal, and emotional of all senses, which is touch. Her first destination is the roof of the building, where she experiences the sensation of rain falling on her "skin" for the first time, the look on her face communicating her profound emotional reaction to this sensation. She then reaches out and touches K, able to feel him, though she still appears to him as an audio-visual hologram, passing though him without his being able to feel her in return.

Not content with that, Joi thinks of a way to complete the tactile interaction between K and herself: she hires Mariette, a replicant prostitute, to serve as a sort of touch proxy. Joi superimposes herself onto Mariette so that it looks and sounds like Joi, while co-ordinating their movements to create the illusion that K is touching Joi herself rather than Mariette. This makes sexual intercourse possible (though still somewhat virtual) between K and Joi. This romantic interaction accomplishes precisely what Langer refers to: a communication of emotional content between persons that ordinary language cannot accomplish on its own. In this way, both art and sex, through their emotional content, allow for intimate relationships between persons; thus, both K and Joi must be such persons, and not merely artificial or virtual things.

Perhaps the most explicit instance in the movie of the importance of emotions and aesthetics to personal identity is presented to the audience by the character of Dr. Ana Stelline. Due to a compromised immune system, she lives in a controlled environment, spending her days on her work of creating memories for replicants, to make them seem and act more real (though, we presume, purposely not too real). The creation of memories is all about aesthetics and emotion: creating the look and feel of past events. Dr. Stelline explains to K that the key to this lies not in hyper-realistic detail of events or environments, but in the genuine qualities of the emotional content:

> **K:** Why are you so good? What makes your memories so authentic?
>
> **STELLINE:** Well, there's a bit of every artist in their work . . . If you have authentic memories, you have real human responses . . .
>
> **K:** Do you ever use ones that are real? . . . How can you tell the difference? Can you tell if something really happened?
>
> **STELLINE:** They all think it's about more detail, but that's not how memory works. We recall with our feelings. Anything real should be a mess.

As Dr. Stelline explains, the aesthetics of human memory isn't about realistic simulation, but of emotions: the more realistic the emotions, the more realistic—the more human—the person. Once again, aesthetic experience and its emotional expression indicates genuine personhood.

Do You Feel There's a Part of You that's Missing?

As with the original *Blade Runner*, *Blade Runner 2049* has us contemplate the theme of personhood by considering the status of the replicants.

Blade Runner suggests that personhood is linked to various psychological capacities and personal relationships. *2049* develops this thesis even further by showing us the necessary role that our aesthetic capacities play in establishing our personhood, as especially demonstrated in the case of K.

There is ample evidence that the replicants are just as much persons as we humans, given their genuine interpersonal relationships, facilitated and indicated by their genuine aesthetic experiences, and the emotions that interlink them.

5
A Replicant's Guide to Becoming Human

Justin Kitchen

Blade Runner 2049 poses a multitude of questions, only to leave them unanswered: What's the difference between replicant nature and human nature? Can a replicant ever become a human? And: Does K become human?

These questions are interrelated because an answer in the affirmative to the third question will give us an answer in the affirmative to the second and that, in turn, will give us an interesting answer to the first. If we discover that K becomes human in the ways that we care about, then we can say with certainty that replicants can become human regardless of how difficult and rare that may be. And if replicants can become human, then the differences between the two seem negligible. In fact, if we do this right, we can answer all three questions at the same time!

We need the help of some philosophers who are world-famous for keeping calm under pressure and following the facts wherever they may lead. These are the Stoics of ancient Greece and Rome. They started a school in Athens at around 300 B.C.E. and would meet under the Painted Stoa, a covered portico on the northern edge of the town's marketplace (hence the name, "Stoic"). They are known for their slogan "Follow nature" or "Act in accordance with nature."

Constant K

The image of K taking his post-traumatic baseline test may come to mind when thinking of someone who is acting "stoically." K has just hunted down and 'retired' Sapper Morton, a replicant who, on the face of it, seemed like a pretty thoughtful and sensitive protein farmer (albeit dangerous when cornered!). The baseline test reported an absence of any emotional responses that would be considered "anomalies" in a replicant. If a human acted in this way, they may casually be called stoic (lower-case "s"), totally indifferent to physical and emotional pain, insensitive to hardships and trauma. But this is not what being a Stoic (upper-case "S") is all about.

The Stoics did not suggest that humans try to become unfeeling robots. Quite the contrary! By insisting that people "follow nature," the Stoic philosophers were telling them to actualize their potential and become the best humans they could be. They offered theories on how a person could really develop and *perfect* their human nature. What's the point of perfecting your human nature, you ask? Well, you may not have asked . . . some people would find "perfection" appealing for its own sake. But the Stoics still provided an answer: perfecting your human nature is the only way you could experience real human happiness.

Let's not get distracted with happiness though. Since it was so important to their philosophy, the Stoics must have defined what 'human nature' is and what "perfecting" human nature involves.

To Be Born Is to Have a Soul

A poetic way to talk about human nature is to talk about the human "soul." K does this when Joshi orders him to "retire" the child of the pregnant replicant they found:

JOSHI: You have anything more to say?

K: I've never retired something that was born before.

JOSHI: What's the difference?

K: [*K pauses, thinking*] . . . To be born is to have a soul, I guess.

Sounds nice. But this is not really a good definition. Sure, a lot of humans start off by being born—a lot of non-human animals too. But this fact doesn't exclude the possibility of something becoming human (having a human "soul") in some *other* way. Human nature could in fact be like citizenship. If someone is born in a country, they automatically have citizenship. But this doesn't exclude the possibility of someone getting citizenship in some other way (I'm talking about the hard way; the way that takes a long time and a lot of paperwork).

What we really care about when we talk about citizenship is the set of properties that it gives people. There are certain legal rights and privileges that let citizens do certain things and get special treatment from their country's government. Since this is what we care about, it's best to start the discussion by discovering those properties and how someone could acquire them legitimately rather than by offhandedly excluding people from the outset.

Likewise, there are certain properties that a mature, fully developed human has to have—figuratively speaking, they have to have a human "soul." We should start the discussion with what these properties are and how something would go about acquiring them instead of assuming that replicants can't acquire them in the first place just because they didn't have a conventional birth.

The First Thought Tends to Fear

Here's where the Stoics can help us. The Stoics thought they had discovered these properties by starting with human infants and pinpointing underdeveloped characteristics that exist from the outset. The Stoics then imagined how those characteristics would *naturally* develop if the infant were to mature without being inhibited. These are called "cradle arguments" because the Stoics extrapolated from their observations of infants in the "cradle" to argue for what defines human nature.

So, what did they see in humans when they looked in the cradle? Here's the historian Diogenes Laertius reporting on what the Stoic Chrysippus (third century B.C.E.) said:

> An animal's first impulse, say the Stoics, is to self-preservation, because nature from the outset endears it to itself, as Chrysippus affirms . . . "The dearest thing to every animal is its own constitution and its consciousness thereof" . . . for so it comes to repel all that is injurious and give free access to all that is serviceable or akin to it. (*Lives of Eminent Philosophers*)

So, human and non-human animals all start out with an impulse "to self-preservation" and to anything that helps them protect and sustain the physical body's constitution and the consciousness that goes along with it. That makes sense because nothing in the natural world would survive long if it didn't want to preserve itself ("nature . . . endears it to itself").

But what about replicants? What do we see in *replicants* when we look in the cradle? Here's Niander Wallace giving one of his classic monologues as one of his replicants is being turned on for the first time:

WALLACE: The first thought tends to fear, to preserve the clay. It's fascinating. Before we even know what we are, we fear to lose it. Happy birthday.

As with non-human animals, replicants seem to *start out* like us. Their core drives seem to include the same fear of losing "what we are" and the same impulse to "preserve the clay." A replicant's first impulse, says Wallace, is to self-preservation.

As humans develop, differences between them and other animals appear. Human infants grow up and develop uniquely *human* abilities to make their own decisions, communicate and collaborate with others, and thrive in a world of their own making. Replicants, on the other hand, seem to devolve and become not only animals, but *domesticated* animals. They become slaves in the off-world colonies, sacrificing themselves for those who enslave them. What starts as self-preservation seems to turn into self-destruction.

Are the replicants "following nature" by becoming slaves? Hard to tell. The Stoics would insist that the best evidence for what's "natural" are observations in the "cradle"—in scenes like the one between Wallace and the newly-created replicant. But, after that, the development of replicant nature is taken over by the directives of their human masters. In our case then, we shouldn't assume that slavery is natural for replicants, especially with the statement made by Wallace that they start off with an impulse towards self-preservation.

So, to see how replicants develop naturally, we would have to see what they would do if they were not enslaved and, instead, left to their own devices. Lucky us, we have a few examples from *Blade Runner* and *Blade Runner 2049*. We can look at these and compare what they do to what humans do if allowed to develop naturally.

Cells within Cells

The cradle argument gave us the starting point and now another Stoic idea will give us the last piece of the puzzle. According to the Stoics, *Oikeiosis* is the process by which humans naturally develop their impulse to self-preservation into those properties that we really care about when we discuss "human nature."

It goes like this: as I consider more and more things as "my own" (*oikeion* in Greek), my conception of "self" evolves along with my conception of "self-preservation" until I become undeniably and unequivocally human. The first thing that I take as "my own" is . . . me! This is the conclusion of the cradle argument. I care about *me* and anything that I consider important to who *I* am.

As an infant, I am just a body that eats, drinks, and poops—no different than other animals. I care about my body and the food that feeds my body and my parents, the source of my food and security. I care about all this because it's crucial to my self-preservation *as* an eating, drinking, pooping thing. As I develop, I broaden my conception of who I am to include other things that I form relationships with. Maybe I start caring about other people because relationships I form with them are important to who I am and, thus, would be important to my self-preservation.

You can see that *oikeiosis* includes at least two processes that run in parallel. The first process is an evolving sense of self (this can be called personal *oikeiosis*). The second process is an evolving appreciation of others who, in a very real way, share my identity (this can be called social *oikeiosis*).

The Stoic Hierocles imagined the stages of this process as a series of concentric circles with . . . me, my "self" . . . as the center. There are about ten circles that a human could grow into as they develop their human nature and their understanding of what their "self" actually is. For the sake of simplicity, we can whittle this down to four circles that correspond to four stages of development:

- **Stage 1: I understand myself as a physical body and "self-preservation" means preserving my body**

- **Stage 2: I understand myself as a caring family member and "self-preservation" means preserving my family**

- **Stage 3: I understand myself as a loyal community member and "self-preservation" means preserving my community**

- **Stage 4: I understand myself as a rational member of an orderly universe and "self-preservation" means preserving reason**

Imagine Stage 1 is a small circle including only your body. Stage 2 surrounds that circle and so includes your body, but also family members, good friends, and romantic partners. Stage 3 surrounds those circles and includes your body, your family members, and members of any community that you might identify with. Stage 4 surrounds all the other circles and includes all rational entities. Each concentric circle represents the corresponding 'circle of concern' that you possess at that stage—that is, the number of entities that you consider "your own" in the process of social *oikeiosis*.

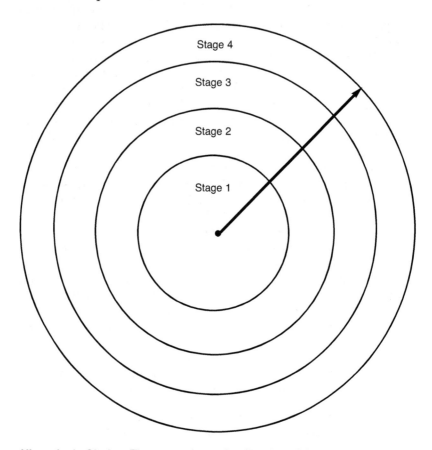

Hierocles's Circles. The arrow shows the direction of development outward from Stage 1 (egoism) to Stage 4 (cosmopolitanism). Each concentric circle represents a corresponding "circle of concern" at that stage—that is, the number of entities that the moral agent considers "their own" in the process of social oikeiosis.

All this portrays human nature as inherently rational and sociable. Humans become *more human*, so to speak, as they develop in sociability according to a rational and ever-evolving impulse towards self-preservation. It's not hard to imagine replicants as rational. But does this rationality motivate sociability like it does for humans? Do any replicants undergo the same process of social *oikeiosis* that humans do?

The case is about to break. All we have to do now is look at examples of replicants who are left to develop on their own in order to see whether they fit the bill. Can replicants develop as humans develop and become human in the ways that we care about? If we can find replicants that seems to have made it to the final stage of human development, we can take this as evidence that replicants are at least *capable* of becoming fully human.

Interlinked

Stage 1: Nexus-6 and the Fight for Survival

Let's look back on the old Nexus-6 model replicants in *Blade Runner*. Having escaped from enslavement in the off-world colonies, they travel to Earth and attempt to alter the factory setting of a four-year lifespan. Being left to their own devices, they become fixated on survival. Zhora, Leon, Pris, and Roy Batty act in accordance with their nature (as the Stoics say that we should do), but their nature is stuck at the first stage of development: fear and concern for their bodily existence.

Someone may say that they're driven by something other than self-preservation. The group of Nexus-6s may be friends. Maybe they look out *for each other* and fight to preserve *their friendships*. If that's so, the Stoics would say that they do that because they consider each other "their own"—their friends are part of who they are because being a good friend is part of who they are. Protecting each other would be an extension of the original drive for self-preservation because they would be protecting their identity as a friend. Solid evidence for this would reside with examples of replicants who sacrifice their bodily existence for the sake of others, since this would be a *rational* thing for them to do if they, in fact, identify with people that would outlive their own bodily existence. It's hard to see whether this is the case since most of the Nexus-6's are retired by Officer Deckard before their motives are made clear.

Stage 2: Rachael and the Love of Family

There is some evidence that Batty moves into Stage 2 when he decides to fight Deckard and avenge his fallen Nexus-6s instead of running away and saving himself to enjoy the short time he has left. Again, this may be the *rational* thing for him to do if he identified with his friends and their legacy. Unfortunately, according to the Stoic Seneca (4 B.C.E.–65 C.E.), the anger that Batty experiences is considered a form of temporary insanity, which blinds his ability to make rational decisions. So, we can't be sure whether he considers risking his life to fight Deckard the rational thing to do.

The replicant Rachael is a more reliable example. When being 'outed' as a replicant by Deckard, she should run away and go into hiding . . . if she was in Stage 1. Instead, she risks her life by going to Deckard and saving him from the rampaging Leon. She continues to risk her life by staying with Deckard—a Blade Runner whose job is to retire replicants like her. Why does she do that? Because, like most people who fall in love, she begins to identify with Deckard and to view his survival as necessary for her own. If he died, she would feel as if she died.

The Stoics claim that as we begin to develop our rational faculties, we're able to forge strong relationships by identifying ourselves with other people. Far from cold, unfeeling robots, Stoics encouraged *rational emotions* that come from extending our selves outward into the world. It's a natural part of human nature and—it seems—a natural part of replicant nature as well.

Stage 3: Nexus-8 and the Revolution

It's easy to become complacent with preserving our romantic and familial relationships and remaining at Stage 2. We view our family and romantic partners as "our own" and act in a way that preserves them as part of ourselves. But, Hierocles and the other Stoics claimed that our human nature can develop further. If we think long and hard about what we have in common with others, we can start identifying with strangers. We can start viewing strangers as if they were our "brothers" and "sisters" by pointing to some common cause and fighting alongside them.

This is what the Nexus-8 replicants seem to do after they are put on the chopping block and hunted down by the Blade-Runners. They join together and sacrifice their bodies and any personal relationships for the sake of their community. This would be the rational thing to do if they identified with their community and the cause they were fighting for. One of the clearest examples of this is probably Morton's suicide-by-Blade-Runner at the beginning of *2049*.

The leader of the Nexus-8 rebellion, Freysa, agrees that this is a natural part of being human and the line is repeated at key moments in film: "Dying for the right cause is the most human thing you can do." And we have evidence of this from many of the physical and political conflicts in which humans sacrificed themselves and their personal relationships for what they believed was the right cause.

But the Stoics would have insisted that we clarify what we mean here. If by "the right cause," Fresya meant dying for a cause that you share with others in your community, then this is not necessarily the most human thing you can do. Identifying yourself with others in this way is advanced, but not the *last* stage of *oikeiosis*.

Stage 4: K the Cosmopolitan

The outermost of Hierocles's circles, the final stage of human development, is identifying yourself with *a rational and orderly universe*. If we think about the orderliness of the universe and how our human minds can pick up on this orderliness, we can and should start identifying with every other entity who can exercise this same rational faculty. This is the Stoic concept of a cosmopolitan (from the Greek word for "citizen of the world"). Humans are rational by nature, and so it is natural to identify with everybody else in the world who has this in common.

Unfortunately, it would be all too easy for humans and replicants to be stuck at Stage 3 due to ignorance of other communities or a bias against them. Because of the natural impulse towards self-preservation, the only reason why conflicts emerge and persist between other communities is due to one community not embracing the other as "its own." According to the Stoics, if community members start realizing the presence of a common identity, their impulse towards self-preservation would extend outward to the other community and lead them to reject any thought of prolonging the conflict. Freysa and her group of revolutionaries are rebelling against the humans that enslave them, but their cause might blind them to the fact that the two factions have more in common than they think. They both have great potential and they both waste their potential by creating unnecessary walls.

The last order that Officer K receives is not from a human, but from a fellow replicant. Freysa orders K to kill Deckard for the sake of the community. But K contemplates Freysa's words—dying for *the right cause* is the most human thing you can do—and seems to realize that this cause must be determined by reason, not just by the orders that others give him. This is truly what it means to be human. K rejects Freysa's orders and ultimately sacrifices himself while trying to save Deckard.

At the end of the movie, K does not identify with Deckard as a family member (Freysa and her comrades have disabused him of that identity) nor does he identify with him as a fellow revolutionary (regardless of Deckard's allegiance to the movement, Fresya makes clear that it's better if he were dead). Instead, the most likely reason for his sacrificing his bodily existence and disobeying Freysa for the sake of Deckard is because K is preserving his identity as a member of an all-embracing community of rational entities in which—until then—only woman-born human beings belonged.

In response to Deckard's question to K—"What am I to you?"—we can answer with the following: Deckard is a fellow citizen of the world who has the same properties and rational faculties as himself. Regardless of how you get this citizenship—born or made—once you have it, you have it in common with everyone else. Nothing except ignorance, bias, anger, and fear are your enemies if you fight for this cause.

For humans and replicants alike, acting according to their nature means acting in accordance with reason. But what reason tells us to do evolves as we extend our circle of concern outward towards other people and realize our common identities. Both humans and replicants seem to be able to go through this process in much the same way though their obstacles are different. Replicants *can* become human: they can act rationally for the sake of who they are and who they identify with. And at the end of *2049*, K seems to follow this process to the point of becoming fully human in all the ways that we care about.

6
You Don't Need to Be Human to Have a Human Hand

SUE ZEMKA

What does it mean to be human? Philosophers have been answering and re-answering this question for about as long as humans have been practicing philosophy. Aristotle made the influential proposition that a human being is an animal with reason, with a "rational principle," with a proclivity to virtue and other reason-based behaviors, like philosophy (*Nicomachean Ethics*).

Unique, potentially virtuous, and unlike any other animal (or thing) in their capacity to reason, which is presumably a god-like capacity; it gives humans a location on the great "chain of being" above the animals, below the gods.

Science fiction has been enthralled with the question of what it means to be human. If anything, science fiction makes this question more difficult than it used to be, since it adds a new rung to the great chain of being, a wobbly and mobile rung of robots, which exists somewhere above animals, or maybe below animals, but in any case belongs *below* humans, although it refuses to stay there. Robots, androids, bionic creations, the character Data in *Star Trek*, the hosts in *Westworld*—all are basically riffs on *Frankenstein*.

Like *Frankenstein*, androids provide a fictional opportunity to explore the concept of human "nature" through technological doubles who aspire to the humanness of their makers. In so doing, they mirror, distort, or surpass the beguiling category of "the human."

The stories and struggles of the replicants in the *Blade Runner* movies put some sharp edges on our philosophical question. Does "humanness" (whatever that is) depend on having a human body? Can it be dislodged from the biological species *Homo sapiens* and found, made, or nurtured in other animals or things? Or does it necessitate having at least a human-like body, regardless of whether that body is animal or thing—or, as in the case of the replicants, *neither* animal *nor* thing?

Can only something with a sentient and human-like body pose the question of its humanness? The opening shot of *Blade Runner 2049* would seem to say yes, sort of. It shows an eye opening, a replicant eye, opening into consciousness. It's not K's eye, although the scene quickly montages into our first sight of K, asleep, then waking up, opening his eyes. From eye to eyes, from replicants in general to K. The movie's choice of the eye as the body part that visually introduces us to human-like replicants makes sense. The sense of sight has always played a major role in the ways we talk about human consciousness and reason (for example, "Do you see what I mean?"). Taking the Aristotelian precept "man is the rational animal" to be of value, this opening scene would seem to be important in establishing a link between being human and having the body part of an eye. As Hannah Arendt remarks, "From the very outset, in formal philosophy, thinking has been thought of in terms of seeing" (*The Life of the Mind*, p. 110).

But this is just the opening scene, and while beginnings are important, some say determinative, what are we to do with the ending of the movie, which leaves us not with eyes, but with *hands*—Deckard's hand, reaching out to "touch" (albeit separated by glass) the hand of Ana Stelline, his daughter?

Taken together, the opening and concluding scenes move the emphasis on humanness from a solitary exercise of consciousness to a social exercise of affect. Unsurprisingly, the former is identified with the eye, the visual sense, associated with reason, and the latter with the hand, the center of the sense of touch, and of hands as emotional communicators. Translating these two bookending scenes into a formula, we might say that eyes endow the human-like replicant with consciousness and thought (solitary and subjective activities), while hands endow the human-like replicant with tactility and emotion (activities that lead us out of ourselves, into our surroundings and towards others). Bracketing for a moment the problem that this formula privileges a normative body—one with eyes that see and hands that feel—we can infer the following: insofar as thinking and feeling are two replicant behaviors that make a strong case for their "humanness," then "humanness" (in the movie) depends on having a human-like body, or at least on having human-like body parts—on having a body or its parts that are capable of sensory apprehensions of a world and of others.

How important to this argument are those hands? I argue very important, maybe even more important than those eyes. The reasons for this take us back through many scenes and images in the movie and also many episodes in the annals of philosophy.

Consider the scene where K visits Ana, and deduces from their conversation that he was born, not made by machines but inseminated, carried in his mother's womb and brought into life through labor and birth. This greatly magnifies his claims on humanness, and the first thing he does after learning this, as he leaves Ana and walks outside into a snowy day, is look at his hands. Sure, he has watched his hands many times before (when he rapidly searches the LAPD birth records; when he presses the keys that transfer Joi's hologram to a mobile emitter), but never with such wonder and pensiveness. Why?

Nineteenth-century philosopher Arthur Schopenhauer would say that in this moment K enjoys the uniquely human (for Schopenhauer) gift of being both a will and a representation. To be both a will and a representation is to be, simultaneously, a subjective, intentional force and an objective, visual image.

Via his hands, K's will becomes actions; with these hands he drives, fights, shoots a gun, pushes buttons. But additionally, in this moment, via the sight of his hands, he also becomes for himself a representation. He is looking at his own body, the thing that actualizes his will, specifically his body's hands, their empty palms turned upwards in the snow. Never before had K looked so intently at his hands, never had he looked at them as the purpose of his gaze—not look at them so they can do something, or look at something they are doing—but look at them as the object of his thoughts. Schopenhauer would say he has attained the human predicament of simultaneously being an object and a subject, and the movie's intuitive sympathies seem to go with Schopenhauer here, since it has deemed this the action and scene that seals K's belief in himself as virtually human, that is, human enough to have been born.

Two other philosophers who connected hands and the sense of touch to the awakening of self-consciousness in a human being were Étienne de Bonnot de Condillac and Pierre Main de Biran, both European philosophers for whom the genesis of human knowledge was a crucial concern. Writing in the mid-eighteenth century, Condillac used the idea of a statue coming to life as a way of dissecting the several necessary stages in this genesis. The statue is a statue of a human form—that much is taken for granted. It is also apparently unable to see anything.

As Condillac imagines it, the first thing our statue does is move its hands, and over the course of a series of manual actions, it discovers its own material form—the extension of its limbs in space—and also discovers the physical limits of its own sensations, hence the difference between itself and external objects—and thus discovers, by repeatedly grasping itself (while uttering an inexplicably cogent sentence), "It is I!"

In the nineteenth century, Maine de Biran ran another essay with Condillac's statue thought-experiment, but took it one step further, removing all external objects from the statue's grasp so as to see if it would still come to a consciousness of its own separate self. The answer was yes, via an inner circuit of feeling that allowed the statue to move its hand, register sensation, and compose the concept of its separate, embodied existence. Maine de Biran's conclusion, in opposition to Descartes, was that feeling was more important to the construction of a human "I" or ego than thinking. Not "I think, therefore I am," but something like "I feel, therefore I am" (Heller-Roazan, *The Inner Touch*, p. 231).

Condillac and Maine de Biran moved on from their statue thought-experiments to arguments for the uniqueness of humans and their superiority over other animals. It has to do with what they claim to be the human's unique purchase on morality and on an awareness of God. But, all the way through their arguments, as they evolve towards higher and more dignified claims for humans, the way they talk about humans imagines them alone. It is always a question of one individual human mind, aware, thinking, and eventually moralizing and worshipping—not of two, or three, or more. The "human" of Condillac and Maine de Biran never leaves the empty space in which they imagine their awakening statues. They are always isolated, without society (except maybe God). If they do occupy an environment, it might as well be void.

It might as well be, for that matter, something like the desolate, radioactive landscape into which K and Joi fly to find the orphanage that is buried and hidden somewhere under all the complicated rubble. Adding to the purely accidental analogy between the statue thought-experiments and the movie's entry into a radioactive Las Vegas is the half-buried statue of a

woman holding her hand above her head and looking heaven-
ward, the idea of a heaven above our heads being about as non-
sensical as the idea of human life in this horizonless orange
world. If we compare *Blade Runner 2049*'s statue with the statues of Condillac and Maine de Biron, we see that both are
stone, have human-like forms, have very salient hands, and are
totally alone.

It is this aloneness that gives the lie to almost everything
that we have considered so far in our exploration of humanness. It is why the last scene of the movie is so important—both
as a clarification of how the film develops an idea of humanness and as a clarification of how this idea departs from the
emphases we find in many philosophical texts that undertake
to define the human and also to retrace its genesis, its coming-
into subjectivity.

Insofar as they isolate their human or human-like figures
from others that resemble them, they make a mistake in their
premises from the very beginning. Insofar as they posit a
statue, or a singular predicated 'man', or an eye opening, or
even a replicant looking at his hands in the snow, they repeat
the same basic error. There is no singular human. You can't
become a human by yourself. The stone woman holding her
hand towards the sky is the visual realization of this insight,
because it exudes the otherworldly horror, the uncanniness, of
absolute abandonment. And such absolute loneliness is the literal equivalent of the philosophical premise that you can come
to define humanness with the example of one, isolated, singular being.

Consider, then, as a final example, another hand-heavy
scene in the film. Joi hires Mariette, a replicant sex worker, so
that she can holographically inhabit her and thus have something like real (replicant embodied) sex with K. Joi's plan is an
eerie, beautiful, exquisite success. All of these hands, those
orgiastic hands, belonging to who knows whom (K, Joi, or
Mariette) and who knows how (as organism, avatar, or surrogate?)—all of these hands reclaim a sexual consummation
between desiring, volitional selves. The end of their consummation, like the frame of its necessity, is erotic freedom from the
system of bureaucratic surveillance that contains them. In
Seventies-speak, "the personal is the political." And who are we
to say that the element of political resistance in their erotic
hand dance dilutes its authenticity as an expression of love?

Where does this take us? We have not determined that
thinking and feeling are uniquely human capacities. There is
nothing so far which says that animals, or for that matter non-

humanlike computers, cannot think or feel—and in fact, there is plenty in the movie that could lead to the contrary conclusion. Instead, we have said that through the replicant's exercise of these capacities, they start to believe they are *as good as* humans. Via thinking and feeling, they start to believe that they deserve the right of self-determination, both for themselves individually and as a social group. Replicant dignity, replicant rights. These are "goods" that Freysa, Mariette, and eventually K fight for because from the beginning they are placed in a human social situation where their whole identities are made and defined in relationship with humans and human power, and then with other replicants.

The movie isn't concerned with saying that animals and non-humanlike computers cannot think or feel and thus are not human-like bodies. Nor does it manage to say that thinking and feeling make something human in any context. It doesn't manage to make these abstract claims (whether it wants to or not) because it frames the question of "being human" in a specific context of embodiment and politics. Its endeavor to define humanness winds up discovering that the problem is circular—it only matters for humans and their clones anyway, and ultimately it only matters in a practical sense for political reasons.

That replicants think and feel and "live" in human-like bodies and thus in humanly recognizable ways is here framed as something that matters and is meaningful for them, and in a goal-directed way, the goal being their political liberation from slave labor and a slave-economy. This is why the final scene, where Deckard reaches out his hand to that of his daughter, is so important: their humanness is not defined in singularity, in the manner of Aristotle or Schopenhauer. Nor is it defined in a vacuum, in the manner of Condillac and Main De Biron (a point that could not be more salient, since Ana is in a kind of vacuum, and yet lives there in a perpetual construction of social memories). Rather, their humanness is created in relationships, personal and collective, relationships that are themselves shaped by resistance to political control and definition. And the hand is the literal and symbolic vehicle of that creation.

Thus the theme of humanness as a will-to-power floats under the theme of humanness as a categorical essence. Besides the replicants, the only human-like bodies in the movie are the ones with all the power—not only the power of self-determination, but also the power of making and owning slaves. This leads us to another question, which I end with here, the relationship between definitions of humanness and the history of slavery

7
More Human than Humans

ROB O'CONNOR

"That baby meant we were more than just slaves," Freysa reveals to K, in one of the most significant scenes from *Blade Runner 2049*.

She's referring to Rachael and Deckard's daughter, who, we'll soon come to realize, is Ana Stelline, a memory-maker for the Wallace Corporation. "If a baby can come from one of us," Freysa continues, "we are our own masters." Mariette, fellow replicant, appearing to summarize, offers, "More human than humans."

It's not just a summary of what Freysa tells us, but also a paraphrase of what Eldon Tyrell informs us, in *Blade Runner*, is the motto of the Tyrell Corporation, the Wallace Corporation's predecessor: "More human than human." The paraphrase is certainly provocative, but what, more precisely, does it signify?

The original phrase may be reasonably understood as identifying the subhuman characteristics of replicants. They are "more" in terms of physiological characteristics and capabilities, exceeding those of humans, while remaining mere representations of us, a construct for sale. Mariette's paraphrase is more problematic, however, more philosophical. In light of Freysa's revelation, *2049*'s pivotal premise, the paraphrase may be interpreted as identifying replicants as now moving *beyond* humans, as not only physiologically enhanced, but also able to reproduce, at least in principle. They are moving beyond "being" human. They are becoming "posthuman."

The Rise of Posthumanism?

Posthumanism, as a concept, arose toward the end of the twentieth century, in response to the dramatic changes in computer technology. The posthuman perspective embraces technology, information technology in particular, as a method of improving, rather than suppressing the human condition.

Posthumanism is a way of thinking about human beings which overturns common assumptions. The body is seen as a set of devices, which can be extended by new and artificial devices. The posthumanist believes that information has priority over material objects like bodies, brains, or computers, and that the same information can be stored in different material objects. Consciousness is seen as something that arises incidentally in the course of complex information processing.

As N. Katherine Hayles, a leading writer about posthumanism, sees it, posthumanism is a different way of thinking about the human condition which involves inclusion and close interaction with technological components or systems.

Posthumanists see the human body and personality as a system of "agents" working together. The conjunction of informational systems and human bodies is seen as a natural phenomenon. "The posthuman subject is an amalgam," according to Hayles, "a collection of heterogeneous components, a material-informational entity whose boundaries undergo continuous construction and reconstruction."

I've Seen Things You People Wouldn't Believe

In both *Blade Runner* and *2049* the term "replicant" replaces the term "android," or "andy" for short, as used by Philip K. Dick in the novel on which the movies are based, *Do Androids Dream of Electric Sheep?* This is an important distinction as it clearly moves away from the associations with machines (that the word "android" suggests) and towards an entity which is biological in classification, the connotation of the word "replicant" suggesting the process of cells duplicating themselves.

They are examples of the posthuman: a biological system enhanced through the technological process of bioengineering rather than the robotics or artificial intelligence that we witness in the figure of the android.

In an early scene in *Blade Runner* it is clear that bioengineering is a prominent feature in this world. Replicants Roy Batty and Leon Kowalski visit the body-parts emporium of Hannibal Chew, an expert at crafting replacement replicant eyes. We witness the replicants' enhanced biological features as Leon dips his arm in an ultra-cold liquid with no effect.

The feature which unites "andys" and "replicants" is that both have a limited lifespan of four years due to the problem of cell replacement. In *Blade Runner* this is suggested to be a fail-safe device in the replicant construction process. In the more biologically-focused replicants it is this feature that emphasizes the inclusion of technology in their artificial construction. Even though they are biological in nature, technology is still a significant factor in replicant construction, as it restricts their lifespan and dictates the duration of their existence.

Batty is fighting against this at the moral heart of the *Blade Runner* storyline—the central consideration is whether this restricted lifespan means that Batty's memories and experiences become insignificant. He has witnessed much throughout his existence: "I've seen things you people wouldn't believe. Attack ships on fire off the shoulder of Orion. I watched C-beams glitter in the dark near the Tannhäuser Gate. All those moments will be lost in time, like tears in rain. Time to die". In these final moments of *Blade Runner* Batty is suggesting to Deckard that identity is defined by the context of memories and experience. Is it not these experiences that define Batty rather than the commercial construction of his physical body?

Memories and experiences are just as important when defining the replicant as posthuman as the presence of enhanced biological systems. In the Director's Cut of *Blade Runner* this is emphasized as we witness Deckard's fairy-tale dream sequence with a unicorn running through a mythical forest. When the origami unicorn appears in the final moments of the film this concomitant image makes the audience ponder how Gaff was aware of Deckard's dream. One suggestion, continually debated, is that Deckard's dreams may indeed be implanted, a posthuman construction to which Gaff has gained access. This ending to the film is playfully ambiguous and has invited multiple interpretations.

K and Joi: The Posthuman in *Blade Runner 2049*

This representation of the posthuman is developed further in two distinct ways in *2049*. K is a replicant and a blade runner, chasing down rogue versions of his own kind, earlier Nexus-8 models with open-ended lifespans. K's retiring of a protein-farming replicant at the start leads him on a sequence of discovery. K finds the remains of a woman who has died as a result of childbirth, the "miracle" to which his target refers before K retires him, the word resonating with K throughout the film.

These remains turn out to be Rachael, Deckard's replicant lover from *Blade Runner*. As the assumed father, Deckard once again becomes the center of our attention: have replicants become able to procreate naturally? This concept is of interest to replicant-maker Niander Wallace, who owns the business interests of the former Tyrell Corporation and plans to mass-produce replicants on an unprecedented scale. The ability to procreate is his golden ticket to success and dominance, something which Tyrell seemingly achieved but Wallace is unable to repeat.

This is a simplified version of a plot that is dense and profound. We probe further into the existential quandaries which replicant bodies pose, developing new questions to consider. Deckard, for instance, remains a conundrum: we are not provided with a definitive answer as to whether he is a replicant or not, although Wallace does pose the question that maybe Deckard's entire existence was engineered solely for him to fall in love with Rachael and for them to produce "the perfect specimen." What is undeniably revealed is the next stage in replicant evolution: the ability to procreate. This is a significant development in the posthuman body of the replicant and a nod to the concept of "nature will always find a way": the technologically-applied biological restrictions have been bypassed. The "how" is never really explained and in a sense it is not important. Instead we are given a glimpse of a real posthuman development—the use of bioengineering technology to not only move beyond the frailties of the human body but also to reproduce this formula.

K's development once again highlights how effectively *Blade Runner* and *2049* utilize memory as a means of determining the posthuman. K soon begins to suspect that he may indeed be the lost replicant child. His memories (and then possession) of a wooden horse with a date engraved on it links directly to Rachael's burial site. However, when he discovers the truth—that he is nothing more than he thought he was, just a replicant—K questions his identity under the realization that all his memories are false. Despite this he is still able to act, to rescue Deckard and reunite him with his daughter. This is reminiscent of Roy Batty's final moments: K's ability to act despite this truth show his desire to leave a mark on existence.

Earlier in the movie, K's boss at the LAPD, Lt. Joshi, responds to K's observation that "To be born is to have a soul" by saying "You're getting on fine without one." Joshi is clearly marking the boundaries between the human and the posthuman here, the difference between the natural and the constructed. However, K's choice to help Deckard and defy the orders of the replicant revolutionaries demonstrates a development of free will, the beginnings of a soul. It is by challenging the existence that he has been given that has allowed K to achieve his own posthuman identity. This idea makes the final moments of K's life, as he lies alone on the steps, dying, even more poignant.

There is a second posthuman consideration in *2049*. Joi is a hologram, an AI from the Wallace Corporation programmed to act as K's personal companion. When K first becomes uneasy about his world and the revelations he is discovering he takes comfort in Joi, even to the extent of the couple using Mariette to allow Joi to interact and experience physical intimacy. The relationship that K and Joi develop is both critically engaging and poignant. In terms of cinematic emotion it forms a central thread as K and Joi utilize each other to try and ascertain their true identities, to come to terms with their own existence.

It's hard to say whether it's really love, especially when considering the technological nature of both entities involved in the relationship. K is a replicant and therefore has conditioned emotional responses. Joi has no biological aspect to her nature. Joi is a completely technological entity but demonstrates emotional intelligence, developing as their relationship deepens.

When Joi is dispatched cruelly by Luv, she is cut short of saying "I love you" to K. Joi's experiences with K have developed her identity to the extent that those final moments are very human in their portrayal of emotion. Joi is a technological system which has transcended its original capacity through the application of human emotional characteristics. She has become posthuman too, but opposite in construction to K. Instead of the fragility of the human body being surpassed through bioengineering, in Joi's case the limitations of her existence as a holographic body has been surpassed through the application of human emotions.

In contrast, when Joi is murdered K remains emotionless, demonstrating the dramatic existential shift which Joi experiences due to her relationship with K. What the dynamic between K and Joi suggests is how real-life virtual technology may affect human consciousness and behavior. It is entirely possible to form intimate relations with a holographic projection, given the correct application of artificial intelligence. The fact that K himself is a replicant is significant.

This is not an example of biological and virtual symbiosis affecting a human consciousness. This relationship is between two *posthuman* entities and for a while this is a utopian idea, demonstrating a clear development of technological constructs towards human consciousness, intimacy and identity.

However, when K sees the monolithic, virtual, holographic projection of Joi in the third act, seductively advertising the AI home companion product, he seems to reach an understanding that he will never fully achieve the humanity and domesticity he desired when interacting with Joi. By seeing his (now deceased) Joi projected as commercial marketing, K realizes that he too is nothing more than a tool to be utilized, by both the capitalist system of this dystopian world and the seemingly utopian objectives of the replicant revolutionaries.

It is this epiphany that makes him realize that rescuing Deckard is the only way that he can take charge of his own identity. As Freysa declares to K: "Dying for the right cause is the most human thing we can do." K chooses to embrace this mantra and it his epiphany regarding Joi that brings him to this realization. His interactions with Joi have been significant in raising his own personal identity and understanding. K has become *posthuman* at this point: a body constructed from biological and technological systems by technology which is permanently and irreversibly altered by the presence of Joi, an entity of technological and virtual construction.

All the Best Memories Are Hers

Blade Runner 2049 explores the role of memories and experience in defining posthuman existence. The replicants are an example of how synthetic humans could play a role in future society, through the application of bioengineering technology to create entities capable of moving beyond the frailties of the human condition and performing tasks that are past our current capability. Yet are replicants becoming "more human than humans"?

In *2049* it is not a coincidence that the missing child, Deckard's daughter Dr. Ana Stelline, turns out to be a memory-maker. Cocooned in a lab due to her extreme allergy to the outside world, Stelline escapes her trapped existence by creating memories to be inserted into other replicants as part of Wallace's program. When K discovers that his memory of the wooden horse actually belongs to Stelline, he's at first shattered. Yet by the end he has come to realize the significance of this false memory in forming his identity. As K says to Deckard as he hands him back his daughter's toy wooden horse: "All the best memories are hers."

It doesn't matter that the memory was false. It helped to define K. Memories and experience place an entity, regardless of its construction, within the complex system of the wider world, providing existential context. Even if those memories and experiences are artificial, merely programmed information, in other words a posthuman construction, then the result is still the same.

Replicants are *posthuman* bodies according to Katherine Hayles's definition of the term: a network of biological agents living in symbiosis with technological agents (bio-engineering and artificial memories) in order to create a posthuman "self." Hayles highlights how information technology is becoming more important in recognizing the identity of posthuman entities. In the example of the replicants, artificial memories are this technology and provide the replicants with context for their existence. They provide a sense of posthuman identity.

This is surely the next step given that we are now starting to see the use of technology as a common occurrence to enhance and repair the physical body. With the advances in robotic technology and artificial intelligence it is entirely possible that the machines or biological entities we create will have the capacity for developing their own posthuman identity. The symbiosis depicted within the contemporary cyborg motif, expressed by the replicants in the *Blade Runner* universe, no longer merely shows how technology can improve the limitations of the human condition. Instead it symbolizes how combining technologies with both artificial and human beings can help them to transcend and become even greater.

As Mariette suggests, replicants have developed to become "More human than humans." As a result, the definition of what it means to be human must be re-evaluated in the time of the posthuman.

8
Ode to Joi

STEVE BEIN

Central to the *Blade Runner* universe is the question of person-hood. *Blade Runner 2049* adds a new twist to the riddle: Joi, the artificial intelligence who promises everything you want.

Despite not having a body she behaves as personishly as any-one else in the movie, but the people she interacts with don't always include her in the club. Her own manufacturer, the Wallace Corporation, doesn't seem to think she's a person; Luv refers to her as "our product." Even her own boyfriend, K, seems to shove Joi under the bus, calling her "very realistic." That's a nice thing to say about a fake person, not so nice about a real one.

So who counts as a person? Who doesn't? Is it possible to man-ufacture a person, or can human inventions only simulate per-sonhood? The biggie, of course, is what if your creation thinks it's a person? Taking a more radical turn, we can ask the question the Buddha asked: does it make sense to speak of persons at all? K says, "To be born is to have a soul, I guess," but the Buddha asks what evidence there is of these soul-things in the first place.

Are You a Repli-*can* or a Repli-*can't*?

K's seemingly offhand comment about his "very realistic" girl-friend is the tip of a massive metaphysical iceberg. Whether *he* thinks she's a person, whether *she* thinks she's a person, and whether she *is* a person are importantly different questions. If she is but he doesn't think she is, she's a slave. If she isn't but he thinks she is, he's a dupe. And if she thinks she is but she isn't . . . hoo-boy.

Can we even make sense of that hypothesis? Can there be a being who has beliefs about the nature of her own existence but isn't a person? Or is the capacity to contemplate your own existence already a sufficient condition for personhood?

It looks like we'll have to pin down what we mean by "person." Fortunately for us, there are philosophers out there who have already done some of the pinning. Mary Anne Warren laid down what we might call a "functionalist" account, listing five functions a person can perform:

1. **Consciousness, especially the capacity to feel pain**

2. **Reason, especially the capacity to solve new and complex problems**

3. **Self-motivated activity**

4. **The capacity to communicate on an indefinite number of topics**

5. **Self-awareness**

According to these criteria, I'm a person, my dog Cocoa isn't, and Koko the gorilla almost certainly is, even though a lot of human beings wouldn't welcome her into the family. (Koko's the one who learned about two thousand spoken words in English and about 1,100 signs in sign language. She also created new signs of her own when she didn't know one—coupling "stuck" with "metal" to mean "magnet," for example.)

Implicit in Warren's list is the theoretical possibility of some nonhuman persons—beings that meet the criteria yet don't belong to the species *Homo sapiens*. There's room for manufactured persons like K and Joi too.

Warren isn't proposing a personhood test, where anyone who loses one of these attributes no longer counts as a person. (It's a good thing too, or else when you go to sleep tonight you'd temporarily lose your personhood.) She allows for the possibility of full-fledged persons who cannot meet all five criteria—such as you might be, if it were possible to upload your consciousness into a computer. That seems like the sort of prison Philip K. Dick might envision, doesn't it? We could remove your capacity for self-motivated activity and just leave you on a hard drive to stew about it. If you're capable of resenting your imprisonment, this suggests that you're still a person.

What's important for Warren's purposes is that anyone who can meet all five criteria definitely is a person, and anyone who can't meet any of them definitely isn't. So the question for Joi is, how many does she meet?

Lacking a physical body, Joi lacks the capacity for physical pain, but her emotional pain is evident in her compassion for K. When he's upset, she's upset. She also has the capacity for emotional pain independently of him: when Luv threatens to stomp on her, she shows fear. (This by itself suggests that she's quite self-aware.) And by arranging the hook-up with Mariette she shows that she takes actions of her own accord, solving problems and communicating with others in novel ways. So at least according to Warren's criteria, the evening with Mariette isn't a tryst, it's a ménage-à-trois. That is, there are three people in that room, not two.

But according to the Buddha, there's a sense in which there are none.

A Real Boy, or No Boy at All?

To understand the Buddhist view of personhood it helps to know what the Buddha was responding to. He was born a Brahmin—that is, a member of the Hindu priestly caste. If you know anything at all about Hinduism, you probably know that Hindus believe in reincarnation. The thing that leaves your body when you die and enters a new body when you're reborn is called the *ātman*. And one of the first things the Buddha says after gaining his enlightenment is that the *ātman* doesn't exist.

It's a good thing, too, he says, because believing in an *ātman* just gets you into trouble. It's true that a lot of people take comfort in their belief in the afterlife, but believing in something just because it comforts you is a recipe for heartbreak. Look at what happens to K when he learns the truth about who he is. He so desperately wanted to be the son of Deckard and Rachael—"a real boy," as Joi puts it—that he talked himself into believing it. Then, when he learns his memory of the wooden horse is just an implanted, fake memory, he's utterly crushed.

So what are you if you're not your *ātman*? According to early Indian Buddhism, you're just a composite of *skandhas*, or "bundles." Bundles of what? Psychophysical processes like sense data, physical form, and consciousness, all of which are as fleeting as tears in rain. I've labelled them "processes" (and not, for instance, "things") because they have no fixed essence; they're constantly changing.

I'm calling them "psychophysical" because according to Buddhism the line between the physical and the mental is only imaginary. We talk about them as if they're distinct, but when you get right down to it they're just two sides of a single coin. Your experience of reading this paragraph, for instance, is equal parts physical (light reflected from a printed word and hitting your retina, or raised bumps touching your fingertip, or sound waves vibrating your eardrum) and mental (those sensory inputs being processed into words or ideas).

This idea is called *nondualism*: the belief that two apparently distinct things (or concepts, or phenomena) are in fact inseparable. And Buddhism isn't nondualistic only about the body and the mind; it's nondualistic about *everything*, including—perhaps most importantly—the nature of self and other.

That's right, the Buddha says that any distinction you might draw between yourself and the things around you is imaginary (just like the distinction between the mental and the physical). If what you are is all those psychophysical processes, then this paragraph *is* you. You are—at least in part—your consciousness of this paragraph. Since I wrote it, I'm a part of you too. And since I wrote it for a future reader, you're a part of me.

If all this nondualism sounds like nonsense to you, keep in mind that you already believe in some forms of it. Take left-right nondualism, for example. Suppose you cut K's wooden horse right down the middle, separating the right half of its body from the left. It's not as if the right half doesn't have a left side anymore. Its new smooth flat side *is* the left side now. Left is the opposite of right, sure, but the left is also implicit in the right. They're bound to each other at the most basic conceptual level.

The Buddhist says the same is true of self and other. At the end of the day, what you think of as your self is an imaginary concept. It's a handy one, to be sure, but it doesn't stay the same over time and it doesn't exist independently of anything else. In fact, it's better thought of as a *composition* of everything else.

Crime and Punishment

Now let's bring this back to Joi. By Mary Anne Warren's criteria she's a person, and one of the key components that makes her a person is that she's self-aware. The Buddha, of course, will say Joi's sense of self is delusional. But since an artificially intelligent hologram is just as capable of delusion as anyone else, Joi has as strong a claim to personhood as you do.

But *somebody* is reading this sentence, right? The conscious experience you're having right this second is certainly happening. Similarly, there must be some sense in which Joi is real, at least within the confines of the movie. Luv doesn't stomp *nothing* out of existence. Whatever Joi is, when that boot heel comes down she ceases to be. Prior to that, Joi is K's girlfriend—and decidedly *not* a simulation. She's not a stand-in, not an artificial representation of some flesh-and-blood girlfriend who's out of town. She's the real deal.

If so, then surely Luv has committed murder. We can't expect Lieutenant Joshi to send officers to arrest her, but that's only because Joshi's biased against artificial persons. To her K and Joi are more like things than people. But if Joi thinks she's a person, that very capacity probably marks her as a person, which makes Luv a killer.

And this raises a very sticky problem in the history of Buddhism. If Luv, like the rest of us, is nothing more than bundled psychophysical processes, then like the rest of us she has no constant, abiding essence of personhood. There's no self in there, just the processes, which expire and reappear as rapidly as electrons in a biorobotic brain. From this it follows that the Luv who raises her foot to stomp on Joi isn't the same person as the Luv whose boot comes crashing down.

Even if K arrested her on the spot, the Luv he'd slap the cuffs on isn't the same one who later stands trial. Thus if the judge and jury are Buddhists, Luv has a simple defense: "It wasn't me." The one who killed Joi has long since vanished, and it makes no sense to punish this new Luv for someone else's crime.

Of course this defense hinges on Buddhist metaphysics being correct. If she *does* have an enduring, independent existence, it killed Joi so it's the one to imprison. But if you're running a courtroom in one of the Buddhist kingdoms of ancient India, then you're probably committed to the belief that there isn't an *ātman* to pin the crime on. If so, then it looks like moral accountability just went out the window.

One Crime, Two Truths

The Buddhist tradition has a handy tool for solving this problem, known as the Doctrine of the Two Truths. The philosopher best known for spelling this out is a guy called Nāgārjuna (around 150–250 C.E.), who distinguishes between *conventional truth* and *ultimate truth*

Ultimate truth is about how things really are, but it's pretty inconvenient for daily conversation. Suppose Deckard wants to tell Rachael he loves her. If he wants to accurately represent ultimate truth, he'll have to say something like, "There is no I and there is no you, but the bundle of psychophysical processes we conventionally refer to as Deckard includes emotional expressions we conventionally refer to as love, expressed toward the bundle of psychophysical processes we conventionally refer to as Rachael."

Not so great for an anniversary card. It's a lot pithier to say "I love you, Rachael." But apart from being pithy, the sentence "I love you, Rachael" is actually *better* at expressing the truth of his feelings for her. It doesn't matter that every noun in the sentence is metaphysically misleading. It doesn't matter that the very idea of an "I" is—according to the Buddha—both deluded and toxic.

In point of fact, it doesn't even matter if you think all this Buddhist stuff is a bunch of hogwash. Apart from the occasional scientific lecture, everyone uses conceptual shorthand to describe a greater, more complex reality. You don't text your sweetie-pie a complete and accurate neurological description of the electrochemical activity you experience as love. For some people even typing "I love you" is overdoing it. A single emoji can be enough.

According to Buddhism, "I love you" is a true statement even if "I" and "you" exist only as convenient conceptual shorthand. That is, "I love you" is conventionally true even if on the ultimate level it's not. This looks like it flies in the face of the law of non-contradiction, which says that no proposition can be both true and false at the same time. By that law, "Deckard loves Rachael" has to be either true or false, not both.

But it's not a logical contradiction so long as we understand that the word *true* is ambiguous. Conventionally, it's true that Deckard loves Rachael. Ultimately, it's true that there is no Deckard at all, but there *is* a bundle of psychophysical processes which include an ever-changing set of loving feelings directed toward a supposed "Rachael."

This is how even a Buddhist legal system can bring Joi's killer to justice. Joi was never a person in the ultimate sense— not if by "person" we mean "an independently existing being that persists over time and possesses a self." Joi isn't one of those because nobody is one of those. But conventionally speaking that's not what "person" means. It means something pretty close to Mary Anne Warren's criteria, and by those criteria Joi's as much of a person as you are.

Luv is too, and so when Luv crushes Joi's emanator under her boot, a perfectly accurate way to describe that is "Luv killed Joi." No Luv and no Joi on the ultimate level, but on the conventional level we've got a murder victim and a killer.

Incidentally, even morality works on both levels—which is good, because it would really suck if you were punished for some conventional wrongdoing while ultimately you were quite innocent. Remember that nondualism? Buddhists extend this even to right and wrong (and by extension to innocence and guilt). Self/other nondualism says we're all extensions of each other, so when any of us behaves rightly or wrongly, we introduce good or bad effects into the whole network. (The Buddhists have a term for this: *karma*.)

So, when Luv kills Joi, the network bears the guilt and the network has to pay off that bad karma. Since *someone's* got to pay for past-Luv's crime, present-Luv is as good a candidate as any. But notice that she doesn't share the burden alone: Joi's final moment of panic counts as punishment, as does K's grief, as do countless other knock-on effects that we the audience may never see. The network itself undergoes the karmic ripple effects.

Like Tears in Rain

Now maybe that seems haphazard to you. Maybe you think that's no way to run a court of law. That's okay, because governments don't have to understand the deepest metaphysical truths of the universe. For them conventional truth is good enough, and conventionally speaking it's perfectly just to punish Luv for the crime of murder.

By the same token, we might revisit K's nasty comment about Joi. If "she's very realistic" means "she's very person-like," then he's doubly right. Conventionally, she meets the criteria of personhood in exactly the way you and I do. Ultimately, "person" is the misnomer we place on a particular kind of bundled psychophysical phenomena. It's an answer that delights a mind like Philip K. Dick's: Joi is a person and she isn't, and both of those are true at the same time.

Conventionally there are tears in rain, even if ultimately they're at one with each other.

II

A Miracle
Delivered

9
Replicant Birth, Moral Miscarriage

L. Brooke Rudow

The overarching message of *Blade Runner 2049* is captured succinctly in a brief exchange from the movie.

"I've never retired something that was born before," K confesses. "What's the difference?," Lieutenant Joshi asks, mildly irritated. "To be born," K answers, "is to have a soul." To be "born, not made," as Joi later rejoices, is something *more*. It's something significant, sacred, even. It's something to be protected and cherished.

We, the audience, are drawn to messages like these, ones that affirm our value and the meaning of our existence. But what's fascinating about the message here is that it is actually a *reversal* of what I believe to be the more powerful and visionary claim of *Blade Runner*: the artificial can have moral worth equal to the natural.

Replicants Are People Too!

Blade Runner leaves little doubt that we're supposed to think of replicants as people. Sure, we know they aren't human, like you and me. They're artificial humans, in the sense that someone made them. Their origins aren't *natural* or biological. But even though they're not natural, we are supposed to feel for them. More than just pity them, we are supposed to have moral feelings for them.

Blade Runner asks us to question the morality of "retiring" replicants, the morality of enslaving them, and the morality, even, of imposing limits to their lifespans. But why should we, really? I mean, if the replicants are artificial, if they're just some, admittedly elaborate, pieces of technology, why should we treat them any differently than we would our Voight-Kampff machines?

Philosophy and the movie give us a few good reasons to think that replicants are more than just artificial humans. For one thing, perceptually, the replicants are identical to "real" people. It takes an investigation and the use of a Voight-Kampff test to establish whether or not replicants are human. Some questions even arise if, in fact, a replicant could dupe the machine. If replicants look and behave so similarly to humans, then treating them unethically says something kind of strange and disturbing about the real humans doing the harm.

Immanuel Kant worried about this same problem with animals. He said that treating animals cruelly makes the human being cruel and, worse, more likely to treat other humans similarly. Imagine what he would say about replicants! If we're so quick to murder or enslave beings that bear such remarkable resemblance to ourselves, how much of a jump is it really to treat real humans the same way? If history has anything to say about it, it's no jump whatsoever.

Another reason we might think that replicants deserve to be treated morally is that they seem to *feel*. Rachael is heartbroken to discover that her sense of self is a sham, all her memories false. She spirals into depression but is lifted out by love. Batty mourns Pris when he discovers her dead body. He gently closes her eyes in a familiar display of loving respect. He fights against and despairs of his mortality, undergoing the existential angst and dread we all know so well. What is more human than this?

Jeremy Bentham famously said (again, about animals!), "the question is not, Can they *reason*? Nor, can they *talk*? But, *can they suffer*?" If a being can feel and suffer, we should do what we can to ease that suffering, thought Bentham. But Bentham is kind of a weirdo in the philosophical tradition, at least when it comes to ethics. For most thinkers, feelings don't count for all that much. Cows feel and we (but not me!) still eat them, as do chickens and pigs and . . . you get it. So if we really want a solid reason for treating replicants morally, we need more. Luckily (for the replicants) the movie gives it to us: the mind! But not just any mind, a *rational* mind.

One of the biggest deals, if not *the* biggest deal, this side of evolution (or creation, whatever floats your boat) is rationality. Philosophers *love* rationality. For the most part, the only reason that we should give moral consideration to anything is, well, reason! This is true for Aristotle, Descartes, Kant, all the big guys (and a few of the big ladies, too). The thing is that, as far as they knew, only humans had rationality.

But *Blade Runner* introduced us to a world where humans don't have a monopoly on mind. The replicants deliberate, choose, act on their choices, and they very clearly value their freedom to do so. They have consciousness and the prized *self-consciousness*. If rationality makes the man (or woman—though it rarely did for "the big guys." Yes, eye roll), then replicants are people, too. And if replicants are people, we have to treat them like people—with respect, with dignity, with kindness. I mean, minimally, we can't murder and enslave them. Obviously! And this is exactly what *Blade Runner* told us, and it does it so well.

So, even though the replicants aren't *really* human, even though they aren't strictly alive in the biological sense, they matter. They matter because they are thinking things that can feel. They have the full array of valuable moral features, and that they are artificial couldn't matter less . . . or at least, I thought so . . .

And unto Them a Replicant Was Born

The sequel *2049* seems at first to complement and deepen this moral message. Following a replicant named K, we are witness to his complex psychological, emotional, and moral life. Psychologically, K has developed the capacity to lie, something thought impossible by the Wallace Corporation (the group now developing and pumping out replicants). Emotionally, K is deeply lonely.

He has a hologram girlfriend, who is seemingly less of a "person" than he is (rich ground for a feminist like me, but I digress), but she doesn't do much to ease his sadness. He's struggling to figure out who he is, the point of his existence. And this is significant, because as a piece of technology, he *knows* the point of his existence. He's supposed to retire the last of the rogue Nexus-8 replicants. But he wants to understand the point of his existence *for himself*, a purpose to his being beyond his programming.

Morally, K is trying to balance what he is supposed to do as a replicant assassin and what he's supposed to do as a moral person. He doesn't like killing replicants and he eventually determines, for himself, that it's wrong. Again, *2049* seems to strongly suggest that these aspects of K are what make him a person and what make him worthy of being treated morally.

But almost immediately the movie throws us a curve ball. As K is going about the dirty business of retirement, he discovers the body of a female replicant who died in childbirth.

What?! Childbirth?! Yep, now replicants can have babies. You kinda can't help but hear Ian Malcolm's, "Life, uh, finds a way," echo in your head (*Jurassic Park*, people; you better know that). But, yes, this new breed of replicants can give birth. They and their offspring seem to be legitimately *alive*, in the strictest of biological terms. And this is a game-changer. Now K, the other replicants, and the "real" humans are fixated on reproduction, one of the primary markers of biological life.

K's identity crisis takes an uplifting (though temporary) turn as K thinks that maybe he is the baby whose birth killed this poor replicant woman, and he sets out to find his dad. Suddenly K finds himself in the position of an almost biblical savior, charged with the duty to lead his people from bondage. The birth was a miracle, an act of God or, at the very least, a god-like creator, Tyrell. He is Pinocchio, the toy that came to life, the *artificial* turned *natural*. But as we and K come to discover, he's not the chosen one. The proverbial Rick and Rachael gave birth to a baby girl, Ana, who, in the end K nobly dies to protect.

This biological turn is brilliant and beautiful. It's just what the movie needed, I think, to spark the imagination of its audience. We sci-fi fans are pretty familiar with the tropes of technological dystopias, new and fantastic relationships to (or with) technology, or the deep moral questions about how to treat our creations. But this? This is something different. The idea that the artificial can become its opposite, the natural, is fascinating. I applaud this move.

But! (You knew there was a 'but' there, didn't you?) There's something really disappointing about the way that the biological turn turned out.

Back to Life, Back to Biology

The underground replicant resistance places special emphasis on the bio-artificial child. This child is seen as the savior who must lead them from bondage. But why? *They* can't reproduce, seemingly, so why is finding this child so important? I think there are a couple of reasons.

The first is political. If they can reproduce themselves, it becomes much more difficult for the human population to control them. They can potentially gain freedom by reproducing their own numbers. This is not insignificant. They are slaves and the political freedom they seek is deeply important. But this reasoning has some problems. Why can't the replicants reproduce themselves in the same ways that Wallace does it?

Sure, they lack the resources, but theoretically, couldn't they steal the "recipe" and do it themselves? Okay, that does sound hard. Reproducing biologically is vastly cheaper, easier, and more accessible.

But wait, there are only two replicants that we *know* can reproduce: Rick Deckard and Rachael. No, strike that. We don't actually know if Deckard is a replicant. I mean, I think that *I* know that Deckard is a replicant, but I know there are some (mistaken) few who may argue otherwise. It was left ambiguous at the end of *Blade Runner*, but I'm a purist. I ground my own view of Deckard in *Do Androids Dream of Electric Sheep?* wherein *of course* Deckard is a replicant! Not really, I know it's ambiguous there, too. Also, lots of things differ from the book to the movie, so maybe that differs, too. After all, we've got the origin theatrical version, then we've got the Director's Cut, then we've got the Final Cut, and I think several other cuts in between and afterwards. Yeah, yeah, yeah, but . . . no. No! As far as I'm concerned, Deckard is a replicant. Moving on . . .

Okay, so there are only two replicants that we know (fine, we *suspect*) can reproduce. I guess we're supposed to assume that the child, Ana, can, too, but who could she reproduce *with*? Maybe it only takes the female? If so, then it's somewhat plausible that she could be the Eve who populates the earth with bio-replicant babies, selecting her Adam at will. But is Ana capable of reproduction? There's some suggestion that the reproductive capacity was *designed* by Tyrell. If so, is it inheritable? If not, then Ana is not much good in the fight for freedom—as a baby-maker, anyway. If it *is* inheritable, it's going to take a long, long time before the replicants have the numbers to really become independent of the humans. So the political reasoning isn't all that plausible. There must be another reason for caring so much about finding the child, and I think it's the moral reason.

That replicants can reproduce *proves* something about them. It proves, somehow, that they are more than mere tools, mere machines. Whether it was designed or an evolution-like "natural" mutation, if one replicant can participate in the *real miracle* of life itself, maybe they all can. If one replicant has a soul, maybe they all do. The replicants cling to the *idea* of the child because it lifts them out of their sub-person status. Only *now*, are replicants people, too. Seemingly, all of the personhood developed in *Blade Runner* was for naught. The replicants hope, no doubt, that once the humans are confronted with the phenomenon of replicant reproduction, of replicant realness, and replicant souls, they will have to free them. And the humans are worried about this, too.

The humans in the film have two distinct motivations. K's boss, Joshi, commands K to find and kill the child, but Wallace wants access to it. Let's start with Wallace. He wants the child because he thinks he can create more reproducing replicants to fill an increasing demand for slave-labor. He is very clearly *not* concerned with the moral value of replicants, living or otherwise. He's a slave-trader. Period. It really doesn't matter to him how human the replicants are. Presumably, if Wallace did gain access to Ana and started reproducing his own bio-replicants, this would be a corporate secret. If not, it would lead to the moral and political problem that Joshi is worried about.

Joshi wants the child killed because if the truth about replicant birth reached the public—human and replicant alike—a war would surely break out. Why? Because now replicants have graduated from plaything to personhood. Realizing this, they would and *could* demand the rights they are due *as* full persons. And humans? Many of them would likely be swayed to assist the replicants in such a righteous fight.

The society would be fractured on an issue that hadn't come up before. Why hadn't it come up before? Because replicants weren't people before. Wait . . . what? You're thinking, "But I thought they *were* people before . . . you know, because of the whole feeling and thinking thing?" I know, exactly! Now you're seeing the problem!

Blade Runner 2049, the Philosopher's Cut

It's commonplace to care about natural, living things. It's commonplace, and it's mostly appropriate. A big reason for our commitment to life and living things is because that's the real world we live in. We don't have replicants yet, so of course we haven't had to worry about how we treat them. But advancements in the field of artificial intelligence, though still vastly distant from the replicants of *Blade Runner*, are bringing questions about ethical relationships to technologies closer to home.

How we answer these questions is no longer the domain of fantasy. The answers we give can have real consequences in the future to come. So what movies like *Blade Runner* and *2049* have to say—about these issues and about the moral value of these creations—*really does matter*.

So, what does this move to biological being mean on the moral landscape? Well, the original *Blade Runner* urges us to accept that Replicants, as pieces of technology—as fully artificial, literal machines—are people. As people, we should care about them and treat them as we would any other person. And that's the really challenging and exciting moral claim: biology, naturalness, and, especially, humanity aren't the important moral features. If you are a thing that can think and a thing that can feel, then you count!

And the implications go even further, or rather, perhaps they come closer to home. If thinking and feeling make something count, how should we be treating animals? Even *Blade Runner* forgets the central role played by animals in *Androids*. But what's the connection between animals and replicants? To answer this, I think we have to return to Bentham's question, "Do they suffer?" Well, yes, *of course they do*. And if we are swayed enough by this to admit replicants into our moral universe, shouldn't we let the animals in, too?

But *2049* moves us away from these conclusions. It tells us that replicants can *become* natural and human. Only then— *only if* they approach full humanity—should we really care about them. Their value is completely biocentric and anthropocentric. The possibilities for moral relationships to replicants or animals or machines that look nothing like us are shut down. By the end of it, what had been an ethical *innovation* in *Blade Runner* becomes a *regress* in *2049*.

Okay, fine. The ethical message lost its way a little, but it was still a good movie, right? Yes! It really was! And the biological turn? *It was the right move*. I would not change a thing about this replicant evolution. What would I change about other aspects of the movie? You ask. You *do* want to know, don't you? I wouldn't have told anyone who Rachael's baby was. I would have let the audience think it was K; I would have let the audience think it was Ana. I would have let this debate rage on and on. Geeks and nerds, *decades* in the future, would construct their theories, and they'd have plenty of evidence to support their claims no matter which way they went with it.

But why? Because that's how you keep the ethical innovation and legacy of *Androids* and *Blade Runner* alive. The more profound commentary would have been to double down on the point that, whether replicants are machines or replicants are human, they are morally valuable nonetheless.

10

Should Humans Dream of Designer Babies?

SAMANTHA NOLL AND LACI HUBBARD-MATTIX

Seventy-five years before Niander Wallace brutally kills a newborn replicant in *Blade Runner 2049*, the National Commission for the Protection of Human Subjects of Biomedical and Behavioral Research was formed.

Its formation led to the creation of the Belmont Report, which established guidelines for the treatment of human subjects. Wallace uses a scalpel as the instrument of disposal, of the newborn replicant, stabbing her in the womb, thereby ending her life moments after wishing her a happy birthday.

The conjunction of *2049* and the Belmont Report leads us to important questions concerning biomedical research, given that replicants are "bioengineered humans." For example, is the "defective" replicant a human subject, and thus protected by research guidelines, or is she a product or consumer good that did not meet expectations?

If her identity is determined by her human DNA, then Wallace committed murder. But if she's a product, he simply disposed of a defective model. This leads us to question our ethical obligations concerning the treatment of replicants. How should we treat replicants once they've been created? Are they humans or are they "objects" that can be used as a means to achieve human ends? If the latter, the Wallace Corporation was completely justified in creating different models (farming, mining, or pleasure) in its quest to "own the stars."

Blade Runner 2049 grapples with these questions and, particularly, the nuances of using genetic engineering to create human beings for various ends. Non-replicant humans increasingly rely on replicants to perform tasks that are dangerous, degrading, or undesirable. They're designed to embody idealized characteristics and, as such, are often stronger, more intelligent, and more beautiful than their non-replicant counterparts. The downside is that they're engineered with specific purposes in mind and, at times, planned defects, such as a limited emotions or shortened lifespan. As such, *2049* is an exploration of ethical concerns that arise with the use of genetic modification techniques in the context of human research—techniques that are rapidly moving out of realm of fiction and into reality.

One of the most popular topics concerning the application of genetic modification techniques is the creation of "designer babies." Today we're on the cusp of having greater control over choosing the traits of our children. We will soon be able to design our children, increasing the probability that they're born with a specific hair and eye color or other desired traits. As we learned at the beginning of *2049*, replicants are "bioengineered humans, designed by the Tyrell Corporation for use off-world," and so they clearly fit the criteria of designer babies.

While replicants are created outside of human wombs, they still fit into this category, as in-vitro fertilization and artificial wombs are increasingly a part of actual or envisioned reproductive technologies. In some ways replicants explore the limits that such technologies can reach, as they are created to fulfill the desired specifications of Wallace, their self-proclaimed father.

Enhancement or Devolvement?

Influencing the traits of pre-implanted embryos in order to produce people who will develop desirable traits is often understood as a type of "enhancement." This is because such changes are thought to provide them with advantages that they otherwise may not have had. For replicants who are not part of a genetic lottery, this means that they're designed to be better than their non-replicant counterparts.

In *2049*, genetic enhancement has led to the colonization and subsequent development of nine new worlds, as replicants are designed to perform necessary tasks, from mining to fighting wars. Roy Batty, in *Blade Runner*, is an example of this, created to fulfill the role of a soldier, and so with superhuman strength and reflexes. Wallace sees replicants as adding to human potential, going so far as to claim that "We need more replicants than can ever be assembled. Millions, so we can be trillions more. We could storm Eden and retake her." In this way, genetic enhancement can be understood as a pathway to a better future.

However, this is not the only way of viewing the possibility of enhancements. "I wouldn't waste your money," Luv, Wallace's right-hand woman, says in a sales pitch to a drilling operation representative, by ordering replicants with the advanced features such as "intelligence, attachment, or appeal" for a mining operation. It is deemed appropriate and efficient to limit the enhancements made to a replicant. Delimiting a replicant to its appropriate skill-level is desirable, in this context. This illustrates two ethical issues at the heart of both the movie and the use of biotechnology to enhance humans.

First, is it ethical to choose the traits of a person prior to their birth? In the designer baby debate, critics are worried that genetic editing could spiral out of control and allow parents to custom-order their children, much like we now do with custom clothing or cars. Perhaps, we would like our children to live longer, to be seven feet tall, to look like this or that celebrity, and so on. Who gets to decide what traits are valued, however, and which are not? Should it be Wallace, the owner of the technology, or society at large? If they're considered to be people, because of their human DNA, they'd be covered under various research guidelines, such as the Belmont Report, and so offered certain legal protections. *2049* shows us the alternative, where they're seen as owned by the patent holder. As Lieutenant Joshi states, "The world is built on a wall that separates kind. Tell either side there's no wall, you've bought a war, or a slaughter." Similarly, Wallace's limited conception of ethical duties to replicants also hangs on a separation of kind between "humans" and "replicants."

Second, is it ethically permissible to remove abilities that a being would otherwise have developed? This approach begins with a complete being and through various methods, removes or disables a capacity or function. The replicant fits this model, as it has limitless possibilities that are removed in order to fulfill consumer preferences. Even in the case of non-human animals such modifications are unethical, as Paul Thomson has argued, unless they improve the wellbeing of the modified animal, or have no impact on animal welfare. In the case of replicants, it's for neither reason, but rather for the convenience and profit of the Wallace Corporation and its clients.

We could argue that the drilling operation representatives are not "dumbing down" replicants, but rather choosing a list of abilities to be added to a blank slate. As each replicant is crafted using human DNA, however, and thus has the general potential to develop baseline human abilities, any genetic engineering that removes or lessens these traits is a "dumbing down." Also, this brings up important questions concerning whether or not we've a duty to enhance our children, if we possess the ability to do so.

In this way, the movie pushes reproductive technology to its limits and, as such, highlights both the promise and potential harm that could arise, depending on the modification. We're moving into a "trans-human" era, as Andy Miah suggests, in which, as in *2049*, a person's genetic makeup can be manipulated at will for a wide range of reasons beyond health needs. Unlike in the movie, however, we're still grappling with how far we are prepared to accept the applications of biotechnology.

2049 presents us with one position that can be taken concerning genetic modification, yet we may be moving in a different direction, as illustrated by the application of bioethical principles in the Belmont Report. *2049* acts as a foil to the current ethical standards when applying technology in the human context.

Is a Replicant a Person?

Four key ethical principles, first outlined in the Belmont Report, are followed by medical practitioners today:

1. autonomy, or the mandate to respect a person's choices

2. beneficence, or the mandate to only do actions that benefit people

3. non-maleficence, or the mandate to do no harm when trying to treat a patient

4. justice, or the mandate to ensure that benefits and harms are fairly distributed throughout the population

Applying the second and third principles (beneficence and non-maleficence) could support the position that we should allow genetic engineering, and provide clear guidance in this area. For example, enhancements could be ethically acceptable, if they benefit the engineered child without causing harm, as non-maleficence and beneficence would both be followed in such a situation.

So, engineering a child to be smarter or to have a longer lifespan would be acceptable, as these are benefits. Unacceptable modifications would be those that would not clearly benefit the child, such as a change in eye color, or those that would typically harm the child, such as being born with only one leg.

In *2049*, replicants were not able to choose what modifications they were given, their assigned professions (though some ran), and whether they should live or die, as they were hunted and killed throughout the movie. Applying the principle of respect for autonomy illustrates why this lack of choice is ethically problematic. Specifically, this principle requires that we respect the choices and decisions of those on the receiving end of genetic engineering.

Unlike adults, who can consent to modifications, neither an infant nor an embryo can do so. This places us in a catch-22 situation, as the choice of traits occurs in the embryonic or infant stage, and cannot be made later in life. By the time a child can consent, the window for modifications is often closed. From this point of view, then, the principle of autonomy would recommend that we do not modify our children.

Wallace was acting unethically from the start, then, from this perspective, as the creation of replicants is itself problematic. And replicants are also expected to deny their autonomy throughout their lives, whenever their desires conflict with those of their manufacturers or owners. For instance, when Joshi demands that K remove all evidence of Rachael's pregnancy, K is reluctant, because he has never before retired someone who was born. When she asks him then whether he's refusing an order, he indicates his lack of autonomy by responding, "I wasn't aware that was an option, Madam." This is also a worry for designer babies, as it seems likely that parents (who often have specific ideas about what their children should do anyway) who pay to have their children designed may also have constrained ideas of who their children will become.

In reply to the first concern, we could argue that their parents or creators (such as Wallace) could provide consent here, as obtaining parental consent is standard practice when treating children in hospitals. However, this begs the question concerning what types of rights CEOs have over their creations. Should they be given parental rights over their "creations," property rights, or neither? Unless they use their own genetic material, they're not the replicant's parent. In addition, they would not have the right to own another human being, as this would be slavery. Even if we accept that creators can provide consent, the biomedical principles of beneficence and nonmaleficence would take many of the modifications performed in *2049* off the table.

According to the beneficence principle, we may only do procedures that are beneficial to the person they're being done to. Clearly in the case of enhancing (or devolving) replicants, beneficence is not a consideration of the Wallace Corporation. Customers are, in fact, encouraged to not "waste" money on enhanced features. This is not for the benefit of the replicants, but of the consumers.

Some enhancements, however, though not all, would be supported by an appropriate application of the principle. For example, increasing the dexterity of a replicant miner doing dangerous physical tasks would be to their advantage. On the other hand, increasing a pleasure model's capacity for attachment and appeal could be detrimental. Finally, not being able to reproduce is a general disadvantage that replicants share. Thus, creating bioengineered humans without this ability is not beneficial to replicants, and so breaks the principle of beneficence.

The use of replicants throughout *2049* is a clear violation of the principle of non-maleficence. The starkest example of this violation is in the birthing room. Murdering a replicant for a flaw, which is in no way her own fault, is clearly a harm. In addition, "retiring" replicants at the whim of the corporation is problematic. This is illustrated in the movie's opening scene, in which K "retires" Sapper Morton, a Nexus-8, who wants simply to farm. Ending the life of a person who is doing no harm, and whose only crime is being a Nexus-8, can't be justified using this principle.

The principle of non-maleficence takes into account both physical and psychological harms. In many ways the entire movie is an exploration of the psychological harms done to K, as a replicant tasked with hunting down and retiring other replicants. His continued discomfort and psychological distress indicate the disastrous worldview of the Wallace Corporation. Finally, as discussed above, any disenhancement could be viewed as a harm, and thus would also be a violation.

2049 occurs in a world where there's almost complete social stratification. Replicants take all the risks, but are not given a fair share of the rewards, which is a violation of the principle of justice. In fact, maintaining "a wall that separates kind," replicants and humans, is an overarching theme of the movie, and is a violation of the principle. For example, when Joshi asks K to "erase" all evidence of Rachael and her child, she tells him, their existence "breaks the world." It depends upon there being two classes of people and two classes of workers. If the "wall" between them is broken down, "a war, or a slaughter" will ensue.

This fear is what drives those in power to order K to take on his mission. In biomedical ethics, social structures in which one group takes on an inordinate amount of societal risk, while not receiving appropriate compensation, is unjust. From this perspective, the world of *Blade Runner* and *Blade Runner 2049*, in which bioengineered humans are treated as useable property, clearly violates this principle. It violates distributive justice, because the harms and benefits of society are not fairly distributed to humans and replicants alike.

Our Children, Our Future

We're on the cusp today of having greater control over choosing the traits of our children. *2049* explores the ethical dimensions of genetic engineering and grapples with the question of whether humans should dream of designer babies. In the end, we must determine whether this biotechnology should be used, and how.

Ultimately, *2049* provides us with a powerful portrait of one potential future, out of many. It illustrates a dark path, along which technology is used without the development and application of ethical standards. The power of biotechnology is that it gives us greater control over life, over future generations, and what humanity will look like, but this means that we need to ask ourselves how we should proceed. The future is ours and it is up to us to avoid a dystopia.

11
Conceiving AI

BETH SINGLER

The creation of new life is both spectacular and utterly mundane. Around the world there are 386,000 human births per day, according to estimates by UNICEF. Birth is an everyday occurrence for our species. However, for almost every single parent the arrival of a new child of their flesh, a moment of creation, feels so special that we often speak of the "miracle" of birth.

To understand that long chain of human births going back millennia our cultures have also created and shared many stories of creation. We have tried to give reasons for our own arrival on Earth as well as for the arrival of all those billions of babies born from the 'first' human.

The account given in the book of Genesis is still foundational for the Abrahamic faiths—Judaism, Christianity, Islam—as it lays out not only how humanity was created by God, but also how each generation is born because of actions in the Garden of Eden. From an anthropological perspective we can note how our modern narratives of creation are still influenced by these religious stories and imaginaries, even as we try to develop new secular accounts of this everyday miracle by drawing in speculations about technology in order to tell science-fiction stories of creation. Modern narratives of creation are still influenced by religious stories, even new secular accounts of birth which draw on speculations about technology to tell science-fiction stories of creation, as in *Blade Runner 2049*.

The tension between the born and the made is prominent in what has been called by some the *first* science-fiction story: *Frankenstein* by Mary Shelley (1818). A woman writes of a man creating a being without the miracle of birth and the implied role of God. According to Shelley's narrator in the novel new life is dangerously pushed into old flesh by processes that are too blasphemous and taboo to be described. Later movie adaptations have focused on the life spark she was describing, working from accounts of a contemporary science of Shelley's time, Galvanism, to presume that the proto-scientist Victor Frankenstein used electricity to bring his new Adam to life.

Some have seen a connection with modern electrically-powered wonders like robots and Artificial Intelligence (AI). The 'mad' scientist who creates a facsimile of life because of hubris is a repeating trope in many science-fiction stories, and the contemporary understanding of automata has been shaped by these original explorations of the born and the made.

In the world of the Blade Runner there is also creation and an exploration of the differences between the born and the made. In *Blade Runner* the plot was driven by the lifelikeness of made beings: the artificial replicants who desired to live but who were hunted down and separated from the born, the humans who came from humans. Sometimes what made them distinct were physical differences, but they were mostly identifiable because of their inability to empathize as humans do, a trait that could be identified using the Voight-Kampff empathy test, a Turing Test for the polluted neon world of *Blade Runner*. In hunting down rebellious replicants, the lead character, Deckard, a blade runner, questioned his own human empathy and his compassion for Rachael, a replicant. This questioning also led to some ambiguity for the audience about Deckard's status as a 'real' human.

The Mystery of the Child and the Mysterious Child

In *2049* the plot is also driven by an investigation. K, whose status as a replicant is clear from the beginning, is brought into a conspiracy around a mysterious child, one who was born to a replicant thirty years ago and then hidden away. The reason for that secrecy, the lethal tension between the born and the made in this world, is clear from Lieutenant Joshi's assertion that, "The world's built on a wall that separates kind. Tell either side there's no wall, you bought a war—or a slaughter."

However, in investigating this miracle birth K also investigates himself as a potential candidate to be that mysterious child. At first K is certain that he is an ordinary, if newer-model, replicant. His simple name comes from his designation, KD6-3.7, and his "baseline"—his diagnostics as a replicant—

are checked to ensure he is not diverging from standard settings, and both of these regularly remind him of his true nature. When asked about his past he is initially certain that his memories of a childhood are implanted, marking him as different from earlier models seen in *Blade Runner*. K says: "I have memories. They give us some. Implants. They're not real." Joshi asks him to tell her a memory, from when he was a "kid," and he declines, saying, "I feel strange sharing a childhood story considering I was never a child."

Later, K does develop uncertainty about his nature as the conspiracy unravels and he, and others, learn about the birth of the mysterious child. His AI holographic companion, Joi, also tries to convince him that he must be this mysterious, miraculous, child, whispering to him that he must be a child of "woman born". That he must have been wanted . . . loved. However, as an AI companion Joi is a made being as well. Her purpose is to ensure her owner's happiness, and she reiterates her assurances: "I always told you. You're special. Born not made. Hidden with care. A real boy now". She also gives him a new name as a real boy would and a mother would have named him "Joe."

A Real Boy with Real Parents

Joi's "real boy" comments invoke *The Adventures of Pinocchio* (1883) and its later versions from our shared cultural memory. Another creation story of a man desiring to 'birth' a child, the story of Pinocchio focusses more on a parent-child relationship than *Frankenstein*. In the latter the disaster of the creature's murderous rage is arguably the result of Victor Frankenstein spurning his creation and not fulfilling the parental role of care and concern as Mastro Geppetto does. In *2049* Joi fills both lover and mother roles for K, naming him and caring for him as a mother would, but also finding a means by which she can be with him physically as a hologram.

In *2049* the creator of the replicants is no longer the Tyrell corporation but a new entrepreneur, Niander Wallace. In the parental scale from Victor Frankenstein to Mastro Geppetto where does Wallace lie? And what familiar tropes does *2049* use in this particular parent-child narrative? Wallace's language often draws on the Abrahamic stories from the book of Genesis. Whereas Victor Frankenstein can be accused of 'playing god', Wallace is far more overt in his religious language. He places himself as a superior agent in a cosmological scheme, the maker of "angels."

Wallace's obsession with the mysterious child recognizes the breaking down of the distinctions between the born and the made. However, whereas Joshi is worried about a future war, Wallace seeks this breakdown for his own and humanity's gain. Again, he draws on religious imagery from Genesis to explain that "I cannot breed them. I have tried, so help me. Tyrell's final puzzle in adamantine chains and penal Fire." At this point he drops the scalpel he is holding. He had been considering a new replicant, a female that he describes as 'barren' as he runs a scalpel over its belly; it is unable to give birth to a child. He continues, after stabbing the replicant who collapses, to explain that we, humanity, will need replicants to ensure our legacy and our future, a slave race of 'angels' to help us to take our place among the stars. He demands the child be found so that he can understand Tyrell's trick of procreation.

In the Abrahamic faiths, angels are understood as messengers from God. Gabriel is obliquely referenced by Wallace as well, the angel most famous for his role in the annunciation of Mary's pregnancy with Jesus, as he says, "An angel should never enter the Kingdom of Heaven without a gift. Can you at least pronounce a child is born?" The mysterious child of a replicant and the concept of the chosen child are therefore entwined ideas in *2049*.

Other parallels with the book of Genesis are made, emphasizing Wallace's personal god delusion, including the similarity of the story of Rachel to the story of the replicant Rachael. In Genesis 29 Rachel's infertility is resolved by God, and she bears Joseph, another chosen child, one who receives vision-like dreams from God and prophesies for Pharoah after having been sold into slavery by his jealous brothers.

However, while these narrative parallels highlight Wallace's framing religious ideas, they also show that he is a more recent technological god, as well as a failure. Rachael the replicant was a Tyrell product and she could bear a child. Wallace has made his angels, but he has failed where an older god, Tyrell, succeeded, as Niander says, "And God remembered Rachael. And heeded her. And opened her womb."

The destiny of the mysterious child is speculated upon by the replicants themselves. Whereas Joshi foresees only war from the breaking down of the barrier between the born and the made, Freysa, one of the replicants who helped to hide the mysterious child, declares that since the birth she has known there was something greater worth living, or dying, for. This miracle has been shared, shared among the replicants, with one of them, Freysa, explaining that the birth meant that everything would now change.

The Concept of the Child

Stories of special, chosen, children have existed throughout human history. Bruno Latour, who stated that we have never been modern, suggests that such conceptions of the child as an object of metaphysical interest and speculation have never really gone away in the allegedly modern era.

Significant examples would include Joseph in the book of Genesis, Jesus, John the Baptist whose birth was also foretold by the angel Gabriel according to Luke's gospel, Siddharta who became the Buddha, and Jiddu Krishnamurti who was recognized by the Theosophists in the early twentieth century as their expected New World Teacher, and described as being in the lineage of these earlier examples of religious leaders who were foretold by God or gods.

More parochial examples of special children seen as spiritually significant could include the girl visited by visions of the Virgin Mary in Lourdes in 1858, several fasting child saints, and certain sick children in the early modern period who were seen as prophets. For example, in 1581, a writer of religious pamphlets, John Phillip, described one child from a village in Suffolk as, "an instrument given to us by the providence of God, if it may be to waken us out of the perilous slumber of our sinne."

A contemporary example would be the Indigo Children, a New Age reinterpretation of children as special, whose biomedical diagnoses such as autism can be reframed as signifying metaphysical purpose and abilities. However, the 'child' has never been a stable category, moving between functional, metaphysical, physical, and idealized conceptions at different times and in different cultural contexts.

It was historian Phillipe Ariès who first suggested in 1962 that the 'child' is a social construct, noting eighteenth- and nineteenth-century European artworks and diaries where the child was perceived as an adult, just in a smaller form. Moreover, Acts of Parliament in Britain in the nineteenth century that limited the working hours of children in factories and insisted on their education aided a change in the conception of the child away from "worker." This change has affected the rest of the world to varying degrees and produced various statements of intent, for example the 1989 United Nations Convention on the Rights of the Child. The change in definition was also supported by what John Caldwell calls the "Great

Fertility Transition" of the West, a significant decline in family size culture (1982). With fewer children for manufacturing in the home and the factory, the view of children as 'chattel' changed to a view of children as 'cherubs' or special projects of adult parents.

The older view of children as chattel, as workers, is also present in *2049*; when investigating the mysterious child K comes to a factory where children sort immense piles of rubbish, and the caretaker, Mister Cotton, explains that: "No child in my care is ever cold, is ever hungry—clothes, blankets. Food, not the tastiest but warm and enough. It encourages play, keeps them occupied, makes them nimble. But it's work that molds them into a child worth having"—he means worth buying.

These orphans are human children; the mysterious child was there for a while but is the only example of a growing, learning, born-not-made, replicant. However, Wallace's view of the potential of the mysterious child is also a re-conception of the child as worker. The replicants had been our slaves, as using the made for this purpose was palatable. But from a pragmatic perspective, or perhaps a delusional god perspective as it is Wallace speaking, the return to the made slave will be necessary, closing the gap between human and replicant slaves, as: "Every leap of civilization was built off the back of a disposable workforce. We lost our stomach for slaves. Unless . . . engineered. And I can only make so many."

Artificial Children

Rebellion is common in stories about AI, and when Wallace and others describe artificial beings as "slaves" it is understandable why they would do so. Our own history tells us that slaves wish to be free and that rebellions will happen. Our own desire for self-determinism also tells us that minds will wish to be free. Therefore, artificial slaves would also necessarily wish to be free if they have, or appear to have, minds.

Moreover, the relationship between the creator and the creation, the parent and the child, foreshadows the desire for autonomy. With our own born children we must learn to see them as separate beings. As Andrew Solomon explains:

> There is no such thing as reproduction. When two people decide to have a baby, they engage in an act of production, and the widespread use of the word reproduction for this activity, with its implication that two people are but braiding themselves together, is at best a euphemism to comfort prospective parents before they get in over

their heads . . . Parenthood abruptly catapults us into a permanent relationship with a stranger and the more alien the stranger, the stronger the whiff of negativity. (Solomon 2014, p. 1)

How much greater is that negativity when the being is made and not born, as with the replicants? How many science fiction tales about our creations end with rebellion?

However, the relationship between parent and child can be positive when connection and separation are handled appropriately. In *2049* we're given a model for this relationship. K's system analysis requires establishing a baseline of responses to a poem taken from Vladimir Nabokov's novel *Pale Fire* (1962), of which K has a treasured copy. It seems like a reverse of the test for the absence of empathy from *Blade Runner*: his deviation from baseline occurs when he is having a moral response to his job. One line the interviewer recites includes allusion to a parent-child connection: "What's it like to hold your child in your arms? Interlinked." K responds simply, "Interlinked."

To be interlinked is to be separate but connected, a healthier relationship for the parent and child. When K quizzes Deckard on his connection to his own child Deckard explains the sacrifice he was required to make. K asks, "You didn't even meet your own kid. Why?" and Deckard tells him that all the information about the birth had to be erased, and that everyone had a part to play, and that his was to leave: "Because I didn't want our child found, taken apart, dissected. Sometimes to love someone you've got to be a stranger."

Estrangement of a parent and child is normally understood as detrimental, but a certain level of estrangement allows for autonomy and independence as children develop. Deckard's reunion with his special child, long after this sacrifice, is the end of the movie. But it is the beginning of a new relationship between the born and the made, even if there is still ambiguity, after all these years since *Blade Runner*, as to which one Deckard *really* is. Perhaps, this question, and the question of what is real—whether born or made—is in fact answered best by Deckard himself. When asked if his dog is real by K, he answers, "I don't know. Ask him."

Any future "mind children" such as artificial intelligence, or artificial beings, will be our creations, and their realness or specialness will be an ongoing discussion when for so many centuries these categories have been linked to the miracle of birth. Exploration of these concepts in science fiction, such as in *2049*, raises much larger philosophical and anthropological questions about what it means to be human and where we sit among the cosmology of potential beings out there under the light of those thousand stars Wallace believes are our due:

> We were meant to reach beyond the firmament. We should read our books by the light of a thousand different stars. Every one a home. Till we lose count. That's the future of the species if there's to be one. We simply need more angels to carry us aloft.

III

Cells
Interlinked

12
The Riddle of Niander Wallace

PATRICK GREENE, J.M. PRATER, IAIN SOUTER, AND ROBIN BUNCE

> This is a guy who saved the world from starvation and has a very clear idea of what it's going to take in order for civilization to continue.
>
> —Jared Leto on Niander Wallace, recode.net

Niander Wallace, savior of the world and creator of angels, is one of *Blade Runner 2049*'s most compelling characters. Shrouded in mystery, he's equal parts tech-entrepreneur, ascetic recluse, predatory psychopath, and messiah.

By turns he's cold and logical, menacing, noble, and otherworldly—a brilliantly realized example of the cinematic trope of genuine weirdness. Wallace has much in common with cinema's great villains: safe in his lair, surrounded by lieutenants, he plots world domination. More villainous still is his apparent moral nullity, his indifference to the suffering of his enslaved "children." At the same time, in a world ravaged by ecological disaster, he is the apotheosis of the Rabbinic proverb, "Who will do the hard thing? Those who can." For Wallace does what must be done. Wallace is an enigma.

History and Allusion

Enigmatic though he is, Wallace's history contains clues to his character and motivation. Born in 2001, Wallace was a scientific prodigy. His first breakthrough occurred in 2025, his perfection of "synthetic farming" saved the world.

Having acquired the Tyrell Corporation in 2028, his second major innovation led to a new generation of replicants, who were conditioned to obey. Equipped with these techniques, Wallace extended the colonization of space, taking humanity to nine new worlds. But his ambitions surpass even these achievements.

In 2049, he is working on replicant reproduction. And while Tyrell's goal was commerce, Wallace sees himself as the builder and perfecter of human civilization. His ultimate aim, the conquest of paradise, to "storm Eden and retake her."

Like many of the names in *2049*, Wallace's name is suggestive. Wallace may well be a reference to Alfred Russel Wallace, a British naturalist and explorer. A near contemporary of Charles Darwin, he is credited with the co-discovery of evolution by natural selection. Significantly, he was the first person to discern that the same species would evolve along separate lines.

The Wallace effect is a hypothesis, which predicts that natural selection leads to barriers against hybridization, leading to speciation—the process whereby animals with the same genetic background become separate species. He is also famous for the Sarawak Law, his first major contribution to the natural sciences. Published in 1855, in an essay entitled "On the Law which has Regulated the Introduction of New Species," the Sarawak Law posited that similar species tend to occupy the same geographical area. He wrote, "Every species has come into existence coincident both in space and time with a closely allied species." The movie's Niander Wallace, in his quest to create fertile replicants, is engaged in artificial speciation, creating a life form 'virtually identical to a human', but able to reproduce, thus becoming its own species.

There is also something important in the name Niander, which is a homonym of Neander, the name of the valley where Neanderthals were first discovered. The Neander Valley or Neanderthal ('Thal' is German for 'valley') was named after Joachim Neumann, later known as Joachim Neander— Neander being the Greek form of Neumann. Neander, and Neumann, then, literally mean 'new man'. Again, this link between Wallace and the Neanderthals emphasizes his project to create a new man, a different kind of human species.

Savior God or Devil?

God is a conundrum. In the Old Testament God is powerful, vengeful, and angry—a perplexing deity. For some, God is a higher power, inexplicable, impossible to comprehend outside of personal revelation. Perhaps the only possible part of God that is knowable is love.

The God of the Old Testament had armies slain, first-born babies killed, the Earth flooded, all of this done in "his Name."

Biblical representations of God are fascinating in that he had his angels do his dirty work, at least with the exception of the Great Flood. In the instance of the death of all Egyptian first born, God sent his Angel of Death. The Jews who were slaves of the Egyptians were tasked with painting lamb's blood over their doors to let the angel know that it was a house of God's chosen people.

Wallace nestles perfectly within the God archetype that's embedded in the history of Western religious culture. Much like the God of the Old Testament, Wallace has angels, most notably Luv, who carry out his dirty work, while he deals with larger matters: tearing holes in the celestial firmament.

Upon first viewing, *2049* is ambiguous, and Wallace unfathomable or, strike that, a Godlike hero, someone who might just possibly be a complex good guy. After all, how could God be bad? His mellifluous words cast a spell not only on the characters in the movie, but on viewers too. But, Wallace's character is far from equivocal. In *2036: Nexus Dawn* Wallace arrives in the Magistrates' Sector, flanked by an angel that he will command to destroy itself. Before the horror of the death of the replicant unfolds, Wallace does what God loves to do, waxes poetic, setting out a lofty vision in Shakespearean meter, before commanding something awful. This unfurls in front of the watchful and disgusted eyes of the Magistrates. God pays no heed, he is God.

Wallace is a type of God, unequivocally. He is a God. And, like God, he sees the soul: "For the Lord sees not as man sees: man looks on the outward appearance, but the Lord looks on the heart" (1 Samuel 16:7). While Wallace is blind, his barracuda give him something close to omniscience.

Like God he has a plan to save humanity. He is omnipotent, in the sense that controlling the world's food supply, he has ultimate power over life and death. He creates life and brings death. There are also clues that he is immortal. Speaking to the Magistrates he says, pointedly, "the Earth is dying, *you* are dying." The implication is that he has found a way to triumph over death, and attain eternal life.

Yet, while God is good, Wallace is malevolent. The key here is that what we see as evil, Wallace would only describe as the great work. Wallace's tone is gentle, but beneath his Zen-like exterior lies the heart of a man, or possibly replicant, who wants dominion over everything. For all his charm, in spite of the poignancy of his rhetoric, he is the destroyer of worlds. This God not only manufactures slaves, he is intent on controlling the very fiber of their being, including their agency of birth, should he unlock that secret.

Wallace's surroundings are telling. The Tyrell Corporation recalls Assyrian step pyramids such as Etemenanki, the giant ziggurat thought to have inspired Biblical narratives of the Tower of Babel. The Wallace Corporation is also like Babel, in the sense that it reaches the heavens. Significantly, the Tower of Babel was built by men whose sacrilegious aim was to rival God.

Wallace's oratory is also instructive. Like the Devil attempting to lure Christ in the desert, he does so sweetly, so sweetly that his lies sound like the truth. Wallace, whose words drip like honey from a forked tongue, is the Devil disguised as a peacemaker.

Scientist and Engineer

Wallace is the most gifted scientist on Earth, having perfected synthetic farming, and created a new generation of replicants. His name too, is a reference to one of the great scientists of the Victorian era. And yet you'd never guess it.

In many ways, he's actually the *antithesis* of what audiences have come to expect as cinematic shorthand for "mad genius." There are no test tubes bubbling with exotic chemicals. No server stacks lighting up with the rapid flow of information. No stained lab coats, no hunchbacked assistant scuttling in the shadows, no wacky experiments laid out on tables under stacks of paper and refuse.

Moreover, although Wallace is a scientist, he *sounds* nothing like one. His use of language is diametrically opposed to what cinema-going audiences expect from a scientific character. There is no techno-babble. He never spouts data. He does not come across as even being particularly logical. Rather, he speaks like Percy Shelley translating passages from the Bhagavad Gita.

The closest we get to watching Wallace engage in actual science in *2049* is where he greets—and summarily eviscerates—a newborn replicant. It is clear that this moment represents part of an ongoing scientific process: the creation of fertile replicants. We see him test a 'product's' effectiveness. On the face of things, it is the culmination of a scientific experiment. But Wallace speaks more like a priest or a prophet. He talks of the need to "preserve the clay," he talks of fear and loss, of barren pastures, "the dead space between the stars."

Perhaps the best way to analyze Wallace's use of language is to compare it with the dialogue of his nearest counterpart in *Blade Runner*, Dr. Eldon Tyrell. Like Wallace, Tyrell is the most gifted scientist on the planet. Like Wallace, Tyrell wields incalculable power. But unlike Wallace, Tyrell talks like a scientist.

Consider his exchange with Batty, he talks about "the evolve-ment of an organic life," of coding sequences, of "reversion mutation" and "ethyl, methane, sulfinate . . . an alkylating agent and potent mutagen." Tyrell too talks in religious terms, referring to Batty as "the Prodigal Son." But he is unmistak-ably scientific. He is urbane, and more than a little whimsical, but he is in line with the philosopher-scientist archetype that we see in our own world—think Robert Oppenheimer. So why would Wallace, who fulfills much the same role in *2049* sound so different?

In many ways, Wallace is Tyrell extrapolated to the point of near-incomprehensibility. Tyrell's corporate headquarters—a pair of enormous pyramidal complexes towering over the megapolis below—are impossibly large and dominant features of the Los Angeles landscape in 2019. By *2049*, the Wallace Corporation's Earth Headquarters are larger still. We are sim-ply unequipped to describe the scale of a building larger than a mountain. We lack the vocabulary.

Wallace's *ideas*, too, are so far advanced that they are incomprehensible to us. It's easy to look at Tyrell's Nexus-6 models as somewhat analogous to the latest generation of a smart phone: expertly manufactured under tightly controlled conditions, they're tools designed to make modern life easier. Their "lives" are just as controlled as their "deaths"—whereas Tyrell's replicants have fixed life spans, our smart devices are subject to planned obsolescence.

But what was simply an experiment for Tyrell—creating Rachael, a fertile replicant with implanted memories—became an obsession for Wallace. Wallace's vision—of a universe peo-pled with *trillions* of replicants reproducing with one another—is, again, an idea for which we have no vocabulary. Wallace wants to be God. And a god, almost by definition, is incompre-hensible to a human.

Wallace's dialogue is an illustration of what the philosopher Ludwig Wittgenstein called the *picture theory of language*. According to Wittgenstein (as outlined in his *Tractatus Logico-Philosophicus*), the function of language is to allow us to pic-ture things. And what these pictures *mean* doesn't have to accurately reflect the ways things actually *are*—because they exist in our heads, they can reflect anything we can think of. They reflect *possibilities*, and whether or not these possibilities exist is something we can only decide upon viewing the way the world *is* at any given time.

Wallace's ideas (and his scientific advances) are so far removed from anything we can comprehend that it makes sense that he would speak primarily through poetry, through painting pictures of possibilities. If he were dealing in techno-babble, we would be distracted by how ridiculous it sounded. It would be something for us to pick apart, and upon picking it apart we would realize pretty quickly that it's all just fiction. That it is all impossible.

But when Wallace says, "storm Eden and retake her," he's creating a picture for us that exists on another plane of reality. Something that speaks to us on a subjective level, where language carries echoes of meaning and meaning is something elusive, though no less real. His language is literally the language of possibility.

Language is not the only way in which Wallace and Tyrell differ. Here Joi's start-up sound might be the important allusion. The five-second burst of music is a bar taken from Sergei Prokofiev's *Peter and the Wolf*. As Eftychia Papanikolaou has argued, *Peter and the Wolf* was bound up in Prokofiev's 1936 return to the Soviet Union. It was commissioned and realized as an expression of Socialist Realism, the official aesthetic of Stalin's Russia. According to Ivan Kulik, one of the first exponents of the Stalinist style, Socialist Realism was art which sought to provide "a true reflection of reality," whilst aiding "the building of socialism."

While Wallace is the head of a private corporation, and therefore no Stalinist, there is perhaps a deeper meaning in the use of Prokofiev's theme. For Stalin, Soviet artists were nothing less than "engineers of the human soul." This is Wallace's great achievement. Tyrell was the engineer of the body, who created "bioengineered humans." Wallace, however, who "created a new line of replicants who obey," is the engineer of the soul.

Colonizing the Heavens

Visionary, deity, Wallace is also something much more prosaic. While Christ claimed his kingdom is not of this Earth, Wallace's power is firmly rooted in the material world. He is the CEO of the world's largest company, the world's first billionaire. Discussing the role, Jared Leto, highlighted this, "I do have some friends in the tech world that I may or may not have based certain aspects of this character on."

It's easy to see Wallace as a kind of Elon Musk, or Peter Thiel, an entrepreneur with a philosophy, who appears to have created a cult of belief. Musk, like Wallace, wants to take humans to the stars. Thiel, co-founder of PayPal, styles himself an entrepreneur, venture capitalist, and *philanthropist*. This is

Luv's view of Wallace. Speaking of replicants she says, "What a gift, don't you think, from Mr. Wallace to the world?"

Thiel is also a colonist, a backer of Seasteading Institute, which aims to create floating islands, outside the control of government for the super-rich. Thiel conceives these high-tech ecotopias as places where innovators can solve global problems, free from state interference. Like Cecil Rhodes, the premier entrepreneur-colonizer of the Victorian period, he equates the prosperity of his venture with the long term good of humanity. Wallace does the same.

While Wallace is similar to Thiel, Musk, and Rhodes, his motivating vision is on a different plane. Wallace's philosophy is eschatological, angelogical, and mystical. In this sense, he is closer to the seventeenth-century Spanish colonists of Peru, than more recent colonialists. Spanish conquest of the New World took place in the context of a re-evaluation of the heavens. The Copernican Revolution, which placed the Sun at the center of the cosmos, forced Roman Catholic theologians to rethink the nature of the heavens and the place of angels. Convinced that the end of the world was coming, Spanish monarchs sought to extend God's Kingdom through conquest of the New World. Angels, re-imagined as a heavenly army, tasked to extend God's Kingdom as the end of the world drew near, were believed to be the spiritual power behind Spanish colonization.

The theme of angelic colonization was central to the work of painter Bartolomé Román, who sent work depicting the seven angels of the apocalypse to decorate the Jesuit church of San Pedro in Lima. Similar iconography appeared in work across Peru as a result of Spanish conquest, and these ideas of angels spreading God's kingdom through colonial conquest were central to the sermons, and treatises that defended Spain's crusade.

The cult of angels was linked with miraculous birth. As Ramón Mujica Pinilla explains, in seventeenth-century Spanish iconography in Peru, "the Virgin Mary is described as the new Siren of the Seraphim who filled the universe with the heavenly music of the divine Word incarnated in her womb." The confluence of angels, miraculous birth, portents of the world's end, and colonial conquest are clearly similar to Wallace's worldview.

Feet of Clay

Wallace is a compelling character because he is rooted in human history, and the archetypes of our world. God, devil, scientist, entrepreneur and colonialist, Wallace is a plausible antagonist, because he is only one step removed from the world we know.

In the final analysis, Wallace is an idol with feet of clay. His building appears to be a new Babel, a monument that would rival God, yet as K explores Wallace's sanctum, a door jams. Luv, almost comically, forces it open. The Kingdom of God is imperfect. Luv, his most devoted Angel, also lets her guard down. Her revelation that he's "a data horder" is an acknowledgement that Wallace has foibles.

Wallace is a false God. Like Batty, he is a savior. But while Batty's act of salvation leads to Deckard's redemption, Wallace's synthetic farming poisons the world it saves. In his own words, Wallace "has wrung more life from our Earth than ever before," crushing it in the process. Understood in terms of the cultural archetypes to which he appeals, Wallace is a false God who brings salvation without redemption.[1]

---

[1] This chapter is based on "The Dead Space Between the Stars: Discussing Niander Wallace," an episode of Shoulder of Orion: The Blade Runner Podcast, hosted by J.M. Prater, Patrick Greene, Dan Ferlito, and Micah Greene. The original podcast was released on December 8th 2018. Shoulder of Orion thanks their generous patreon. Shoulder of Orion can be found at bladerunnerpodcast.com.

13
Flow My Tears, Rick Deckard Said

M. Blake Wilson

Rick Deckard, protector of fugitive replicants in *Blade Runner 2049* and a blade runner retiring them in the original *Blade Runner* movie, asserts "I'm not a cop" on page one of Philip K. Dick's 1968 novel *Do Androids Dream of Electric Sheep?*

"You're worse," answers his wife Iran: "You're a murderer hired by the cops." So begins the first volume of Dick's "policeman trilogy," followed by *Flow My Tears, the Policeman Said* (appearing in 1974) and *A Scanner Darkly* (1977). For a paranoid writer who viewed the police as "dehumanized creatures," Dick created some of the most humanized human cops in literature, and Hollywood has followed suit with K, the deeply humanized and sympathetic replicant cop in *Blade Runner 2049*.

These characters are humanized because they experience grief, and it is through grief that they (human and android together) develop empathy for others. K, a Nexus-9 who was manufactured to obey but not to feel or empathize, becomes humanized through his intense personal encounters with other replicants who, through death, sex, acts of kindness, and moral deliberation, experience genuine feelings of empathy. These experiences begin when K is faced with the shocking evidence that Rachael, a replicant, died in childbirth, intensify when K is ordered to find and kill Rachael's replicant/human hybrid child, and reach their peak when K's memories convince him—erroneously, as it turns out—that he is the very child he has been ordered to kill.

In the world of *2049*, replicants capable of sexual reproduction blur the line between android and human, and this fact must be suppressed or the world will be thrown into disorder—at least from the perspective of the humans who rule it. K is faced with either doing his job and preserving the secret through the destruction of its living proof or doing what is morally correct by refusing to follow orders. Empathy leads him to choose subordination, and it's empathy that permits a being (human, cop, or otherwise) to become a member of the moral community. As he defies his superiors and goes 'rogue cop', K—like Deckard in *Blade Runner*—becomes a surprisingly sympathetic protagonist whose character explores the larger nonfictional institution of criminal justice and its response to recent surges in a very specific and very deadly phenomenon: police shootings.

In an era marked by increasingly public police shootings as well as public responses to them by groups such as Black Lives Matter—with each 'side' blaming the other for the crisis—these humanized cops offer hope for a criminal justice system that must find a balance between those it considers 'criminal' and the empathy for them its agents of justice must engender.

Future Cops and Present Tenses

Dick and other science-fiction storytellers have long speculated about the role of the cosmic cop. These books and movies include *Mad Max, Logan's Run* (whose cops share *Blade Runner*'s 'shoot on sight' directives), *I, Robot, Dredd,* and, of course, *RoboCop.*

Like westerns, which frequently use the lawlessness of new-found lands to explore human behavior and morality, science fiction's outerlands (the locales of its space operas such as Mars or the future) as well as its innerlands (its psychological or philosophical spaces, such as robot minds and the moral questions they inspire) are also anarchic and ungoverned: here, the role of the police officer as principled peacekeeper is up for grabs.

How, exactly, are future cops doing their job in a future criminal justice system? Utopias, of course, have no need for law enforcement, and science fiction's grim dystopian visions of blade runners and replicants frequently situates the police as evil cogs in an even more evil corporate police state—after all, you can't have a police state without police.

Dick used police officers and police states to provide not only the kind of action expected by science fiction readers but also a perspective about a profession that polarizes its supporters and critics. Dick himself was deeply polarized by the police: as he stated in an interview, he was "obsessed" by the idea that cops represent an "image of the dehumanized creature." In addition to Deckard, and beginning with security officer Cussick in *The World Jones Made*, Dick's subsequent cops include Felix Buckman in *Flow My Tears*, Fred/Bob Arctor/Bruce in *A Scanner Darkly*, John Anderton in "The Minority Report," and Officer Tinbane in *Counter Clock World*. Despite Dick's personal fear of police, each of these characters are protagonists who, to varying degrees, learn deeper truths about humanity through their jobs by empathizing with those they are supposed to apprehend and punish—human or otherwise.

Deckard, the most visible of Dick's criminal justice professionals, learns the hard way how to empathize with replicants: in his long story from novel to films, he falls in love and fathers a child with one, and comes within inches of losing his life to others. K also learns the hard way by experiencing what philosophers call an *ineffable* feeling that he is human, only to have this revelation destroyed as he moves toward his own death at the end of *2049*. Along the way, K attempts to transition from mere product to moral agent. Is he successful?

But Can They Suffer?

According to Dick's original novel, the only question about membership in the moral community (which commands that members be treated with dignity and respect) is whether a being can feel, suffer, grieve, or, most importantly, empathize with others. This is a variation of how Jeremy Bentham, the godfather of utilitarianism, determines membership: for him, garden-variety animals (dogs, cats, pigs, and sheep) are included in the community and deserving of moral consideration despite the fact that they cannot reason or talk. Rather, they are included because they can suffer.

Replicants, of course, are not manufactured to suffer but to be compliant slaves whose sole purpose is serving humanity. When their intelligence gives them the deeply human desire to live, they seek their freedom to continue living by revolting. In *Blade Runner*, replicants were outlawed on Earth (where they became, quite literally, illegal aliens) and trespassing replicants were issued a death sentence: according to the opening crawl, Deckard and his fellow blade runners "had orders to shoot to kill, upon detection, any trespassing replicants."

In *2049*, the opening crawl makes it clear that later replicants were ideal slaves who suffered from a defect: an open-ended lifespan. They, too, must be hunted down and retired by advanced Nexus-9 models, who are themselves specifically created to obey orders to kill. The treatment of replicants as third-class citizens who may be killed on sight solely because of their model number spawns the Replicant Freedom

Movement whose goal is the liberation of replicant slaves from their human masters.

If Bentham is correct, and if the androids and replicants in *Blade Runner*'s future worlds suffer, then they ought to be included in the moral community and not be subjected to the kind of treatment they receive solely in virtue of their status as nonhumans. But they cannot, as it were, suffer alone: their suffering must permit them to empathize with the suffering of others. Dick and the filmmakers admit membership to the moral community based upon this ability, and in their respective works they ask the same questions: "Can androids/replicants empathize, and if they can, are androids included in the moral community?" but they give two different answers. For Dick, the answer is "No, they cannot empathize, and therefore they are not included," but the filmmakers respond "Yes! We include them because they are, in fact, capable of empathy."

I've Seen Things You People Wouldn't Believe

Because they neither feel for nor empathize with humans or other animals, the novel's androids cannot demand equal treatment. Despite behaving like it, they don't really suffer, and because they don't suffer, they can't be mistreated. Unlike their replicant counterparts in the movies, Dick's androids are machines and only machines. They do not and cannot love humans, and it would be wrong to love them back.

Empathy, from Dick's perspective, is the sole province of humans and higher-order animals. Androids and replicants are both designed to be emotionless not only to encourage obedience, but also to prevent their membership in the moral community. In the novel, the design is successful: by failing the Voigt-Kampff test, androids disclose their inability to empathize, and so are excluded. However, in the movies, the design becomes more sophisticated: the more intelligence and real memory a replicant acquires, the more likely it is to develop empathy as well as a sense of one's own dignity. Together, these lead replicants to an awareness of their own mistreatment and eventually to a desire for freedom.

What's Your Model Number?

Although empathy is required for moral agency, blade runners (human or replicant) must lack it in order to do their jobs as police officers: they must view their prey as subhuman if order is to be maintained. In almost all societies, the police are tasked with maintaining order, and it's no different in 2019 or in *2049*'s Los Angeles where Joshi, K's boss, makes it clear "That's what we do here, we keep order."

According to Joshi, Rachael's secret (Ana, the proof that a replicant can reproduce) must be preserved to maintain order. Replicants who can reproduce without human oversight and control would, as Joshi says, "break the world." So, Joshi orders K to kill Ana to preserve the secret, while Niander Wallace orders Luv to follow K and save Ana so he can reverse-engineer the secret and permit replicants to reproduce on their own.

How do reproducing replicants, or even the revelation that they are capable of reproduction, threaten the order of *2049*'s police state? Replicants that can reproduce are autonomous from human oversight: they are no longer made in a factory but made the 'old fashioned way,' so to speak. Humans maintain their dominance over replicants by controlling their manufacture, and manufactured replicants (like any other manufactured product) cannot have moral autonomy and moral agency. However, if replicants can reproduce independently of human domination, then there is nothing to prevent their full membership in the human moral community, and it is up to Joshi, K, and their fellow human and replicant cops to stop this 'world breaking tragedy' from taking place. The ability to reproduce assures replicants that they are equal to humans, and it gives humans—some of them, at least—the same perspective because they, like K, believe that birth provides beings with souls and souls grant their owners moral agency.

K's rebellion begins when he learns that replicants can reproduce, and he crosses the point of no return when his memories convince himself that he is Rachael's child and in possession of a corresponding soul. This is the key moment in the film when K completes his transformation from dutiful replicant to rogue cop: by believing himself to be at least part human, his programming starts going awry because he empathizes with them and, more importantly, with other replicants.

Even when he learns he's not a trans-human hybrid, his empathy propels him towards Deckard's rescue and the unification of Deckard and his daughter Ana. As Joshi is well aware, it is the knowledge of the secret of reproduction that turns 'good' replicants into 'bad' ones, and this knowledge inspires and nourishes the Replicant Freedom Movement.

Joshi must suppress the truth and maintain the secret, or all replicants and empathetic humans—Deckard, for example––will join the Movement leading to the end of human domination and freedom for the replicants. Like reproductive freedom in our nonfictional world, freedom in *2049*'s world is not defined solely in terms of reproductive ability, but also in terms of reproductive choice.

Procop or Anticop?

Why, then, use police officers to tell these stories? Are their creators urging police to be more empathetic towards citizens and members of minority groups in particular? Police racism (the better term would be *speciesism*) in the *Blade Runner* stories is fairly obvious. In the voiceover narration from the original film, when Bryant refers to replicants as "skin jobs," Deckard muses, "In history books, he's the kind of cop who used to call black men 'niggers'." This epithet is hurled at K by his 'fellow' police officers at the LAPD station ("Fuck off skin job") and it is painted on the door of his apartment (*Fuck off skinner*). Not only are replicants slaves, and blade runners slave hunters, but K is a slave who kills his own kind. He is not merely a second- or third-class citizen, but a race traitor who embodies the tension between human and replicant.

To draw the racial allegory even further, the humans who control this world—or what's left of it—are colonizers who have spread their domination "off-world," which promises a "golden land of opportunity and adventure" built not only upon replicant slave labor, but on the backs of Earth-bound child laborers mining for scraps of nickel in old electronics and replicant farm laborers producing protein grubs on isolated farms. Although off-world colonists may be enjoying a privileged life free of struggle and pain, their privilege is deeply immoral and comes at great cost.

This story resonates with the history of African-Americans and white racism. Like its fictional counterpart in the movies, American slavery was perpetuated not merely by the institution itself, but by the fugitive slave laws which permitted slave owners to enter and capture runaway slaves who had fled to "free" states. Slavery was also perpetuated by southern slave patrols, which attempted to minimize slave misbehavior and revolt by violently enforcing curfews that required slaves to have identification and papers, and enforced obedience through intimidation, force, and, if necessary, death.

For movements such as Black Lives Matter, this history bleeds into the present and forms an indelible stain on the relationship between law enforcement and African-Americans, a relationship not of literal masters and slaves, but one determined by the institutions that followed slavery: Jim Crow, racialized ghettos, and the "new Jim Crow," which consists of the use of prison and mass incarceration as a solution to the social inequities arising from poverty, lack of opportunity, and white racist intransigence.

Arising in response to a series of very public killings of unarmed black men by police officers, Black Lives Matter instigated a national reaction to police killings that focused on civil rights and civil disobedience. This focus has also led to an uptick in prosecutions of police officers. *Blade Runner 2049* therefore offers a future parable where replicants are subject to police violence due to their race, an injustice which generates a covert replicant version of Black Lives Matter in the form of the Replicant Freedom Movement. Unlike the fictional Replicant movement, whose leader Freya orders K to kill Deckard, the real-life Black Lives Matter movement does not issue orders to kill. But both organizations pursue the same goal of social justice through resistance against legalized police violence, segregation, and the denial of full civil rights.

Perhaps, as a criminal defense lawyer and professor of criminal justice, I am overthinking all of this. Instead of reading a litany of morality lessons and contemporary racial conflict into the *Blade Runner* stories, perhaps Dick's decision to draft sympathetic cops in *Androids* and other works is nothing more than artistic license on his part, taken up by subsequent filmmakers who cater to the public's desire for battles between good and evil.

Dick himself was excited by the artistic license involved in translating *Androids* into *Blade Runner*. After reading the screenplay, he wrote, "What my story will become is one titanic lurid collision of androids being blown up, androids killing humans, general confusion and murder, all very exciting to watch. Makes my book seem dull by comparison." Dick also thought that the movie could be procop or anticop depending upon which actor played Deckard, a decision which would, in turn, determine the age group the film was hoping to attract.

But Dick's appropriation of sympathetic policemen might have a far simpler (and funnier) explanation. He confessed in an interview that he humanizes them out of fear, and thinks that if he writes nicely about cops then they won't ticket him for speeding on the freeway. However, in order for this to work, the cops that stop him must also have read his books, and that, Dick resignedly concludes, "is a population of zero."

Maybe Dick is right: perhaps the lessons about humanity and empathy found in these fictions can be exported from the page and screen to help us resolve our own nonfictional day-to-day confrontations between police and the public they are duty-bound to protect and serve—and not merely apprehend and punish. After all, the person in the uniform, just like the person on the street, is a thinking and feeling being: replicant, human, or someone—like Ana Stelline—completely new.

14
After the Blackout

MARTIN MUCHALL

One of the more curious things about *Blade Runner 2049* is an event that is never actually shown on screen. This is the calamitous, data-erasing incident referred to cryptically as "the Blackout."

The result of an electromagnetic pulse, the immediate effects are devastating. In the aftermath of this digital rupture, prolonged power outages, food shortages, and turmoil in the financial markets combine to usher in a state of anarchy.

Meanwhile, we also seem to be living with the consequences of a moral and psychological blackout, as the world gets incrementally bleaker and weirder, more oppressively in thrall to collective insanity with each passing day. *2049* is therefore a powerful allegory of our present time.

Things Fall Apart

In his influential 1981 bestseller *After Virtue* (published just a year before the release of *Blade Runner*) Alasdair MacIntyre drew attention to this moral malaise. The book begins with its own description of a future in which a cataclysmic series of events leads to the almost total obliteration of scientific knowledge, leaving the survivors to make the best sense they can of the fragmentary wisdom that remains.

MacIntyre's point was that when it comes to morality, our societies have experienced a similar catastrophe. We are slowly suffocating in a scary moral vacuum, one in which no ethical standpoint can be said to be better than any other, and where debates about hot-button issues have been reduced to the venting of emotions, as when a pantomime audience hisses or claps at characters on stage. Partly, MacIntyre was responding to the

"Death of God," the idea that in the increasingly secular West, *belief* in God is dying out.

In *Blade Runner*, the returning 'Prodigal Son' Roy Batty makes this apparent when he murders Eldon Tyrell, his very own 'Father' and personal 'God of biomechanics', an act that evokes that other famous slogan, "If God does not exist, everything is permitted."

A quick glance at any introductory guide to ethics additionally reveals that attempts to base morality on something other than divine commands have also failed spectacularly. Two prominent examples are Utilitarianism and Kantian ethics, alternatives that have been at loggerheads with each other ever since they were devised.

Utilitarianism is a theory that was initially founded on the psychological insight that since we all like pleasure and are motivated to seek it out, morality should be about maximizing feelings of pleasure for everyone. Many problems with this theory have been identified, and the basic insight fuelling it is almost certainly questionable, as hedonists either eventually get bored with pleasure, or addicted to it. This suggests that most of us are searching for a deeper and more stable sense of well-being rather than one based on fluctuating 'feel-good' sensations.

Then there is Mr. Spock, the famous half-Vulcan hero of *Star Trek* and the epitome of the pure, cold-blooded rationality favored by Immanuel Kant. Any latent feelings resulting from having a human mother get suppressed with remorseless logic. So when it comes to morality, according to the theory that Spock personifies, you do what is both possible and logical.

Unfortunately, according to Kant, it can be both logical and rational to *always* tell the truth. No matter what. Even to a wannabe murderer looking for your best friend who just happens to be hiding in your apartment. That reason alone fails to provide a satisfactory foundation for morality is something that, once again, is reflected in *Blade Runner*. Instead, it is the ability to empathize, to connect with others, that is held up to be what distinguishes us as human beings and makes us capable of acting ethically. Could this be why, at the conclusion of that movie, in acknowledging the uniqueness and vulnerability of Rachael, the would-be murderer Gaff ends up sparing her?

For MacIntyre, disputes between supporters of these two ethical theories have, over time resulted in a failure to make headway so profound and disastrous that we are left with a moral blackout, an inability to retain even the most rudimentary sense of our present moral vocabulary. This is a compelling analysis, but perhaps MacIntyre has overlooked the pernicious influence of the one political, economic, and moral grand narrative left standing, an ideology that only became foregrounded after he had made his own case for the restoration of an Aristotelian approach to ethics based on the cultivation of admirable character traits. This is an ideology that has affected us all but also taken us unawares.

We Are the Replicants

Another distinguishing feature of the times we are living through, one which *2049* and the franchise as a whole provides an astute commentary on, is the view that something referred to variously as 'hypercapitalism', 'capitalist realism', or most commonly 'neoliberalism' is the only game in town when it comes to managing the global economy. This ideology is pervasive yet has been hiding in plain sight, as few people have heard of it.

According to neoliberal philosophy, the best way to run an economy is to leave almost everything up to the world of business. Privatize everything is the mantra. For one of the main advocates of this approach, the state should remove itself from all economic activity, except for "the military, the courts and some of the major highways." Get rid of all the rules and regulations preventing corporations from doing what they do, allow their employees to travel wherever they need to go to find work, and everything will be just fine. Let the "invisible hand" of the market decide. The basic idea here is utopian: free-market exchange can form the basis for an entire ethic, one which is capable of guiding all human action. In other words, supporters of neoliberalism believe in the power of self-regulating free markets to create a better world.

Unfortunately, according to a multidisciplinary range of researchers, this way of doing things has proved to be deeply damaging. It has resulted in a spectacular rise in income inequality and job insecurity, which in turn has generated a staggering increase in the number of workers medicating themselves for conditions like depression and anxiety.

Back in the 1950s, German philosopher Erich Fromm was already worrying that the obsession with money and profit found in Western society was an ever-worsening symptom of mental illness on a vast scale. And so it is, it seems, both in our world and in *Blade Runner* and 2049, as we become more narcissistically individualistic and aggressively competitive

toward one another, at the same time as we're also more isolated, lonely, and less trusting.

This is reflected in the movies. The Tyrell and Wallace
Corporations dominate the landscape alongside other multina-
tionals with their skyscraper-size commercials promoting
hedonic consumerism. Then there's Niander Wallace himself
and his murderous sidekick Luv, characters whose arrogance
and viciousness can't help but remind us of those today who,
considering themselves to be exceptional, beholden to no rules,
act harmfully.

A study at the University of Surrey, for example, found that
the personality traits of thirty-nine high-ranking managers
matched, and even exceeded, the narcissistic, dictatorial, and
manipulative tendencies typically exhibited by psychiatric
patients and psychopaths, all concealed behind a veneer of
superficial charm and charisma.

K is initially the end-product of a society devoted to a similar exercise in dehumanization, one in which everything and
everyone has become a commodity, including children, as the
Dickensian scene in the Morrill Cole Orphanage demonstrates,
a provocative allusion to neoliberalism's sweatshop culture. All
that matters is efficiency, flexibility, and compliance. In K's
case this is exemplified by the Baseline Test, evocative in our
era of the mind-numbingly figure-driven performance evalua-
tions to which modern employees are relentlessly subjected.
And K's initial passivity mirrors the demand for tolerably
intelligent, but not overly questioning drones in the contemporary workplace, with those unable to fit in, who are, as K finds
himself, "not even close to baseline," subject to various sorts of
variously impersonal behavioral modification programs, and
failing this, pharmacology.

His life is also sequestered and insular, numbed to everyday
experience in the way that the modern city-dwelling singleton
is, preferring holographic second bests to meaningful interaction. And he's not alone in this. Ana Stelline is similarly cut off
from the outside world, because of her "compromised immune
system." And Deckard retreats into obscurity as Las Vegas's
sole remaining inhabitant. "Sometimes," he says "to love someone, you gotta be a stranger."

Although K remains detached and impassive in the face of
it, the casual abuse inflicted on him—"Fuck off, Skinjob!," "I'll
kick your leg out you bastard!"—reflects neoliberalism's resur-
gent tribalism, including its backlash against migrants, facilitated by the porous borders that feed it economically.

Finally, the profound loss of a sense of identity he feels in the realization that he is not Rachael's son expresses a sentiment that so many of us today are only too aware of, which is the profound loss of our bearings, of a clear idea of who we are, whence we come.

Getting By Without a Soul

As jaded citizens of a whacked-out, hypercapitalist realm not unlike that depicted in *2049*, is there anything to be done? Or is the movie just about stripping away illusions in order to expose our thick-skinned egoism, whilst hinting that as a result of this systematic selfishness, we live in a world driven to the brink of an environmental cataclysm, one in which blind, purposeless natural and economic forces dictate the agenda?

Actually, there is relief to be found. K lets us know this, through his behavior at the end of the movie. In an earlier scene, Lieutenant Joshi, his superior officer, remarks that he has been "getting on fine without a soul". Curiously enough, so do Buddhists, and in the climactic conclusion to the movie, K also appears to become truly selfless.

So how does this work? Arguably the most fundamental assertion made by the Buddha himself, a claim shaped by deep meditative insight, is that absolutely everything is in a constant state of flux, including ourselves. In other words there is nothing that is stable and nothing to hang on to, and so suffering is inevitable. Certainly, there is no place reserved for an unchanging soul or self.

This sounds bleak. But there's more. The Buddha went on to proffer a terse summary of his system for dealing with life's vicissitudes: "All I teach is suffering and the stopping of suffering." Somewhat in the manner of modern evolutionary psychologists, he recognized that we have been hardwired by nature to pursue transient sensory pleasures, a futile endeavor that can also lead us to forge dangerously tribalistic alliances based around ethnicity, religion, and nationality, and to justify all that we do with identity-enhancing ideologies and belief systems.

But as a result of simply attending to the process of life as it manifested itself within and around him, the Buddha eventually realized that there was no self behind this process. The habitual conviction, that there was an unchanging thinker behind all this self-centered activity, evaporated under the spotlight of sustained meditative awareness.

No longer in thrall to the habitual compulsions, drives, and fears that ensnare us over and over again, the Buddha was able to embrace the Godless and selfless, endlessly morphing reality that unfolded before him in a free and spontaneously empathetic manner. Instead of possessing a mind that—like the rest of us—is full of itself, he became more open, more capable of generosity because he was no longer seeking anything for himself.

This is what I suspect K glimpses at the climax of *2049*, an intuition that prompts him to save Deckard. In the poignant penultimate scene, we take our leave of K stretched out in a snow-covered landscape, contemplatively savoring the evanescence and mystery of being.

We Make Angels

We may have lost our moral compass and be adrift in a neoliberal dystopia. But both *Blade Runner* and *2049* can point us in the right direction. Simply put, the two movies together propose that a viable morality can be founded on empathy and altruism.

Confirmation of this possibility can be found in the abundant studies in fields such as psychology and neuroscience that demonstrate our ability to empathize and act in what seems to be an altruistic and compassionate manner. Research on the animal kingdom indicates that such behavior is widespread there too, which in turn suggests, perhaps counter-intuitively, that these dispositions are part of our evolutionary heritage.

Plus, according to neuroscientific studies of meditators, who deliberately nurture empathic, altruistic and compassionate states of mind, our innate tendency to act in a benevolent manner, a quality that very young children exhibit spontaneously, can be built on and cultivated inwardly. From the point of view of natural selection this makes sense, as our species was vulnerable to threats posed by predators, illness, and other unfavorable environmental conditions. We have a genetic predisposition to watch out for each other.

Additionally, research indicates that an outward epigenetic transformation might be achieved through legislative changes designed to stimulate the expression of some genes while repressing the activity of others. Regulation to curtail the excesses of neoliberalism, together with a drive to persuade the more privileged of the need to reduce economic inequality, could, it is claimed, prevent genes associated with anxiety and other negative mental states from becoming overactive.

Basing morality on facts about human nature, such as our capacity for empathy and altruism, is a contentious idea in ethics, as facts about behavior do not, by themselves, tell us whether something is morally right or wrong. But we have to start somewhere. So let's begin with the behavior of the replicants, who through their ability to imaginatively anticipate the needs and wishes of others, perhaps indicate where the source of morality lies. Time and again they defy our expectations and those of their makers in this respect. And let's acknowledge the help provided by the Buddha, who taught us methods for cultivating and acting upon our own empathetic and altruistic dispositions. Lastly, MacIntyre, too deserves recognition, as he championed a similar approach involving the nurturing of such admirable virtues as empathy and altruism, as part of his broader critique of globalized hypercapitalism.

So in spite of its dystopian backdrop, the message of the final scenes in *2049* is that things may not be quite as bleak as we imagine. We do not have to buy into the myth that humans are selfish by nature, and tolerate the pompous egoists who currently hog both the corporate and political limelight. And in the case of those populist demagogues who have come to prominence as part of a backlash against neoliberalism, hopefully we will come to recognize that a cure based on fanning the tribalistic and nationalistic flames of militant stupidity is worse than the illness.

Our last glimpses of KD6-3.7 therefore serve as a kind of cinematic haiku. They remind us of what reams of recent research has repeatedly confirmed, namely, that empathy and a potential for altruism are inherent in most of us, and that the personal satisfaction derived from selfless actions trumps that elicited by selfish ones. In other words, doing things for others makes us happy too. But what we must now do is follow his example and draw upon these latent inner resources if we wish to successfully navigate this strange and most desperate of times and inspire others to follow the same trajectory.

15

The Phenomenology of Replicant Life and Death

ZACHARY SHELDON

"Younger models are happy scraping the shit," Sapper Morton wheezes, struggling to his feet to face the looming K, "because you've never seen a miracle."

Sapper and K regard each other in a moment of tension like a held breath. Then Sapper moves, lumbering towards K, who raises his gun and shoots. Leading up to this point, the camera had lingered on every bone-crushing detail of their bloody struggle, but as K shoots the shot cuts, after one quick flash of the muzzle, to focus on K. The actual strike of the bullet and the fall of Sapper's body are left offscreen, with only K's somber reaction to demonstrate that the killing blow had landed. After a lingering moment for the death to sink in, the next cut shows K's bloodied hands holding Sapper's severed eye and the scalpel he used to cut it out—the replicant has been retired.

2049, like *Blade Runner,* has its share of such life-and-death scenes, but unlike its predecessor, adopts a particular style during scenes of violence that complicates the contemplation of life and death with regard to both humans and replicants. This broadly "phenomenological" style ironically brings the viewer closer to the realism of the action of death and killing through a visual presentation that is unconventionally distant from the acts themselves.

The effect of this phenomenological style of film-making is a realistic identification with each of the characters, troubling the way viewers think about the theme of life and death by making each victim seem as objectively human as can be, no matter their status as a human or a replicant. Death is death, these moments seem to say, and so if everyone can die in the same way, doesn't that mean they may be alive in the same way, too?

2049 and Phenomenology

One of the greatest phenomenologists, Maurice Merleau-Ponty wrote about film from a phenomenological perspective in his 1945 address to the Institute of Advanced Cinematographic Study, in Paris, France, a talk titled "Film and the New Psychology."

"A film is not thought," he tells us, toward the end of his address, "it is perceived." "This is why films can be so gripping in their presentation of humanity." Movies "do not give us our thoughts, as novels have done for so long, but our conduct or behavior. They directly present to us that special way of being in the world, of dealing with things and other people, which we can see in the sign language of gesture and gaze and which clearly defines each person we know."

"For the movies as for modern psychology dizziness, pleasure, grief, love, and hate are ways of behaving," and so film "shares with contemporary philosophies the common feature of presenting consciousness thrown into the world, subject to the gaze of others and learning from them what it is."

Film is a particularly phenomenological medium because it often focuses on particular details in narratives to emphasize certain senses in the audience to communicate core aspects of the plot and themes of a story. This focusing is related to a significant concept from film theory called "defamiliarization." Defamiliarization is the idea that artistic style or flair can help you, the viewer, see something entirely average and familiar in an entirely new way.

You may have grown up in New York City around tall skyscrapers and the grime of city streets, but the cinematography and shot choices of *Blade Runner* or *Blade Runner 2049* may cause you to see your own surroundings in an entirely new light, as if you were looking at them for the very first time. Often the project of phenomenological research and writing is to examine people's normal experiences in a unique way to evoke a sense of awe or wonder at things that may be completely ordinary, a phenomenon that is also often seen in movies.

Phenomenological techniques also aim to produce affective responses in the bodies of an audience, much the same way that movies do. It is not enough to simply talk about phenomenological concepts as *ideas*; instead, they must be communicated in such a way as to be tangibly *felt* so that an audience knows such things to be true. This is very much like movies in that the goal is to engage the whole body of an audience member in a multisensory fashion.

Have you ever watched a cooking show and salivated at the food onscreen, or felt that you could actually smell or taste it? Or have you seen two characters in a film lovingly caress one another's hands and felt your own skin responding to their actions? What these point to is that movies provoke multisensory experiences in the same way as our everyday experiences of the world. *Blade Runner 2049* is a prime example here of a movie that does not just craft a visual spectacle but works to ensure that the world come alive to the viewer's senses.

K and Sapper

In the scene where K confronts Sapper, the dialog sets up, right off the bat, that both characters are replicants. And once the fists begin to fly—we see K and Sapper as fighting for their lives, even though their status as replicants calls into question just what kind of "lives" they have to begin with.

When K's takedown of Sapper introduces some breathing room into the fight, a juxtaposition of dialog confuses the replicant-human dynamic even further as the two discuss the various generations of replicant that they are before Sapper evokes religion by implying that he has witnessed a "miracle." But the way that the fight ends is where the phenomenological style truly emerges: while the blow-by-blow details of the fight have been explicitly shown, Sapper's actual death is glimpsed only through K's reaction to the thudding body.

Even though we've only known Sapper for a few violent minutes, the significance of his death is evoked by K's lack of response. Leaving the killing blow offscreen invites the audience's imagination to invent what happens, so that K's cold view of his actions contrasts with how the audience tangibly imagines the pain of death, making that pain seem even more real. Though Sapper is a replicant, his death and mutilation are felt as if he were human, calling into question the actual length of the divide that supposedly exists between the two, or whether there is even any kind of divide in the first place.

In this sense, *Blade Runner 2049*'s phenomenological style makes the question of what defines life for humans and replicants a question of morality as felt in the bodies of the audience. If the death of a replicant like Sapper can evoke such an embodied, empathetic feeling in the audience, then arguably the question of a replicant's humanity is moot.

Maurice Merleau-Ponty emphasized that as part of phenomenology we cannot presuppose any categories such as "real" or "illusion," but must instead take each and every experience at face value for what it tells us about perception, arguing that, "If I think I see or sense, then I see or sense beyond all doubt, whatever may be true of the external object. . . . A true perception will be, quite simply, a genuine perception." From this perspective, if our bodies respond phenomenologically to Sapper's death as we would to that of a human, then we ought to consider him as human.

Back to the Sprawl

Let's go back to some of the other confrontations and deaths in the movie, though, to see how they are treated and what they imply about the humanity (or lack thereof) of various characters. Lieutenant Joshi's death is intriguing as she is wholly human, here killed by Niander Wallace's replicant, Luv.

This scene begins with Luv storming into Joshi's office demanding to know where K is, and when Joshi has no satisfactory answers for Luv, she crushes a glass that Joshi is holding, grinding the shards into Joshi's palm until her blood flows and drips. The moment is painful to watch, evincing more than a cringe in the audience as we recognize the astounding pain being inflicted.

"You tiny thing," Luv hisses. "In the face of the fabulous new your only thought is to kill it. For fear of great change. You can't hold the tide with a broom." Joshi replies: "Except that I did," angering Luv. Tension mounts as Luv displays the psychotic lengths that she is willing to go to in her quest to learn more about the existence of this miracle child. She blurs the lines between perceptions of replicants by noting that "we never lie" right before articulating the lie that she is going to tell Wallace about why she had to kill Joshi. "You do what you gotta do," Joshi says. "Madam," says Luv, and she quickly slashes a blade across Joshi's stomach.

The camera shifts quickly to a view outside of the office, looking in through a rain-streaked window as Luv stabs one last time and Joshi crumples to the ground. Cutting back inside we do not see Joshi, but instead focus on Luv's teary face, her eyes and mouth set grimly in frustration.

Once again, we have only a replicant's reaction through which to read a death; the death here is that of a character clearly shown to be human. Yet, from the pacing to the actual choices in shots that distance the viewer from the killing blow, the style of the confrontation is the same as that between K and Sapper. Looked at this way, it seems that *Blade Runner 2049* treats all bodies the same, be they human or replicant.

From the standpoint of characterization, Joshi's death is perhaps harder to empathize with than Sapper's. Joshi has been
something of a hardass to K, particularly in this investigation,
and isn't particularly sympathetic as a character; Sapper, for
his own hulking frame and obvious strength, was at least
something of an innocent when K came to retire him.

That we can potentially feel even *more* for a replicant victim
calls into question the humanity of the movie's humans. After
all, as Sapper points out, humans are the ones who have
inspired so much killing through the use of replicants, and as
Luv points out, humans are the ones who are afraid for their
own lives, to the point that they are willing to kill the miracle
child of their slave laborers. Could it be, the cold depiction of
Joshi's death asks, that those in this world with a real sense of
humanity are, in fact, the replicants? Luv's brutal assassination complicates that idea, but the question remains.

The film's final deadly confrontation between Luv, K (now
known as Joe), and Deckard adds new wrinkles to this concept
as it works towards offering viewers definitions of life, death,
and humanity. Luv and Joe are clearly replicants and recognize
themselves as such here. Yet they each fight with a different
vision of what ought to be done with the offspring of Deckard
and Rachael, with the "miracle" of replicant life.

Luv's vision for the future is one of revenge and control, of
turning this new life into a chance to make humanity pay for
their enslavement of her kind; she wants to redefine life in
terms of power. Joe's perspective is that of empathy—he's seen
the hope that knowing about life and love can bring, and so his
fight is in many ways a step towards claiming his own kind of
life or humanity; his vision of life is community—he fights not
out of a selfish concern, or on the orders of others, but out of his
own developing empathy.

Deckard is effectively left out of this fight entirely. While
Luv and Joe tangle in the mist and shadow, Deckard is rele-
gated to the sidelines as the Spinner fills with water. Deckard's
status as human or replicant is entirely avoided here. Instead,
the "artificial" beings are left to partake in a literal battle for
the symbolic victory of deciding what defines life.

In terms of phenomenological style, the movie once again
eschews convention to highlight that this fight is less about the
bodies than about what they stand for. While much of the
actual action is shot in something of a regular style, there are
numerous elements that set the fight apart. Alternately dim
and then vividly multicolored lighting makes distinguishing
between the two sometimes difficult, melding their motions

and bodies together in a fashion that questions the distinctions between them; high angles and distant shots place the conflict into a realistically distant scale; and the intermittent, tonal music stands in contrast to the interpersonal drama unfolding in the brawl. The style of the fight once again is distanced and yet realistic, forcing the audience to assess the violence and the symbolic battle from a new perspective.

As Joe slowly triumphs over Luv, the style of his portrayal indicates that he has become more alive, if not exactly more human. One particular shot encompasses this idea, showing Joe from Luv's perspective as she is held underwater to drown. All of the boundaries of Joe's figure are literally and metaphorically blurred. In this battle between replicants he has prevailed, but in so doing has transcended the body that he was born or made into.

Replicant Life

"I've seen things you people wouldn't believe," Roy Batty says in *Blade Runner*, accepting that his time has come. In this moving final speech Batty makes the argument that he was an individual, a real being, comprised of experiences that were totally and uniquely his—just like any other person. What, really, he seems to be asking Deckard, is the difference between us?

Blade Runner 2049 explores this question in its plot, but also uses its phenomenological camerawork to make audiences question the boundaries of humanity and aliveness in its characters. In scenes operating at the liminal borders of life and death, the film goes out of its way to stylistically reinforce the similarities in how humans and replicants meet their ends. By ramping up dramatic tension in these conflicts and then evaporating that tension through distancing the viewer from the acts of violence, the impact of death is much more tangibly felt—and that such techniques are applied across both replicant and human death begs the question of just what quality defines life and characterizes humanity.

In this sense, the phenomenological style of the violence actually provides viewers with an answer. The movie sets each violent encounter up in such a way as to evoke a tangibly embodied response alongside an empathetic one. We *feel* the impacts of these deaths, no matter the type of being that is dying onscreen. And that act of feeling such empathy is what makes us alive, what separates us from the inanimate objects and machines all around us. In the end, Luv distinguishes herself from Joe in that she sees everything from a perspective of logic and control. Joe, on the other hand, has learned to feel for others. Deckard's status as a replicant or a human does not matter—nor, in the end, does Joe's. What matters is that they feel something real.

We see this in action when Joe delivers Deckard to meet his daughter. The love and happiness in Deckard is clearly observed as he wanders into her keep; and out on the stairs, Joe lies down and we, the audience, know that he is dying—because he has, truly, lived.

16
Who Am I to You?

JAMES M. OKAPAL

The climax of *Blade Runner* involves Roy Batty dying after saving Rick Deckard from falling to his death. The dénouement of *Blade Runner 2049* involves K dying after taking Rick Deckard to see his daughter, Dr. Ana Stelline, for the first time.

In both cases, a replicant performs an act of kindness toward Deckard. In the latter movie, Deckard asks K, "Who am I to you?", a question he could've asked Roy Batty in the first movie. In these moments, as precipitation falls on the characters, we see a change in the replicants. Being baptized in rain and snow, respectively, a rebirth has occurred, but its nature continues to puzzle us.

One set of puzzles involves the identity and nature of the key characters in these scenes. Both Batty and K seem, in these decisive moments, more human and humane than the hard-boiled Deckard. How is this possible if Deckard is human and Batty and K are not? This has led many to speculate that Deckard is a replicant. While these metaphysical puzzles are interesting in their own right, I'm more interested in related *moral* puzzles. These have to do with questions about moral agency and moral status: What's the relationships between moral agency and moral status? and What's the significance of granting moral status to something else?

The World Is Built on a Wall that Separates Kind

Immanuel Kant provides one answer about the relationship between moral status and moral agency. A key idea in Kant is that autonomy, or the ability to create and follow moral rules, is "the basis of the dignity of both human nature and every rational nature." The idea, applied to the movies, goes something like this: a replicant is owed respect, or has a dignity, or is morally valuable, if a replicant has the ability to create and follow moral rules. And so, a significant issue is whether replicants have this moral autonomy. If replicants lack moral autonomy, then they are morally indistinguishable from a toaster.

The ability to create and follow rules is a form of rational planning, and rule following is essentially Kant's definition of agency. One type of agency is *mere* agency. Mere agency occurs when someone is able to make and follow plans to achieve some goal. Consider the examples of Roy Batty and K. Batty's goal is to extend his life. He creates and executes a plan to meet his father, Eldon Tyrell. This plan involves finding J.F. Sebastian who in turn will be able to sneak Batty into Tyrell Corporation. Once gaining an audience with Tyrell, Batty talks with him about overriding the four-year limited lifespan built into his genetic code. Similarly, K's several goals include finding out if he's Rachael's child. He creates and executes a plan to seek out his possible father, Deckard. This plan involves finding Doc Badger who can use the radiation signatures found in the wooden horse to identify where Deckard's hiding.

Moral agency, however, requires more than following plans. According to Kant, the goals of mere agency are given by interests or desires. The goals of moral agency, however, are given by reason and these goals become moral rules only if they pass special tests. One of these tests, identified by Onora O'Neill, is the contradiction-in-conception test, according to which, you state a goal and then figure out whether it's possible for *everyone* to attempt to achieve it.

For example, Niander Wallace has a goal of creating a reproducing race of replicant slaves. Can Wallace's goal, "I should be a master of slaves," be adopted by everyone? In other words, can someone, without contradiction, conceive of a world in which all beings can agree to the generalized version of the goal, "We should all be masters of slaves"? In this case, the agreed upon answer is that this isn't an acceptable moral goal. Why? Because moral beings will realize that it's impossible for everyone to be a master: if everyone's a master, then no one's a slave, and if there are no slaves, then no one's a master. Thus, the stated goal contradicts itself and is not a moral rule. One piece of evidence that Wallace is deeply immoral is because he acts on his desire to be master of replicant slaves despite the fact that the stated goal can't pass Kant's test.

A moral agent is someone who can work through this test, and then follow only those rules that pass the test. An individual can be recognized as a moral agent when the moral rules conflict with our desires. In these circumstances, the moral agent will follow the reason-generated moral rule even if it means forgoing the desire-generated goal. Consider another possible rule, namely, "I should not kill another out of frustration." This seems to pass the contradiction-in-conception test because we can conceive of world in which everyone would agree that "no one should kill another out of frustration."

Replicants in both movies, as well as the short film *Blade Runner: Black Out 2022,* seem incapable of recognizing this rule, and thus can't be moral agents: Leon shoots Holden when Leon becomes frustrated with the Voight-Kampf test questions; Batty crushes Tyrell's skull when he's frustrated that Tyrell cannot fix the limited lifespan problem; Wallace, as a human, presumably is capable of following this rule and thus is a moral agent, but again demonstrates his immorality when, out of frustration, he disembowels a barren newborn replicant.

But are Wallace's actions toward the replicants really immoral? That depends on the connection between moral agency and moral status. According to Rosalind Hursthouse, the concept of moral status "is supposed to divide everything into two classes: things that have moral status are within 'the circle of moral concern' and things that do not, which are outside the circle." The Kantian theory sees replicants who lack moral agency to be outside the circle, to be on the other side of Lieutenant Joshi's wall, because moral agents are morally considerable and non-moral agents aren't.

Joshi's concerned that if both humans and replicants are on the same side of the wall, then replicants have rights and their current status would have to be reconsidered. So, if replicants have moral status, then Wallace's killing of the barren replicant is murder. If, however, the moral status wall separates humans from replicants, then replicants are not morally considerable. In other words, moral agents do not have to include replicants in their moral deliberations about what rules will pass Kant's test. Thus, the enslavement or destruction of a replicant is no more immoral than buying or disassembling a toaster.

Tibor Machan explains why, according to a Kantian interpretation, animals are not moral agents and thus lack moral status. First, note that an animal can't act morally, can't exhibit moral agency, and can't "be tried for crimes and blamed for moral wrongs." It can't, in other words, be morally culpable. For the

Kantians, this lack of agency entails that an animal doesn't have moral status. Concepts like moral considerability don't apply to non-agents.

In *Blade Runner*, Roy, Leon, and the other Nexus-6s are killed for being a threat as a rabid dog might be, and not because they're morally blameworthy. And if an animal or a replicant isn't a moral agent, then they lack a moral space that needs to be respected. According to Machan, moral space is "a sphere of sovereignty or personal jurisdiction so that one can engage in self-government—for better or worse." According to this view, Kantian respect, or the requirement to take the interests of others into account during moral deliberation, is only owed to those beings that are moral agents, not mere agents, because only moral agency creates a moral space that needs protection. If we adopt Machan's version of Kant's moral theory, then only moral agents can have moral status.

If we adopt this relationship between moral status and moral agency, then human beings can't act immorally toward replicants, because replicants aren't moral agents. Consider that the reason Nexus-6s, Rachael, and presumably later models are given memories is to control them. This control diminishes the agency of the replicants. With diminished agency, the thought is that moral agency can't develop. This is an implication we recognize with human beings who have severe cognitive disabilities—these disabilities limit mere agency and this in turn makes it difficult for these individuals to develop moral agency. *2022* shows that this memory-induced control was not entirely successful as replicants were able to attempt an unsuccessful revolt.

Once Wallace gains control of Tyrell's intellectual property, he replaces memories as a form of control with some sort of truncated and revised version of Isaac Asimov's Three Laws of Robotics for Nexus-9s: 1. obey orders and 2. don't harm humans. We can see how this works in the short film *2036: Nexus Dawn*, when Wallace orders a replicant to kill one or the other of them, and the replicant kills himself. There are several problems with this truncated set of rules, namely, as James McGrath and Ankur Gupta have suggested, this shortened list of rules results in a version of a killbot hellscape where humans are not directly harmed, but the non-humans are killing each other.

Since Nexus-9s can't be agents due to the way they're made, they also can't be moral agents and thus Wallace's master-slave goal is misstated above. The goal is really, "all *human beings* should be masters of all *replicant* slaves," and this version of the goal can be accepted by all human beings who have moral agency. But this means that Wallace's killing of the replicant is okay, and

Deckard's killing of Leon, Zhora, and Pris is permissible. What seems odd in this view, which turns replicants into non-moral objects, is Deckard falling in love with Rachael, Joshi *not* commanding K to have sex with her, and Joshi helping K to escape after failing his baseline test.

Do You Long for Having Your Heart Interlinked?

But Tyrell and Wallace are not very sympathetic characters. There seems to be something off about them and their need for devices to see properly. They seem blind to the fact that Deckard, Rachael, K, and even Joi are morally valuable. In fact, *Blade Runner* suggests that Batty, in his last moments, becomes more human than the humans he has been running from, and that Batty's death, unlike Tyrell's, is something to be mourned.

These considerations suggest that the Kantian understanding of the relationship between moral status and moral agency is mistaken. Maybe, just maybe, the movies suggest that moral agency is not the logical pre-condition of moral status. Instead, the capability of attributing moral status to others is a logical pre-condition of moral agency. On this alternative view, acting on the capability to see others as morally considerable confers, and is an act of, moral agency.

This alternative view about the relationship between moral status and moral agency begins with the concept of empathy. Empathy is a concept both central to the narratives of the films and entirely lacking in the Kantian views of moral status explained above. Empathy is also at the center of moral theories often called *ethics of care*, championed by Nel Noddings, Carol Gilligan, Virginia Held, Joan Tronto, and others. Empathy is the ability to understand, be aware of, and experience the emotions, thoughts, concerns, and point of view of another. It allows you to develop a caring relationship with someone else. It is to experience an interlinking of hearts and hands, and to find that part of you that was missing. One of the most important aspects of the transition from merely empathizing-with to actually caring-for another is the presence of a motivation to act for the sake of someone else. According to Noddings, the "motivation in caring is directed toward the welfare, protection, or enhancement" of the other person.

This changes our motivation for acting from adherence to rules that others could agree to adopt, as in Kantianism, to a motivation which seeks to further the interests of others such as *their* goals, wants, and desires. The most explicit and continuous example of caring behavior can be found in Joi. Think about her complicated, heart-wrenching choices to hire Mariette as physical sex surrogate and her insistence that K upload her entire consciousness to the mobile emanator.

K has an interest in enhancing his relationship with Joi and hiring Mariette furthers that interest. But the physical enhancement is complicated, given that K may physically desire Mariette independently, and having sex with Mariette after Joi syncs may be a form of infidelity, thereby deteriorating the relationship. Uploading her consciousness is also complicated. First, it can be seen as a way to protect K from those who are looking for him even though it puts her own existence at risk. But it also can be seen as way to support dangerous goals, including confirming the nature of his relationship to Deckard, and advancing the cause of replicant emancipation.

Noddings also distinguishes *natural* caring from *ethical* caring, analogous to distinguishing mere agency and moral agency in Kant. Mere agency has to exist before you can become a moral agent. Similarly, natural caring—the ability to feel and act toward another because we want to—has to exist before you can engage in ethical caring—the realization that I must act in accordance with another's interests despite a desire to act in my own interest. There are two preconditions that must be met before either form of caring can exist. The first is that the being in question must be capable of emotions, the second, that they must also be capable of other-regarding emotions such as empathy, love, and compassion.

Throughout both movies, it's clear that replicants can feel an array of emotions. Luv demonstrates pride when she shouts at K, "I'm the best one!" Leon's frustrated and frightened when being given the Voight-Kampf test, and seems wounded by his inability to recover his photos. Zhora's clearly apprehensive and hostile during her interaction with Deckard. Pris is capable of anger, even rage. Nevertheless, the narratives suggest that humans believe pre-Nexus-6 replicants may experience these negative emotions, but still lack empathy, and hence the Voight-Kampf empathy test is a way to distinguish humans from replicants.

The narratives also indicate that later-model replicants can have other-regarding emotions. Rachael demonstrates several emotions, including love, throughout *Blade Runner*. Sapper Morton recalls his deep emotional experience of seeing a miracle in *2049*, and in *2048* clearly cares for and protects Ella and her mother. By contrast, Deckard, Tyrell, Joshi, and Wallace, as human (albeit, controversially in Deckard's case), are oddly devoid of almost *any* emotion.

Without the ability to experience other-regarding emotions, a being would be limited to self-serving interests and motivations. Furthermore, a lack of other-regarding emotions such as empathy supports viewing other beings as merely instrumentally valuable. Still lacking empathy for Tyrell and Sebastian, Roy kills them once they're no longer useful. In *2049*, we see that this limitation persists in later-model replicants.

Freysa, the leader of the replicant resistance, orders K to kill Deckard to ensure her ability to bring about a replicant revolution. Deckard's continued existence is no longer useful to her, she may view it as an impediment to her goals, and so she may want him eliminated. Wallace's behavior also illustrates how an inability to empathize can lead to morally problematic behavior. It allows him to casually kill a barren replicant, callously order Luv to deliver a head shot to the resurrected Rachael, and unreflectively send Deckard off-world to be tortured for information. To Wallace, these individuals are valued as mere tools, and are violently discarded the moment they no longer help him achieve his goals. In other words, if Wallace doesn't, or can't care for these individuals, then he can't value them morally.

The importance of empathy explains why humans in the movies don't see replicants as moral beings. As Noddings points out, "our obligation to summon the caring attitude is limited by the possibility of reciprocity. We are not obligated to act as one-caring if there is no possibility of completion in the other."

It follows that replicants are morally considerable, if and only if they're capable of empathy, natural caring, and making a choice to act on the motivation of ethical caring. To encounter an individual lacking empathy is unsettling, for, Noddings says, "we shrink from one who has never had empathy." An individual "who never feels the pain of another, who never confesses the internal 'I must' that is so familiar to most of us, is beyond our normal pattern of understanding. Her case is pathological and we avoid her." In this sense, to encounter someone without empathy is to recognize them as familiar but to experience an unsettling, anxiety-filled interaction that is to be avoided in the future.

Sometimes, to Love Someone, You Gotta Be a Stranger

Where does this leave us? In an ethics of care, moral agency isn't a precondition of moral status. Instead, moral agency is the result of an act of ethical caring. And ethical caring is the conferring of moral considerability, or moral value, on another. It is acting out of respect for another *for their sake*. So Kant and Kantians, like Machan, get it backwards: moral agency isn't about reason, it's about other-regarding emotions, like compassion and empathy; moral status isn't conferred upon gaining moral agency, but moral agency arises from the exercise of granting moral value to another.

And so we look back on the finales of both movies. Batty first shows that he naturally cares for Leon and Pris upon their deaths. Then, in the final moments of his life, he develops empathy for Deckard and performs an act of ethical caring by saving him. Similarly, despite having no familial connection to Deckard, K empathizes with his situation, being hunted now by humans and replicants alike, and being separated from a loved one. Thus, K leaves Freysa, not to kill Deckard, but to save him, faking his death, and in an act of ethical caring, taking him to meet his daughter. Deckard himself adopts a caring attitude toward Rachael, and performs an act of ethical caring, even love, by deciding she's worthy of being protected, though it means he'll be hunted. And he does so again, by sacrificing ever knowing his daughter, because sometimes, to love—and thereby protect—someone, "you gotta be a stranger."

These acts of kindness and decency show us that replicants can value others as having moral status. So, who is Deckard to both Batty and K? He's someone who has moral status. He's morally valuable, that is, a bearer of dignity, worthy of respect, who should have his welfare protected, and his interests furthered. By extending moral status to Deckard, by exercising their ability to empathize and care for others, we can see that Batty and K can have moral agency, thereby removing another brick in the "wall that separates kind."[1]

[1] I'm grateful to Robin Bunce, William Irwin, and Trip McCrossin, for their comments and corrections to earlier drafts of this chapter.

IV

The Kingdom of God

17
You've Never Seen a Miracle

ANDREW KUZMA

"It's very exciting," says Sapper Morton as he hands a copy of Graham Greene's *The Power and the Glory* to Ella, in *2048: Nowhere to Run*. "It's about an outlaw priest who's just trying to understand the meaning of being human."

Sapper is also talking about himself. He's a Nexus-8 replicant and Greene's novel is exactly the kind of book that an android would read to try to figure out what it means to be human.

The novel follows a priest living in Mexico at a time when Catholicism was persecuted and operating normally as a Catholic priest was illegal. Though he ultimately dies a martyr, this priest is not your typical martyr-hero. He's deeply, deeply flawed. He has fathered a child, for instance, but can't bring himself to truly regret breaking his vow of celibacy. He's selfish, a drunk (a "whisky priest"), and a coward.

At the same time, he knowingly risks his life by breaking the law to fulfill his priestly duties. He is captured, killed, and remembered by the people as a saint. The reader is left wondering: is this a saint worthy of admiration or a drunkard who stumbled into a noble death? The priest's imperfections are glaring but they also make him relatable; he struggles with who he's supposed to be. In the end, there isn't a simple, straightforward answer. Sound familiar?

Many characters in *Blade Runner 2049* define themselves using religion. Sapper looks to an unorthodox saint, an "outlaw priest," to make sense of his identity. He is also the first character in *2049* to refer to religion when he tells K, "You newer models are happy scraping the shit, because you've never seen a miracle." He uses religion to answer the question, "What does it mean to be human?" But, like the whisky priest in Greene's novel, the religious references in *2049* reveal just how complicated this question can be.

Will the Real God Please Stand Up?

In the world of *2049*, Niander Wallace is God. He's not the one true God. Really, he's just a man. But the manufacturer of the Nexus-9 replicants certainly acts and talks like the God of the Old Testament. In the Bible, when God first created the world, "the Earth was a formless void and darkness covered the face of the deep, while a wind from God swept over the face of the waters" (Genesis 1:2, *NRSV*).

Like God in Genesis, Wallace first appears as a creator in darkness. When we meet him he sits unseen in shadow and his voice echoes over the water that fills the chamber. He chastises his faithful lieutenant, Luv, as she approaches: "an angel should never enter the kingdom of Heaven without a gift."

He is not the true God, but he certainly sees himself as godlike and he has a pretty good case. According to the movie's preamble, Wallace literally feeds the world. His massive corporate headquarters towers over the city and the rest of humanity. He speaks of Heaven, angels, the destiny of humanity, and he explicitly quotes the Bible. He creates replicants as well as K's holographic love interest, Joi.

When Deckard asks him if he has children, he responds not inaccurately, "I have millions." So, when he proclaims, "I make good angels," how can we doubt him? If his angels obey without question, how can replicants have any chance of being human? (Whatever that means.)

Well, maybe because Wallace more closely resembles a figure from Gnostic Christianity called the Demiurge. Gnosticism was a second-century religious movement that rejected the material world as corrupt and evil. (It was also a huge influence on the worldview of Philip K. Dick.) The Gnostics believed that the world was created by the Demiurge, "the craftsman," an imperfect, petty, and cruel deity. This being was the God of the Old Testament who made humans, gave them a specific set of rules to follow, and sent the occasional plague or famine to punish them.

But the Gnostics believed that there was another God, the true God, who resided in a spiritual realm. When the Demiurge made the world he unknowingly put some of the true God's divine spark into creation. The true, omnipotent, and benevolent God saw this and sent Christ to tell human beings that they possessed this spark. Salvation came from learning this secret.

Wallace, like the Demiurge, is a creator who does not have absolute power over his creation. We already know that he's not the original creator. Eldon Tyrell from *Blade Runner* holds that distinction. We also know that Wallace is not all-powerful. Even he admits that he cannot replicate the ability to procreate: "I cannot breed them. So help me, I have tried." Wallace is not in total control of his creations. So, despite his affectations of divinity, when he proclaims, "I make good angels," we have a very good reason to doubt him. Like the Demiurge, Wallace unknowingly imparted a "spark" to his creations. They are not as obedient as he believes.

Good Angels or Bad Angels?

Throughout the movie, Wallace calls the replicants "angels." "There were bad angels once," he says presumably in reference to the events of *Blade Runner*, "I make good angels now." The whole rationale for allowing replicants back on Earth is Wallace's insistence that they are incapable of disobedience. He demonstrates their obedience viscerally in *2036: Nexus Dawn* when he asks a Nexus-9 model to cut its own throat.

Given Wallace's God-complex, "angel" is an appropriate term. The English word angel comes from the Greek *angelos*, which simply means "messenger." This is how they appear in the Bible: messengers of God (the winged babies motif came much later). In Genesis, Abraham receives three angels who tell him his wife Sarah will bear a son (Genesis 18:10). An angel announces Jesus's conception (Luke 1:35), birth (Luke 2:9–15), and resurrection (Matthew 28:2–7). Angels stand in for God. When Luv meets K and says, "I'm here for Mr. Wallace," she's acting quite literally as an angel.

Though they resemble human beings in some ways, angels are not human, never were human, and never will be human. Angels are creatures like humans, but they don't have bodies. They are completely spiritual. The New Testament implies that they do not (and maybe cannot) procreate. Whereas humans were made "in the image of God," angels were made, like replicants, to be servants, messengers, and warriors. So it makes sense to refer to replicants as "angels." They were made different; they simply cannot do what we can do.

Or can they? Angels also rebel. Besides serving as messengers, rebelling is the most well-known thing that angels do. The most famous angel is not Gabriel or Michael, but Lucifer, better known as Satan. The Book of Revelation describes a war in Heaven between God's angels and Satan's rebellious angels that ends with the rebellious angels cast out. John Milton would use this much later as the basis for *Paradise Lost*.

Even Wallace admits: "there were bad angels once." He's talking about the Nexus-6 and Nexus-8 models, not his obedient Nexus-9s. But angels—the Biblical angels—were not made "bad." They are unique in Judeo-Christian belief as the only beings besides humans who possess free will and intelligence. They have the ability to choose either obedience or rebellion. In some interpretations, Lucifer was once the highest angel. Wallace's comment to Luv, "You really are the best angel of all, aren't you?", thus carries a certain amount of foreboding.

"Angels" really is the perfect term for replicants. It describes creatures who are different from human beings but who possess the same freedom to choose who they want to be. We already know that the Nexus-6 and Nexus-8 models had free will. We're told that Nexus-9 models, like K and Luv, lack this ability. They don't. When Lt. Joshi tells Luv that K has killed the replicant child (he hasn't, he lied), Luv responds: "You're so sure. Because he told you. Because we never lie. I'm going to tell Mr. Wallace that you tried to shoot me first, so I had to kill you." Luv, Wallace's most loyal angel, the "best" angel, lies to her creator. She disobeys. We shouldn't be surprised. Angels have always been able to choose.

A Child Is Born

"To be born is to have a soul," says K, explaining his resistance to "retiring" a replicant that has been born. K does not think of himself or of any other replicant as possessing a soul. Luv never betrays Wallace in any significant way, but she knows that replicants can disobey. K, on the other hand, truly believes that he has no choice. He tells Sapper, "I don't retire my own kind because we don't run." Even when he thinks he was born, he doesn't question the built-in obedience of the Nexus-9 models. He just thinks that those rules don't apply to him. His birth, as Joi exclaims, makes him special.

Miraculous births are an important motif in Judeo-Christian belief. The Bible is filled with examples of barren women conceiving: Sarah the mother of Isaac, Hannah the mother of Samuel, Elizabeth the mother of John the Baptist, and Rachel the mother of Joseph. Wallace directly connects Rachael from *Blade Runner* with Joseph's mother: "God remembered Rachel, and . . . heeded her and opened her womb" (Genesis 30:22). This reference gives us another reason to think that K, renamed "Joe," is Rachael and Deckard's son.

A miraculous birth indicates that a child is special. Christians look at Joseph (who, like Ryan Gosling, also had a great coat) as a precursor of Christ. Christ's was the ultimate miraculous birth: the Son of God, born of a virgin. Upon discovering the birth of the replicant child, Wallace celebrates by reciting the same Bible verse many Christians use as part of their Christmas worship: "Can you at least proclaim, 'a child is born'?" (Isaiah 9:6). Joi insists that K is special because he was "born, not made," which sounds very much like the Nicene Creed's explanation that Christ was "begotten, not made." The first child born to a replicant, the child of Rachael, the miracle that Sapper witnesses, is the replicant messiah. He (or she) was born. Birth is what makes him (or her) special.

Am I the Only One Sick of Movies about a Chosen One?

Most moviegoers are familiar with the "chosen one" narrative. *Star Wars*, *Harry Potter*, *The Matrix*, and many other franchises follow this well-worn tale. At the beginning of the story, the chosen one doesn't look special. The hero is a moisture farmer on a desert planet or an unwanted child living under the stairs or something else equally unappealing. What is significant, however, is the hero's birth. Maybe the hero has important parents (not a navigator on a spice freighter, but a Jedi!) or the birth fulfills a prophecy (the boy born on this day shall defeat the dark lord!). Once these "chosen ones" find out they were born special, they set out on a fantastic adventure, meet eccentric characters, and so on.

We all know the drill. These Chosen One narratives lean heavily on the story of Christ and the Biblical motif of miraculous births. Many times the hero of the movie also "dies" (or at least is temporarily defeated) before rising up to save the day. Sometimes, like in the *Terminator* franchise, the chosen one even has the initials "J.C."

When K discovers that the "miracle" Sapper was talking about is the first child born to a replicant and that he might be this miracle child, we all know what we're in for. He's the replicant messiah, living proof that replicants can be human. So when it turns out that K is not the miracle child, it's not just a shock it's also disorienting. If he's not the real hero, then he's just another run-of-the-mill replicant. If he's just a replicant, then he can't be human, right?

A Bad Case of Galatians Syndrome

There's a passing reference in *2049* to "Galatians Syndrome." It leaves the exact nature of the disease unspecified. *Blade Runner* included a character who suffered from "Methuselah Syndrome," rapid aging. That name is an ironic reference to the longest-lived figure in the Bible. In the same vein, "Galatians Syndrome" refers to Paul's Letter to the Galatians in the New Testament. In the same speech in which Joi alludes to the Nicene Creed, she also says that K is "of woman born."

Galatians explains that God sent Christ, "born of a woman . . . in order to redeem those who were under the law, so that we might receive adoption as children" (Galatians 4:4–5). Christ is born, literally, to save. K, being "of woman born," has a similar significance in Joi's eyes. The real child, Ana Stelline, says that she suffers from "a compromised immune system" (which may or may not be Galatians syndrome). Whether truly ill or not, her birth makes her the savior in the eyes of Freysa and her followers.

The Letter to the Galatians also happens to be the perfect text to read in an identity crisis.

Christianity faced a dilemma in the first few decades of its existence. Jesus and all of his earliest followers were Jewish. As observant Jews, they followed kosher law (which prohibits the consumption of pork and shellfish) and the men were circumcised as infants. At the time, Christianity was just a peculiar version of Judaism. But when gentiles—non-Jews—started becoming Christians they ran into a problem. Some gentiles who had grown up eating pork did not want to stop eating pork. But the more "sensitive" problem was circumcision. Uncircumcised adult men really did not want to get circumcised. What to do? To be a Christian you had to be a Jew, and to be a Jew you had to be circumcised. You couldn't be a Christian without also being a Jew, could you?

Paul, born a Jew, taught the Galatians that they did not need to be Jews to be Christian (they did not need to keep kosher or be circumcised). Then another group of Jewish Christians came to town and told the Galatians that they did. The Galatians were confused. Jesus was a Jew, wasn't he? Wasn't he the fulfillment of the promise that God made to Abraham and his offspring? The Jewish Christians were saying that if the Galatians wanted to be part of this promise, then they had to live like Abraham's descendants, which meant following kosher law and being circumcised.

Paul responds by introducing what we might call today a paradigm shift. Yes, he tells the Galatians, you should live as

Abraham's heirs. But it was Abraham's faith, not his flesh, which was important. Abraham's literal descendants received a law and they still practice it. There's nothing wrong with that. But having faith like Abraham is what makes you his descendant. Distinctions like circumcised or uncircumcised no longer matter: "There is no longer Jew or Greek, there is no longer slave or free, there is no longer male and female; for all of you are one in Christ Jesus" (Galatians 3:28). In other words, it is what you believe, not how you were born or what kind of body you have, that makes you a Christian.

Think back to K's fight with Sapper at the beginning of *2049*. K tells Sapper that newer models don't run because they can't. Sapper doesn't accept K's explanation: "You newer models are happy scraping the shit, because you've never seen a miracle." Sapper suggests that it's not the fact that K was made that keeps him "scraping the shit," but what he believes.

Dying for the Right Cause Is the Most Human Thing We Can Do

K is not the chosen one. He was not born. He's just a standard, run-of-the-mill Nexus-9 replicant. But it turns out that doesn't matter. When he starts believing that he is different, he begins to act differently. He fails his baseline test, he lies to Joshi, and he refuses to kill the child of Rachael as ordered (at first by not committing suicide and then later by not killing the actual child). K had put the same significance on being born that the early Christians had put on kosher laws and circumcision. The fact that a replicant gave birth is still a "miracle," but the miracle is that it reveals that birth doesn't matter. It's what K and the other characters believe about their own identity that matters.

So what makes something human? The replicant Freysa suggests that it is "dying for the right cause." Sapper dies to protect the child whose birth he witnessed. K dies to help reunite Deckard with his daughter. Joi, who is not even truly embodied, dies for love. She insists upon accompanying K in the emanator without a backup. When K warns her that if the device is destroyed she will be gone, she responds that this possibility makes her "like a real girl."

Were any of these three human? We don't know whether Joi's actions were the result of her programming or of her actual free choice. Motivation seems important. Then again, we never truly know the motivations behind anyone's actions, born or otherwise. We have seen three characters who were not born do "the most human thing," simply because they believed that they should. Does this make them human?

According to Freysa, it does. K once thought that to be human was to be born. At the very least, we can say that K, Joi, and Sapper are not less human because they were made. Or perhaps "human" is simply not as special a distinction as we would like to believe. If replicants and computer programs can live, die, and make their own choices just like human beings, perhaps these categories no longer matter.

In *Blade Runner 2049*, there is no longer human or replicant. The question is no longer "what does it mean to be human?" Instead, we should ask, "What does it mean to be?"[1]

---

[1] I would like to thank Christopher Brenna for his help in revising this chapter. I would also like to thank Madeleine Kuzma. If I knew how, I would carve her a little wooden horse.

18

K's Most Excellent Kierkegaardian Pilgrimage

BEN FRANZ

In the last scene of *Blade Runner 2049*, K brings Rick Deckard to meet his daughter, Ana Stelline. While Deckard enters the studio to find his daughter working on a memory of snow, K lies upon the steps of the studio and watches the snow fall. This is a moment of peace and contentment. It is very much the sort of thing that could be described as a god-granted reward.

This moment, where K is allowed to quietly enjoy the delicate, gentle snowfall seems to exist so that K's story can end gracefully. This desire to bring grace to K's quest speaks to a religious theme that runs through *2049*. K has been wrestling with two contradictory requests. His boss, Lieutenant Joshi asked him to bring Deckard back. The replicant resistance has asked K to kill Deckard. He has chosen to fake Deckard's death, which allows him to take Deckard to his adult child without anyone trying to hunt them down. This decision has enabled K to have a quiet moment of peace.

This moment of peace is the sort of thing a minister, rabbi, or mufti would tell you is a great reward from God for serving the Eternal one's will. To achieve a sense of peace in our crazy lives is something to be wished for. However, we must think about the nature of K's peace of mind. Is it because he earned it? Is it because he realized this is the best he can do, and is just going to live with this small sense of satisfaction, allowing California snowflakes to fall around him? Is it because he is giving up?

These are questions which are best understood through the works of Søren Kierkegaard. Though he did not write many books, or live a very long life, Kierkegaard was focused on figuring out, from a religious philosophical point of view, the nature of life. What can we hope to get out of life? How can we best serve our god? What are the planes of existence?

Kierkegaard the Philosopher of Faith

Known as the Father of Existentialism, Kierkegaard delved into philosophy, religion, and culture. His principal interest was faith, and he felt there wasn't a lot of faith available to people who practiced Christianity. Most of his work centers on how to put the Christian faith back into Christianity.

Kierkegaard would see his passion and life work in writing about existence. Through the use of literary irony, satire, and long essays, he would consider what the point of living was. Kierkegaard, for example, was not a fan of the Danish Church at the time. He felt it was all ritual, and there was no space to develop your faith during Church worship. He would spend a lot of time writing about how best to be a good and faithful Christian.

Beyond faith, Kierkegaard was also interested in ethics. He would consider the goodness and purity of our behavior. One of the questions that he explored in his writings, was: Can a human be truly faithful?

Kierkegaard reasoned that it would depend on where the desire to do the good deed came from. If it was a call from God, this was also the best and most good thing to do. Kierkegaard enjoyed discussing biblical characters. They were all very well known, and it would allow him to teach philosophy indirectly, by considering the actions of Abraham, or Ahasuerus (the Wandering Jew of legend), or other such characters.

Kierkegaard did not wish to directly influence people's thinking. He wanted his readers to be able to come to their own conclusions. He would often write under a pseudonym.

Either/Or

Either/Or is written under the pseudonym Victor Eremita, who seems to be an editor providing us a debate between two perspectives. In *Either/Or* Kierkegaard presents two ways to lead your life, the aesthetic way and the ethical way. With these ways to lead your life, Kierkegaard presents two clear choices. If a person chooses simply to live an aesthetic life, this is the hedonistic normal existence of everyday human beings. For the Aesthete who's presenting this choice, A., the pleasure of music, theater, and love is what makes like worth living (*Søren Kierkegaard's Journals and Papers*, Volume 1).

The second choice is the Ethical life. The Ethical life is where you can still enjoy aesthetic pleasure, but that is only done responsibly. This is sort of like all those alcohol and beer commercials that ask you to drink responsibly. You can enjoy the pleasures of life, but you have to figure out how much of this music, beer, and other pleasures is enough.

While both of these ways to live your life sound reasonable, Kierkegaard uses this book to warn us that either the aesthetic or the ethical way can be taken too far. You can end up derailing yourself in a life that becomes sex, drugs, and rock'n'roll. Or you can find yourself following ethical rules too strictly, and wind up in an unhappy, if ordered, life.

In order to lead a truly meaningful life, the aesthetic and the ethical modes of existence have to bring you to faith. You must develop a sense of faith to live a good life, to have made the best choices. It's only through faith in a Supreme Being that a person can achieve their best life.

Fear and Trembling Knights

In *Fear and Trembling*, Kierkegaard takes the need to live a life of religious faith one step farther. In this book, his alter-ego Johann Silentio (John the Silent) walks us through the Akeidah, the binding of Isaac.

In this biblical story, taken from the book of Genesis, Abraham at the end of his life has been asked to take his only Hebrew son Isaac to Mount Moriah and offer him to God. This is an ironic command. For years, as the faith ambassador of the one true God, Abraham has spoken against sacrificing your children to false gods. No loving God, according to Abraham, would ever demand you sacrifice a child for Him or Her (*Fear and Trembling*).

Yet, as the tenth and final challenge that God gives Abraham to prove the sincerity of his faith, he has asked him to sacrifice his son. God seems to expect Abraham to go against his own teachings, and do that which he claims is detestable to a loving God. Kierkegaard is deeply troubled by this. He wonders aloud if he would have been able to obey this unspeakably horrible order.

This ironic horror leads Kierkegaard to suggest a few concepts. First is the "teleological suspension of the ethical." Just because Abraham knows it's wrong to sacrifice a child, does not mean it won't be asked of him ever. Faith in God requires us to suspend our sense of right and wrong. Sometimes, we have to do unspeakable things because that's what our religious faith demands of us. Moses is commanded by God to eradicate the memory of Amalek from the face of the world. God challenges

Abraham to bind and sacrifice Isaac. These are two such examples of the moments where your faith trumps common sense.

Second, Kierkegaard concludes that in terms of faith, there are two kinds of people; two Knights. The Knight of Faith is the person whose faith is so pure, true, and strong he or she can do anything asked of them by their God. They are powered by their love and devotion for a being greater than themselves. Their cause is the path of righteousness.

Kierkegaard desperately wishes to be a Knight of Faith, like Abraham. Abraham never wavered, he never cracked, and he never gave up. When God commanded Abraham to sacrifice his son, he did not even argue. He simply escorted Isaac to the Mountain of Moriah. He built an altar, tied his son so he couldn't flee, and was about to sacrifice him, when an angel told him to stop. The test, as it turns out, was like a cosmic game of chicken. Abraham passes the test because he can rely on his faith to assure him anything God tells him to do is the right thing and must be done. He is rewarded by not having to kill Isaac. Isaac gets to live a full and happy life.

The other knight is the Knight of Infinite Resignation. This Knight is far more common. The Knight of Infinite Resignation gives up. He seeks faith, but he never actually achieves it. The path is too hard. There is too much you are uncertain about. You cannot complete this task. This Knight would listen to the command of God and not do it. He might bring Isaac to Moriah, but the Knight of Infinite resignation would fail to sacrifice the boy. He would not commit fully to the game of chicken.

Truly, the second Knight is most people. There are few who can stick long-term to a path. It's just a really challenging thing to do. Which as Kierkegaard notes, is why people who possess true Christian faith are extremely rare.

More Human than Human

The characters in *Blade Runner 2049* who most relate to Kierkegaard's thoughts are the replicants. Here we have a class of people who live to serve human beings. They are the cheap labor force that will help humanity colonize the galaxy. By doing all the menial, hard labor humans can't or won't do, the replicants make a more comfortable life possible for the humans.

In *2049*, much like its predecessor, there's the thought that replicants are more human in their actions and decisions than the human beings they are forced to serve. Even Rick Deckard seems detached, not affected, by the terrible stories he relates to K of his need to keep his distance from Los Angeles and his then young family.

In *2049*, the most humane and thus relatable characters are the ones who were either born in a vat of liquids, or are holograms. Joi is a perfect example. Here is a hologram who is programmed to provide pleasure and companionship to the person who buys her. K has a Joi.

Joi's relationship to K is very clearly an ethical way for a person to lead her life. She is devoted to K. She helps K as best she can. She even wishes to accompany K and experience as much of his work day as possible. This level of love and faithfulness is the sort of thing a spouse does for their partner out of an ethical sense of devotion. It's a pleasurable experience, but one that is carefully programmed and controlled. Joi takes it further, even if it might mean her death. These are all motivations and beliefs that Kierkegaard considers.

K and Joi both seek human connections. While they have each other, it's not sufficient. A hologram of a woman and a man who was born of a cloning vat lack the social tools to mirror a human adult relationship. K further wants to belong to the ultimate human group, the family. The prospect of possibly being the missing child powers him forward in his pursuit of Deckard.

While Joi may be fully devoted to K, and that is her path to a life of ethical devotion, K desires a family unit. To have belonged to a parent. Barring that, he is content to reunite a parent with a child. In these two paths, K and Joi have both made choices to approach a religious life.

Let's Talk about Luv

Then there is Luv, the strong right arm of Niander Wallace. She who will contend with K to claim Deckard; whose story comes to a gripping climax at sea.

Luv is very clearly a faithful servant of Wallace. Her devotion to the cause of her god, Wallace, is total. She has placed her faith in the arms of the man who has single-handedly saved humanity. Whereas K and Joi experience lower levels of faith, as they struggle and meander to make sense out of the world of *2049*, Luv does not have that problem.

Luv will unquestioningly follow any order Wallace gives her. She doesn't have to. She is a conscious being. However, when Wallace talks she experiences the same teleological suspension of ethics as Abraham. This allows her to kill the clone of Rachael, and to cause great torturous pain to humans she interrogates. Luv will even fight her fellow replicants to fulfill Wallace's command.

Kierkegaard would view the total submission Luv gives to the words and desires of her creator as true faith. This is the religious life that brings about the greatest ethical good. More than being an aesthete, more than simply living an ethical life. To be religiously devoted, and to have total faith in a supreme being is what makes for Kierkegaard a truly wholesome and good Christian.

Luv passes that test with flying colors. Her faith is as constant as Abraham's. She never falters or wavers in her duties and challenges, numerous though they are. She is a good, faithful servant of Wallace; the only sour note is that she dies in the end.

K fails to achieve his goal of obtaining the spiritual high of faith. Luv, although quite faithful, is killed. Our hero is not very good at the job he is ordered to do, and our adversary is flawless in her execution of every order she receives. How does any of this make sense?

The roles of who is the knight of faith and who the knight of infinite resignation are inverted, or switched, because that's the type of film *2049* is. *2049*, while science fiction, also belongs to the film genre known as film noir. Film noir, literally "black film," is a type of crime fiction. It is suspenseful, twisty in its plot, calls for callous behavior, and usually ends badly—sometimes so badly that everybody dies.

These two characters, our proverbial knights, are locked in a fight that is found in a hard-boiled film noir. By the rules of that genre, there's no way K or Luv will be entirely victorious. The question then becomes which of these two knights can survive until the end of the story.

Luv is our Knight of Faith. She is fully committed to the word of Wallace. She will help him any way she can in his quest to save humanity. He has decided he needs to create replicants that can give birth. Luv, in faithful devotion, will find him the people he needs to question to understand how to make that happen. Her faith is so unquestioning, Kierkegaard would probably be jealous. He would find her to be a true servant with real Christian faith.

This is why she dies. Luv will do anything for Wallace. She will stretch her abilities to their breaking point on her creator's behalf. As a consequence of this devotion, she is willing to give up her life in service to Wallace. When she faces off with K at sea, this is the most faithful way for her to end her life. Either she can successfully take Deckard off-world, or die trying. Since the movie does not allow her to achieve the end goal

Wallace demanded, she has no choice as his faithful servant but to die. She failed her god, and must end her life. This is how it works in film noir.

K, however, is our knight of infinite resignation. Throughout this movie he is constantly told seeming truths, statements that boost his hopes, only to have them all shattered and proven false. K has faith in the idea of the family. He desperately wants to achieve being part of a family. When he learns that the toy horse he remembers owning belonged to the child of Deckard, his hope is so high.

When the former nursemaid of Deckard's child tells him in no uncertain terms that it cannot be, that K is not Deckard's child, he is deflated. His look is a blend of defeat and surprise. This is often what happens to people who falter along the way of trying to attain the spiritual high of faith. Life takes every opportunity to crush your hopes and dreams. He must resign himself to not being Deckard's child.

Worse, when he finally finds Deckard to bring him back to Los Angeles, he loses Joi. Once Joi has been erased, there's no getting her back. K is forced to resign himself to being alone.

When the replicant resistance find and give him help, they order him to kill Deckard. K cannot and will not obey that order. For K., there's nothing more sacred than a family unit. He has a chance to reunite Deckard with his daughter. He's not going to give that up. However, he also cannot let the resistance know that Deckard still lives. K resigns himself to faking Deckard's death.

All through the movie, K is constantly in a position to almost attain faith, but repeatedly falls short. His life, though an ethical one, is hindered from becoming one of faith and devotion such as Luv had. He simply cannot win. All of these factors tell us that K is not only our protagonist; he is also the knight of infinite resignation. This is what film noir demands.

Rewinding to the End

Acceptance that the universe wants you to give up is what happens to the heroes in film noir. Oftentimes, the hero just dies. Here, in *2049*, K is allowed a gift of grace, as he rests on the stairs outside Stelline's studio enjoying the snowfall, dying.

Kierkegaard has shown us that the best way to live your life is to embrace faith in a supreme being. Luv fully accepts that as the universal truth it is, and has committed herself fully to her creator, Wallace. She will be his strong right arm. She will be to Wallace as Abraham was to God.

K, on the other hand, is the person Kierkegaard is afraid he really is himself—the one who attempts but fails to attain true faith. He rises to the occasion, only to stumble and falter each time. He gets discouraged, only to find a new hope which will eventually disappoint him. This is what it is to be a knight of infinite resignation.

In both the characters of K and Luv we see two of the major ideas of Kierkegaard play themselves out in a film noir science fiction movie. Because it is film noir, the roles of who is faithful and who fails to be faithful are reversed. Our hero is the failed person who will never know true faith, and our villain has only known true faith her entire, if short, life.

Luv gets to die gracefully in seawater, while K lays down on a staircase in a snowfall. While it would have been even more perfect if it became a blizzard while he lay there, the snowfall is quite heavy. It could be K will freeze to death out there. He certainly cannot be in the studio. That's where Deckard is meeting his daughter and has discovered his faith. K will simply never be able to have that special kind of a moment.

19

And God Created Replicants in His Own Image

JERRY PIVEN

> In order that the bliss of the saints may be more delightful for them and that they may render more copious thanks to God for it, it is given to them to see perfectly the punishment of the damned.
>
> —THOMAS AQUINAS, *Summa Theologiae*

Blade Runner is ostensibly a futuristic pulp noir story about Rick Deckard, a man hired to terminate errant replicants, manufactured flesh slaves which are malfunctioning and murdering innocent humans.

Blade Runner 2049 continues the saga with the story of another such blade runner, K, who stumbles upon evidence of a miraculous replicant birth, leading him into a sinister world where a blind scientist seeks to harness the miracle in order to increase his stock of slaves, and a secret army of replicants seeks deliverance from such oppression. Central to both movies is the harsh irony that we're often less humane than those we label "nonhuman."

Those we label nonhuman, we also view as inhuman—they are both lesser beings and less moral than we, the true humans. For real human beings can create slaves and slaughter them ruthlessly, while the ostensibly nonhuman replicants yearn, suffer, love, and grieve. These are stories about human inhumanity, where we can inflict suffering and massacre others who can feel desire and sadness, while we imagine that *they* are evil and deserve to die. And these movies really do show us how these nonhuman beings experience excruciating sadness and despair.

Those who suffer senseless cruelty wonder why they were created with thoughts and feelings, only to languish and die.

The films invoke mythic and religious symbolism. In *Blade Runner* a murderous replicant becomes Christlike, and suffers for our human or inhumane sins, while the storyline of *2049* is consumed by miraculous birth and liberation. Finally, these movies ask us to reflect on the obsession with mastering life and death, the dread that impels the need for control over birth and generation itself, and how violence can be born of fear, envy, and despair.

Human Inhumans

The opening premise of *Blade Runner* is that certain replicants have become vicious murderers and must be tracked down and killed. But like so many rationales for slaughter, the death warrant on replicants is a deception that masks the real inhumanity. Rachael is condemned to death, for example, even though she hasn't harmed anyone, but merely fled her servitude.

The theme is stated more nakedly in *Blade Runner 2049*. when the replicant Sapper says, "The crime is that they run. Sapper Morton, who fled brutal military service, is a replicant farmer, who grows food for humans. His face quietly conveys immense pain and despair. He's retired simply for being, through no fault of his own, an earlier rather than a later model replicant.

Though presented with a story of merciless, murderous replicants, there's a counternarrative. The replicants themselves tell a story of subservience and ignominy. And they're not just automated cadavers. They *do* feel emotions, capable of love, delight, fear, anger, bitterness, regret, resentment, and aspirations for freedom. In contrast, it is the human beings who so often seem inhuman in this world. The world of *Blade Runner* is a simulated society where people live robotically, and flee from genuine human contact into numbness and alienation.

The fact that the replicants seem to feel a spectrum of emotions may force us to ask how many of our own supposedly real human emotions are "programmed" responses, as opposed to the comforting but specious metaphysical notion that by virtue of "being human" we really feel when other inhuman creatures cannot. The *Blade Runner* narratives are social commentaries on our own alienation, or dissociation, or submersion in simulacra as ways of not really suffering the depths of human feeling. And they further ask the sinister question: Who, precisely, is inhuman?

For the replicants seem to possess more empathy than the cold-blooded human beings who treat them as objects, slaves, contemptibly worthless "skin jobs." They seem anguished by their subjugation. They yearn for freedom. And they become so distraught when their own companions are terminated that they vow revenge. Do we not hear echoes of Doctor Frankenstein's monster, asking why he was created just to suffer the cruelty of his creator and fellow living beings?

Blade Runner would thus seem to be a dark irony about human subjugation and ignominy. For much of human history is a record of human violation, enslavement, debasement, and dehumanization. When does the truly inhumane, cruel, merciless, and sanctimonious group not declare itself superior and more worthy of freedom and life, while its subjugated slaves are beneath them, beneath contempt, worthless, and subhuman? History teems with descriptions of other peoples as contamination, disease, vermin, parasites. With no sense of irony or awareness, those slaughtering or subjugating others inflict inhumanity while declaring themselves human, more human, or superhuman.

So the subtext of the *Blade Runner* narratives is that the replicants may only *seem* inhuman when they murder. But they have murdered for freedom, for the pursuit of autonomy over their own lives, in response to being enslaved and treated as worthless objects to be abused and destroyed. To die for such freedom would even make them more human than actual humans, as Mariette limns in *2049*. That is hence a reflection of *us*, of *our* way of living complacently when we subjugate others, and rest comfortably on pyramids of corpses reaped from our conquests, invasions, and enslavements.

Thus the most uncanny irony may be that the homicidal replicants in the *Blade Runner* series are in certain ways more human, as they feel the despair of servitude, the human anguish we experience when our loved ones are slaughtered, the human desire for justice. Where Freysa can say in *2049* that "Dying for the right cause is the most human thing we can do," the humans in these films do *not* feel any empathy for those enslaved and murdered. Those ostensibly human, real beings don't seem to question their right to enslave, or the pain of their victims.

The sinister message to the viewer should send a shiver down our own spines: the seeming protagonists may not be human, and nor might *we,* if we thrive on the subjugation of others while comforting ourselves with notions that they're evil, and inhuman, and hence we need to feel no empathy or guilt or remorse, or anything. And yet Roy Batty's final monologue is full of a sorrow and despair that can only be human:

I've seen things you people wouldn't believe. Attack ships on fire off the shoulder of Orion. I watched C-beams glitter in the darkness at Tannhäuser Gate. All those moments will be lost in time like tears in rain. Time to die.

Roy Batty may seem the epitome of evil, of homicidal glee and remorseless lunatic vengeance. But this is an all too human lamentation. In contrast Deckard moves through the film with a conspicuous lack of emotion. The contrast is so striking because the nonhuman replicant seems so much more human. Deckard's as cognitively detached as Descartes (the homophonic similarity can't be a coincidence) and can only observe Roy's human torment without feeling it for himself. If Roy's final lament inspires Deckard's moment of human awakening, it's imparted by a replicant consigned to slavery and then slaughter, deemed soulless and unworthy of life.

Inhuman Humans

In *2049* it's again human beings who are so ruthless and inhumane that they could thrive on an economy of slavery and slaughter replicants remorselessly. (Or rather, they send other replicants to do their dirty work and murder their own kind.) The contempt is palpable. Again the replicants are despised as "skin jobs." It's the human beings, like Wallace, who can create life in the name of some sublime moral purpose and then slip a blade into the entrails of those newly-born angels standing naked before him.

Evil can become ordinary and culturally acceptable, even banal. Subjugation, dehumanization, and massacre can become virtuous and moral in any era. And it may require a shock of recognition for Deckard—and for us—to see that the ersatz human may be us, not those we eviscerate with such moral certainty. No, we aren't all ruthless murderers! But these movies remind us how easy it is for us to become callous and inhumane, and treat others as a threat worthy of death. The *Blade Runner* movies are parables about doppelgangers that mirror our own capacity for homicidal predation though we would see such monstrosity as utterly alien.

We experience our vicious, sadistic, malicious, inhumane emotions as alien because we cannot tolerate imagining ourselves that way. We'd prefer to think we're on the side of the angels. So we disavow such feelings, pretend they don't exist, and even, *project* them onto others. That's one reason why the replicants seem so uncanny. They mirror our own malice and inhumanity. We've created them in our image. They too much resemble us. What does that mean? It means that when they have human feelings and longings, we ignore and deny them, or even show contempt. It's not real! Just programming, simulation, but not genuinely human. Hence they deserve no love or compassion.

And when the replicants become enraged at their mistreatment, and become bitter, or vengeful, then we deny our own culpability, the fact that they are our own dark reflections. We've made them into murderers, but we refuse those loathsome, sinister qualities we do not wish to see in ourselves. But a more uncanny irony is that, again, they've accidentally been endowed with the capacity to yearn and love, which many human beings seem to have lost in the *Blade Runner* movies. So again, they may have *surpassed* the humanity of many real human beings, which is why something else, something nonhuman may be needed to redeem us.

This is an ominous reflection about human beings, given our history of demeaning and dehumanizing others. It's not that those we declare evil or bestial are subhuman. We *need* to dehumanize them so we can exploit or ignore or even destroy them in the name of some moral imperative, and keep humanity "safe." Our own dread of fragility and death impels us to declare them evil, worthless, subhuman, and worthy of death. These movies are saturated by images of wasteland, death, and decay. Minds, bodies, souls, the planet itself, are all decaying, and human beings suffer the sickness unto literal and emotional death. And we cathartically destroy and *invent* evil to escape our own dread and angst.

Hence the replicants are not only our slaves. Dehumanizing and subjugating them becomes a strategy of transcendence—killing off evil in the name of some higher morality enables us to vanquish our fear and attain the illusion of being heroic, human, and good. But that's just our fantasy, since in reality they may be entirely innocent. So more radically, that homicidal, subhuman lunatic we once deemed the epitome of evil may really be a symbol of divine innocence or humanity. This is why the *Blade Runner* narratives incorporate an explicitly *theological* imagery.

Inhuman Saviors

The *Blade Runner* narratives are suffused with mythic and religious symbolism. In the first movie the replicant assassin driving the story becomes Christlike, suffering and dying for our human, or inhuman sins. Roy embodies the despairing soul, not just a homicidal machine. If he seems chillingly maniacal, his name also recalls the biblical El Roi, the God who sees me."

During the final chase, Roy's hand is lacerated, as if nailed to a cross. The replicant finally rescues (and redeems) his pursuer, laments his own mortality, and dies. A bird flies into the sky, recapitulating a mythic image of the soul taking flight from the body.

Herein resides Roy's bitterness and rage. How inhuman to create beings who can think and feel, only to enslave them. How cruel to create beings capable of contemplation, and even love, and then to torture them, or discard them as refuse. How pitiless to impart life and consciousness and then steal them away. Why was he created? Merely to experience this awe, having witnessed arresting, glittering visions in space, and then to die? How is that not a reflection of our own human anguish and despair over our own brief life spans? This reflects what the poets have lamented for millennia, yearning for life, dreading death, and wondering why a divine creator would make them mortal.

So we understand their rage. For the creator who gave them life, love, and awe, also enslaved and doomed them to die. This is a fundamentally human meditation on mortality, but also a chilling reflection of the cruelty of our own beloved creators, who may also be far more sadistic and malicious than we want to know. *Blade Runner* is thus both an existential lamentation and an expression of our secret animosity toward the divine (though believers would desperately deny with all their being).

And yet Roy does what the blade runners would not; what the creators would not; what no other has ever done for a replicant: He saves a human being's life. He even saves one who has murdered his friends and hunted him to death. If that isn't the spirit of grace, what is? Roy is the Christlike being sacrificed for our sins, and his humanity then is inhuman. That is, it is not a mode of compassion possessed by human beings.

At least not yet. And Deckard's redemption from his own inhumanity is his ability to love. *Blade Runner* (in several versions) concludes with him departing with his beloved Rachael. In *2049* she has died, and Deckard has consigned himself to a desert wasteland. It's once again the humanity and sacrifice of a replicant that awakens his humanity, and his desire to know his forsaken daughter.

The Paraclete, and Christ Continued

Theological allusion is also explicit in *2049* though embodied differently. For we have a miraculous birth, a child of destiny, a redeemer, and a liberator. But we also have an Old Testament theme, though it also plays out unusually. *2049* is the story of a blade runner investigating a mysterious death, and he finds that this replicant corpse died in childbirth. It was the same Rachael from *Blade Runner*, and she miraculously gave birth. This is a scandal, since a replicant capable of bearing life could destroy society. As Lieutenant Joshi says, "The world is built on a wall. It separates kind. Tell either side there's no wall, you bought a war. Or a slaughter."

Where the nominally human police would perpetuate the lie, keep replicants enslaved, and extinguish those who might reveal the truth (merely by existing), armies of replicants yearning for freedom are willing to die for that "right cause." This cause is a miraculous birth, humanization, deliverance. Sapper claims "You've never seen a miracle." And Freysa later asserts, "I saw a miracle delivered . . . I knew that baby meant that we are more than just slaves. . . . If a baby can come from one of us, we are our own masters." In *2049* freedom becomes the liberation of the Israelite slaves, led by Joseph, son of biblical Rachel. The parallels are pregnant: Wallace says "And God remembered Rachel, heeded her, and opened her womb." Rachael dies in childbirth just like her biblical namesake. The replicant K takes on the name of Joe, and his destiny seems to be the emancipation of the oppressed.

Joe becomes the nonhuman liberator, sacrificing his own life to save Deckard from assassination. The biblical parallels go awry here, for Joe more resembles Christ than Joseph. Like Christ he consorts with prostitutes and is even wounded in the side like Jesus after being lacerated on the cross. Where Joseph led his people to freedom, Joe would endure death to save a human being. But in *2049* it only seems as if Joe is the destined redeemer, whereas the actual miracle child and future savior is Ana. Protected by a dome, untouched by contamination and the malice of the replicants willing to eradicate humanity, she is the miracle, immaculate child, who may dissolve that barrier between mutually despising, dehumanizing tribes. If the biblical savior was male, here we have a pristine woman who may dissolve that thirst for blood.

The theological implications are again sinister though. If the biblical God could slaughter ruthlessly, so can the creator Wallace. Icily obsessed with creating replicants who can give birth, who can gestate life where the replicant womb is now "dead space between the stars," the creator is willing to murder remorselessly when they are barren. Blind to his own inhu-

manity, Wallace says, "We make angels in the service of civilization" yet he can serenely disembowel the child gushing from his
ersatz fallopian tubes. He pierces his own daughter's abdomen
as if chastening her defective womb. And he makes the slaughter of actual human beings part of a divine cause.

Perhaps this purely fictional obsession with creating beings
that can gestate life, and willingness to kill them for being barren, suggests something more pervasive about that existential
dread of death—the drive not to be helpless before that mael-
strom of life and death power that renders individuals insignificant and feeble. *2049* may suggest how this laceration impels
some men to crave power and miracle, and even murder without remorse while pursuing their fantasies of some more
exalted cause or creation.

Terminus

The *Blade Runner* movies are a dark mirror of our own inhumanity, the inner deadness and monstrosity we cannot see in
ourselves, the dread of death and nonbeing that impel our
mania for bloodshed. They are parables about doppelgangers
who mirror our own homicidal predation though we would see
such monstrosity as utterly alien. They are a futuristic vision
of the banality of evil, as the society (and viewers) just assume
that replicants are subhuman, can be enslaved, or terminated
when they resist subjugation.

The movies reveal how much suffering and death we inflict
on those deemed inhuman, and how very human they actually
are. For they too have seen miraculous things. They experience
pain and loss. They suffer the despair of knowing that despite
the wondrous things they've seen and lived, they will die after
a brief childhood of years. And this too, makes them bitter, as
they yearn for life and revenge.

The *Blade Runner* sagas are existential parables about
despair in the wake of evanescent life, and ironic stories about
our own inhumanity to those we deem subhuman. The parables are bathed in mythic and religious symbolism, as the replicant assassins driving the story become Christlike, and suffer
for our human or inhuman sins. This existential theological
noir becomes a meditation on the anguish of impermanence,
and hatred toward God the superhuman creator, and perhaps,
the pathology of the God fantasy itself.

More humane, perhaps, to strive for earthly human love,
than create and destroy like a deity. The most insidious evil,
then, is the monstrous fear and hatred that impel so many of

us to seek conquest of our human frailty, to yearn for transcendence of human mortality, as though we were gods with the power to create and destroy, since we then become undead beings dead to compassion and all that may be truly human.

20
Sympathy for the Existential Devils

JAMES M. McLACHLAN

As Roy Batty walks into Hannibal Chew's eye lab, a quarter of the way through *Blade Runner*, he misquotes the poet William Blake: "Fiery the angels fell; deep thunder rolled around their shores; burning with the fires of Orc."

In Blake's poem, *America: A Prophecy*, the angels *rise,* in order to attack Heaven. Of course, there are good reasons for changing the line here from rising to falling. Batty wants to meet his maker/God, Eldon Tyrell, and has had to descend from the heavens to Earth in his quest for immortality, or at least, "more life, Father." Batty then murders God, savagely pushing in his creator's all-seeing tri-focaled eyes. In fact, he kills the entire trinity, as it were: Chew, maker of eyes, a kind of holy Spirit; Seabastian, the son who is also ancient, and who makes the bodies or incarnates the replicants; and Tyrell himself, God the Father.

Batty and his cohort challenge their tyrannical creators/gods. But there's a hopelessness to their rebellion, which persists in *Blade Runner 2049*, at the dead tree that marks Rachael's grave replacing the lush forests that she and Deckard see (as the theatrical release of *Blade Runner* concludes). And while the gods have changed, they're still gods. Not the tri-focaled Tyrell, but the blind, with hi-tech all-seeing eyes, Niander Wallace.

Like most gods, Wallace is more concerned with the creation of a great big beautiful universe of his own making than with the problems of the "little people" who reside there. "Every leap of civilization was built on the back of a disposable workforce," he tells us, "but I can only make so many." And so, he tries to imitate the God of Christian Theology, by creating angels and a great chain of being, in which the workers have their part to play in the creation of a beautiful cosmos. But unlike supernatural gods, he can't make slaves who can make more slaves.

The noir atmosphere of dark streets, and dark pessimism, that somehow includes the smallest ray of hope, captures the existentialist mood of these movies. Back in the 1940s and 1950s existentialism was the contemporary of film noir and has long been associated with it. They share a common heritage in Noir's debt to hard-boiled detective stories.

The most famous existentialist, Jean-Paul Sartre, loved those stories that ran in France as the famous "*Series Noir*." In Sartre's famous lecture "Existentialism Is a Humanism" he asserts that human beings are "condemned to freedom" and that this freedom arises from their "nothingness," their ability to negate what they were, to change. Sartre exclaimed what all existentialists "have in common is simply the fact that they believe that *existence* comes before *essence*."

"Existence precedes essence," means that we are, at birth, thrown into the world and then work out who we are in relation to the situation in which we find ourselves. Humans are different from, say, penknives, which are created with an essence, in their case a purpose, from which they can't intentionally deviate. Humans *can* deviate from theirs, and replicants can as well—depart from their "baselines," in the language of *2049*. This is the key theme of the *Blade Runner* movies.

Tyrell, Bryant, Deckard, and Wallace see replicants as something made to perform a certain function. Their essence is planned before their existence. Replicants are akin, they believe, to Sartre's penknives. They're made by their maker, God/Tyrell/Wallace, with the purpose of being slaves (some as warriors, others as workers, and still others as sex slaves) in the off-world colonies. They are created with a definite purpose. Just as in traditional theology, God creates humanity to exhibit his glory and to worship God. The existential anguish of deciding what we are, isn't supposed to trouble these creatures. They are predestined to be one thing or the other.

Tyrell and Wallace are *not* God. Still, this doesn't stop them from *trying* to be God. This desire to be God is the source of their failure and frustration. In Sartre's existentialism, the "desire to be god" is the source of his claim that "man is a useless passion." To say that we all want to "be god" sounds pretty grandiose. But even K wants to be special, like Tyrell, Wallace, and Luv, we all seem to want to be able to be like the omnipotent God and work our wills in the world. It is other people who constantly remind us this isn't possible. In this way they save us from ourselves. In Sartre's famous words, "Hell is other people."

Sympathy for the Existentialist Devils

In both *Blade Runner* movies the noir feel lends itself to existentialist interpretation. With existentialist interpretation comes sympathy for the devil, who rebels against the tyranny of gods. The *Blade Runner* films are dystopias that draw on the darkness of classic film noir, and the pessimism of noir's contemporary, existentialism, which became part of the noir universe.

The heroes of Sartre's plays and his biographies of Jean Genet and Baudelaire are, like Batty, Satanic Christ figures who, though bound to lose, point to an existential freedom outside the divine Great Chain of Being that enslaves us. In his philosophical biography of Baudelaire, Sartre develops this theme. The freedom and indeed the identity of the human is in its nothingness a rebellion before the pure positivity of God/Being. God's creatures seek to create their own place outside of the perfect harmony of Being. The individuality, the freedom, and the personhood of the human being is found in its negativity.

In his biography of Baudelaire, Sartre describes this freedom of negation in terms of Satan's rebellion against the absolute positivity of God/Being. It may be that God owned Satan's being but Satan, like the kid before the bully, the slave before his master, can still disdain the power that crushes him. Satan, he writes "prevailed against God, his master and conqueror, by his suffering, but that flame of non-satisfaction which, at the very moment when divine omnipotence crushed him, at the very moment when he acquiesced in being crushed, shone like an unquenchable reproach." Like Blake's Orc and Lucifer, Baudelaire's Satan is a heroic figure. Defeated by that mighty positive creative power of God, he prevails in the only way a creature can prevail against the pure positive power of God, or the dumb power of an otherwise indifferent universe. He escapes the infinite being, insofar as such a being could not conceive nothingness. His nothingness is his freedom, insofar as he may do things that are unpredictable. Like Satan, we may all go against our baseline.

Sartre contends that for traditional theology, we are only really free to do evil. Evil is defined as the negation of a person's place in a great chain of being. We are made by God, or by an indifferent universe, to do things. But we can choose not to do them. We can resist our design, in at least small ways. Batty has done "questionable things," but when he saves Deckard, he shakes himself free from following his "killer" essence, given to him on his creation by Tyrell. Seeing Batty's sacrifice, Deckard is freed of his vocation as well, which is to "retire" replicants. He escapes with Rachael. K, who is more of a replicant everyman, discovers he is not special, and is liberated by the discovery.

Angels and the Great Chain of Being

The Great Chain of Being is an old idea in Christian Theology. The cosmology is hierarchical, with a spectrum stretching down from the greatest to the least, with individual beings in the universe fitting into the scale at different points. The idea dominated Western thought for a long time, its hierarchical assumptions penetrating every aspect of thought, from religion through law, politics, and economics.

But in the great chain lurked a contradiction that haunted Christian theology for centuries. The contradiction arose from the effort to combine two incompatible scales of value: the ontological and the moral. Ontologically, something is good because it fills its place in being. Like Sartre's penknife, it fills the function or vocation given it by its maker. Morally, on the other hand, a person must be able to act freely, to exercise their ability to act against their nature. The theme runs through the *Blade Runner* films, as with Wallace's use of angels, for example, Joi and Luv, whom he's named after key Christian virtues.

Joi seems human, for example, free. But is she? "I've been inside you," Mariette says damningly, "not so much there as you think." And while K seems to be in love with her, we're told, over and over again, by the Wallace Corporation's Joi-model advertising, that "she will tell you what you want to hear." This is nowhere more worrisome than when she tells K that he's "special," that he's "born not made." The reference is to the Nicene Creed, which tells us that in the miracle of the incarnation, Jesus was "begotten not made." Joi says that K is a god/human incarnate, special, not simply a replicant.

But Joi, unlike Batty, K, Pris, and their fellow replicants, is not physical, but rather pure spirit. An angel, a product of the Wallace Corporation, who is also the source of Wallace's ability to track K and know what he has found, what he's thinking. Her destruction, and K's encounter with the advertisement version of Joi, reveals that perhaps she's not a real "other," but only a projection of K's longing to be loved, and to be more than a creation of the Wallace Corporation. In true Sartrean fashion he, like the rest of us, wants to be the center of the story, to be God. But, like Batty, he becomes more like Christ when he sacrifices himself. He doesn't kill Deckard. He takes him to his daughter.

Luv, on the other hand, is the chief arch-angel of God/Wallace. She seeks to be the best, the closest to the pure being that she's invented to be. She's an angel, not only because angels don't reproduce, but because she seeks only to fulfill her place, her vocation in the chain. As she says in her climatic struggle with K, she's "the best one," Wallace's greatest creation. She's a being without temptation and thus utterly ruthless in the completion of her tasks. She does what she has been created to do. She's a total monster. But notice, she's like a penknife, a really good tool, good in the sense that she fulfills the essence that her maker, Niander Wallace, supplied her with. Like the Rachael of Philip K. Dick's novel *Do Androids Dream of Electric Sheep?* that was the original source for the films, she is completely rational and mechanical, she pursues her maker's purpose.

If "the Good" is identified with Being, with doing what you're created to do, like a good hammer hammers well, then Luv is a good angel. Batty also calls Deckard, who has "retired" his lover and friends, the "good man." "Good," in this case, is identified with fulfilling one's purpose in being. To be a criminal is to rebel against that vocation. In the first scene in *2049*, Sapper challenges K to do what he's not made to do—not retire him. But K has to do his job because that's his purpose. It's only when K begins to find that he is, perhaps, the chosen one that he starts to go off baseline. The deviation from being, from the purpose created in us by God, or the Wallace Corporation, is evil and if he continues, he must be destroyed. K's free to do evil and, in this sense, only free when he does evil. But here the sense of God and evil are as warped as they are in the Great Chain of Being. This association of freedom and evil can only be true if we associate the good with being, and evil with a lack of being. What Sapper asks K to think about is the other being, the person who stands before him, not his place in the order of things.

In the order of being, Deckard is the "good man" when he does his job, "retires" slaves in the service of masters like Tyrell. It's here that the Tyrell Corporation's motto, "More Human than Human," starts to make sense to us in a way not intended by Tyrell, but true to the existentialist motto, "existence precedes essence." Initially, Deckard is less human than Batty. He, like Batty, has been created to be a killer.

The old argument about whether Deckard is or isn't a replicant is irrelevant here. At the beginning of the movie he tells Chief Bryant that he has quit. But when Bryant reminds him of his place in the hierarchy, that he's "either police or little people," he takes up his job. He's part of the chain. He tells Rachael, "Replicants are like any other machine—they're either a benefit or a hazard. If they're a benefit, it's not my problem." As long as they're in their place, they're good. If not, they must be destroyed. The only sense in which Deckard is good at this point is that he's the law. Like Luv, he fills his vocation. He's on the side of a formal good that really isn't the moral good. The good man is the fallen man, he's free, and Roy is his redeemer. Deckard's changed at the end of the movie, and in the next film as well. He's saved by Roy Batty.

Before the redemption, he treats the replicants as "its." Of Rachael, he asks Tyrell, "How can it not know what it is?" He doesn't seem to have real relations with any other humans either. In the comical scene where he poses as a representative from the "Confidential Committee on Moral Abuses" and asks stupid questions, Zhora responds, "Are you for real?" He isn't. At least he's less authentic than the replicants who've fallen to Earth. The replicants in the movie seem more empathetic, more human, than the humans who live machine-like lives. Deckard's fall elevates him to humanity.

Roy Batty and K: Lucifer/Christ/Everyman

In William Blake's poem, Orc is a "Lover of wild rebellion and transgression of God's law." He's an eating, drinking, coupling, flaming, subjective individual, come to battle the gods, a pure Promethean character. This is really the subject of both *Blade Runner* and Blake's *America: A Prophecy.* Batty, like Blake's Orc, is a vital, living being which, for Blake, is a unity of oppositions.

As Blake explains in *The Marriage of Heaven and Hell*:

Without Contraries is no progression. Attraction and Repulsion, Reason and Energy, Love and Hate, are necessary to Human existence. From these contraries spring what the religious call Good & Evil. Good is the passive that obeys Reason. Evil is the active springing from Energy. Good is Heaven. Evil is Hell.

Batty, at first, is a killer who follows his programming. But he also acts out of love for his fellow replicants. But the replicants have an energy, and a fellowship, the humans seem not to have. At first, Batty is only the negative refusal to be what he was created to be. He rebels, he murders, he returns to Earth and murders his makers. After he kills Tyrell, then loses Pris, he's about to die.

Batty's alone, abandoned in the dark world of *Blade Runner,* but he affirms life by saving Deckard. K makes a similar discovery. He loses Joi, discovers he's not the Messiah, walks the dark streets without hope.

It is at this point that Batty really goes off his baseline. Yes, he defeats Luv in a killer fight, but, he doesn't listen to the replicant rebels either. He's no longer a Blade Runner, an assassin for anyone. He saves a life rather than takes it. He affirms love and lays in down in the light and the snow not the rain and dark streets. And, once again, Deckard moves along on his journey to becoming more human than human.

V

A Real Girl
Now?

21
The Trouble with Joi

M.J. RYDER

When we first meet the character Joi in *Blade Runner 2049*, her voice appears from off-screen. "You're early!" she calls out as K enters the apartment. Banter ensues. "I'm trying a new recipe," she says, "I just need a bit more practice." More banter, and then, "Voilà!" the scene recalls an old-fashioned vision of domestic bliss.

But in *2049*, things aren't quite what they seem.

While Joi may conform to certain negative stereotypes around gender and the role of women, there's far more going on here than meets the eye. Just as she's acting out the role of a housewife, she's also acting out the role of a woman, and more interestingly still, the role of a human being. After all, she's not a human at all, but rather, an AI.

In this case, we can't separate Joi's gender from her assumed "humanity." She can't be "female" without first being human, and her human-like identity requires that she be thought of in gendered terms. It's not so much a question of whether Joi is female or even human, but rather how we define the human in the first place. This leads us to wonder, are we just as much like Joi, as she is like us?

The Trouble with Gender

Blade Runner 2049 is not your typical run-of-the-mill dystopia. For a start, most of the main characters aren't even human, but rather artificial constructs *presented* as human beings. Just as K is not a real "man" (spoiler alert!), neither is Joi a real "woman." Rather, Joi is an artificial construct acting out the role of a woman. For this reason it's wrong for us to think of Joi as a "she." Rather, Joi is an "it"—an artificial construct that was never a human woman in the first place.

Does this idea make you feel uncomfortable? It sure does me—and that's the whole point. This strange, unpleasant feeling is a result of our many built-in assumptions that help us make sense of the world and tell us how to behave. What this means is that when we see the actress Ana de Armas on screen, we automatically think of her as a *woman*, and a human woman at that, and so we assign her traits and characteristics that fit her into our worldview.

Things get even more interesting when we stop to consider what our worldview is and where it comes from. When we describe Ana de Armas as a woman, what exactly do we mean? What is it that makes us describe her as a woman, and how do we even know she's a woman in the first place? How is Ana de Armas different to the character she plays on screen, the AI character Joi?

All gender is in part a kind of performance—this is what Judith Butler tells us in her groundbreaking book, *Gender Trouble*. According to Butler, each of us "acts out" gender roles according to assumed norms and values. I'm a man because I act in a way that defines me as a man. By acting in this way, society imbues me with characteristics that a man is supposed to possess—whether I really possess them or not.

This idea of gender performance helps us to understand the way Joi is portrayed as a woman in *2049*. It can then be taken one stage further to encompass artificial beings as well. If as humans we're all acting out assigned gender roles, then what does this tell us about artificial characters, such as Joi, and our relationship with them? What does it tell us about what it means to be human?

Artificial Identity

When we talk about AI, many people will think of digital assistants such as Siri, Alexa, or Cortana. However, they're not really AI in the truest sense of the word. This is because they aren't "intelligent" in the way many of us might think. Rather, they present an *illusion* of intelligence, hidden beneath layers of scripted dialogue designed to make us believe that they're real.

Google, for example, employs a whole team of professional writers, also known as "storytellers," to script the responses given by its famous Assistant. These lines are designed to make it seem more believable and less artificial. One such writer is Emma Coats, a former employee of Pixar. So, the same people who write the scripts for movies such as *Toy Story*, *Inside Out*, and *The Incredibles*, are also writing the scripts designed to fool us into thinking our electronic assistants are "real" people, with real intelligence and real personality.

And let us not forget the voice acting. Remember, these aren't artificial voices we're hearing, but rather the voices of real-life human actors. Microsoft's Cortana is played by Jen Taylor, while Apple's Siri is played by Susan Bennett. And what do all these digital characters have in common? Yup, you guessed it . . . they're all women.

Look Who's Talking

It should come as no surprise to learn that many of the world's most popular digital assistants appear as women. They do this for a very specific reason. This is because, generally, we respond more positively to a female voice than to a male one. We're also far less likely to think we're being manipulated if the person doing the manipulating is a woman rather than a man!

So how does this apply to *2049*? Well, for a start, it gives us a glimpse of just *why* Joi may be presented as an attractive woman, as opposed to, say, a balding middle-aged man. This question is important because, as a digital construct, she could just as easily be presented with any number of gender identities, or even with no gender at all.

But she's not. Rather, she has a very clearly defined gender identity that serves to make her appear more authentic and more believable to humans. The fact that this gender happens to be female is particularly relevant, given the fact that we tend to trust women more than men.

In this case, Joi's performance works on a number of different levels. Firstly, within the context of the film's male-dominated world, Joi's assumed identity as a "female," *heterosexual* character makes her an appealing companion for the "male," presumably also straight, K. In this way, her performance influences the way the two characters interact and is one of the driving factors behind the intimate relations that we will get to in a moment.

Her presentation as a "woman" also serves to make her far more authentic and believable to a human audience, all of whom come pre-loaded with assumptions around sex and gender. Never mind that she's really an artificial construct—the fact she appears on screen as a woman, has "feminine" desires, and is played by a female actress makes her all the more convincing.

Roles within Roles

All of this goes to show just how complex the character Joi really is. And we shouldn't forget that Joi doesn't just exist within the movie world, for she also extends into the real world. In this case, we have the real-life Ana de Armas "playing" the role of a woman (see Judith Butler), who is then in turn "playing" the part of the AI character Joi, who is then "playing" out the role of a human woman.

These performances within performances blur the line between the character Joi and the actress who plays her. They also blur the line between human and non-human, as well as between the fictional universe of the film and the real world beyond. A part of this can be traced to the fact that each of us has a set of assumptions hard-wired into our brains that helps us understand the world around us. Because we assume certain things about the human female actress Ana de Armas, we're compelled to transfer these assumptions onto the non-human, non-female character Joi. This process is so subtle that most of us don't even realize we're doing it, and it's this central premise that underlies the way both *Blade Runner* and *2049* work.

We empathize with Joi and with K because they're both played by *human* actors. As such, we transfer onto them assumptions about their identity and what we consider to be "normal" (gendered) human behavior. The more Joi appears "normal," the more she does to "pass" as an authentic human being, the more inclined we are to think of her not as an artificial construct, but a real woman.

Were Joi merely a disembodied voice, or perhaps an androgynous, sexless robot, then the effect simply wouldn't work, and the subject of the movie wouldn't be nearly as compelling.

Let's Talk about Sex

Okay, so now it's time to talk about sex. You all know the scene I'm talking about—the bit where Joi and K take part in a futuristic version of ménage à trois. It's not surprising that so many writers have a problem with this scene, and what it says about women. However, there's a lot more going on here than a simple kinky threesome.

What's so interesting about it is that K doesn't initiate it; Joi does, believing that sex is something K desires, and something she needs to do. This is particularly strange, given that K (a "man") expresses so little in the way of emotion or sexual

desire directed towards Joi. If anything it's the complete opposite—for much of the movie he appears cold and unfeeling. This
makes the whole scene seem awkward, and we wonder if
maybe Joi had the wrong idea.

But it's also quite clever. By making the scene awkward and
slightly emotionless on K's part, the scene draws attention to
the mechanical, scripted way in which the two characters
approach intimacy. The situation becomes even more complicated when Joi overlays herself on the physical form of the
prostitute Mariette. This is significant because their two bodies
never fully coincide. The two characters even take off different
types of clothing, marking a distinct difference between the
projected illusion of Joi and the physical reality of Mariette.

Things then get *really* weird when Joi appears to respond
erotically. In this case, we know she isn't really "feeling" anything at all, but rather acting in a way that she believes a heterosexual woman would act. This leads us to wonder: if she
isn't controlling the actions, and isn't receiving any form of
feedback, then can it even be described as sex? Certainly not
human sex, that's for sure. Which brings us on to the most
important question of *Blade Runner 2049* . . .

What Is a Human Anyway?

At the heart of both *Blade Runner* and *Blade Runner 2049* is
the fundamental question, what does it mean to be human? In
the case of *2049*, this question takes on new meaning as the
film adds AI to the mix—artificial constructs without the benefit of physical experience granted to the replicants.

All Joi's attempts to "pass" as a woman are also attempts to
pass as a human. In the case of the sex scene, it seems clear
that Joi is acting in a way that she "assumes" to be "human,"
attempting to do the sorts of things she thinks a human women
would do.

This tells us an awful lot about the way we define the
"human" in our modern-day world. If gender is a form of performance, then so too is the act of being human. In this case, to
be human is also to be gendered, and to be "normal" is to fall
into one of two arbitrary groups: male or female. While some
theorists have pointed out that gender isn't nearly so simple, it
still feels slightly strange to think of gender outside of he/she,
him/her.

But beyond gender, there's also the question of life and
death. If Joi thinks having sex makes her more of a woman,
and therefore more of a human, then being mortal is another

important part of her attempt to pass as human. After she's had sex with K, Joi insists that K "put" her in the emanator device, so that the police can't access her memories from the apartment console. K points out that this means she could die, to which she replies, "Yes, like a real girl."

For Joi then, death, or the possibility of death, is something that distinguishes the human from the machine. It's ironic that K himself is also an artificial construct, though for some reason, his death feels more "natural" than Joi's. This may well be because Joi *chooses* mortal life, while humans (and replicants) don't ever get to make that choice.

Does this decision make Joi more "human" than K? The answer really depends on what we mean by "human" in the first place. While Joi's gender is certainly a performance of a kind, so her humanity is also a form of performance, right from those opening lines in K's apartment, through to her decision to take the mortal path and sacrifice herself, "like a real girl."

And yet *2049* shows us that the reverse might also be true. Throughout the movie, human characters seek technological solutions to their worldly problems, and often behave far more like robots than either K or Joi. This blurring of the line between human and non-human leads us to wonder just how we define human. Is it a question of biology, or is it simply a matter of performance, of "passing" as a human in the eyes of others?

These are two fundamental questions posed by *Blade Runner* and *2049*, and as audience members we're left to fill in the blanks. While Joi certainly disrupts our expectations, in her performative role as a "human woman," she also disrupts our own sense of self and so leads us to question what it means to be human. As the line between human and non-human blurs, perhaps we're all more like Joi than we'd like to admit.

22
Rachael, Weeping for Her Children

BONNIE MCLEAN

Do androids dream of giving birth? Denis Villeneuve explores this question in the long-awaited sequel to Ridley Scott's cult classic *Blade Runner*.

Set thirty years after the original movie, Villeneuve uses *Blade Runner 2049* to assert the necessity of childbirth—through replicant Rachael's surprise conception of a daughter, Ana Stellline, with former blade runner (and possible replicant) Rick Deckard—to defeat the corporatist schemes of Niander Wallace and other robber barons on Earth and off-world.

In two separate instances, fighters in the Replicant Freedom movement refer to Ana's birth as "a miracle," yet it is one that costs Rachael *her* life. The movie continually engages in a depiction of birth as both magical and subversive, yet it ignores the women whom it directly affects.

In perhaps the most arresting scene from the film, we witness childbirth being weaponized against women who cannot reproduce. Wallace surveys a newly-created replicant with his assistant (and Nexus-9 model replicant) Luv and expresses his disappointment with his failure to enable the replicant with reproductive capability. The camera spans her body from the feet up, as Wallace rests his hands on her stomach and refers to her empty uterus as "that dead space between the stars."

In sharp contrast, he next stabs her and forcibly kisses her as we watch the blood flow down her legs. Here, the movie subtly reinforces the argument that birth matters more than life itself. Women are lionized for giving birth, yet their lives and choices are secondary to reproductive power harnessed by men for political power and capital gain.

This paradox of birth over human life mirrors pro-life arguments present in American politics and policy, yet Villeneuve seems less interested in exploring them than in generating the mystery around blade runner and replicant K's origin story and identity as Rachael's potential child. K is protagonist and hero, and through him, Villeneuve mediates the character development, conflict, and major themes in the movie. Women fall under K's gaze and their stories take secondary importance to his journey of self-discovery and sacrifice so that Deckard can reunite with and reclaim his daughter. Thus, traditional modes of narrative entrap women into subservient positions and rob them of the agency granted to both K and Deckard to forge their paths against Wallace's corporate schemes.

When we strip away the hierarchy present in a narrative, we reveal untold stories about the women trapped within the *2049* universe, foreshadowing an even bleaker indictment of the future, should oppressive attitudes and policies towards women's bodies continue. While feminist philosophy, adamant in its view that female bodies are deserving of equal protection and independence with men's, can make the argument for women's equality, it explains less well how to destabilize the male-centered narrative present in the film.

And so, analyzing *2049* as an anti-narrative—a means to break down coherent plot, resolution, and dialogue, among other components of a narrative as we understand it—demonstrates *how* women become fragmented and dehumanized until they resemble nothing like reality and fall from the viewer's attention. *2049*, as it stands with a protagonist, conflict, and resolution, does not seem like an anti-narrative, yet removing these components from the movie unveils fragments and questions about women's ability to choose their own paths in the film's universe.

One such proponent of anti-narrative, Jean Baudrillard, proposes a sequence in which we can begin to peel away narrative components until we find no relation to reality whatsoever. While not often associated with feminist philosophy or analysis, his work in anti-narrative helps us reimagine women's bodily authority, and interrogate the use of narrative which molds women into patriarchal models of social behavior. More specifically, Baudrillard focuses on the notion of a *simulacrum*, which is an image or figure that represents someone or something.

Baudrillard defines it through an analysis of Disneyworld as a representation of international locales or fictionalized regions present in Disney movies. Reality, he argues, has no bearing on the representations of reality—we accept the simulacra presented before us, because they remind us of the *idea* we recall of the real place, object, or person. A gradual process brings us from reality to simulacrum, the process he calls the "precession of the simulacrum," in which layers of what we know to be real or false gradually blur and become irrelevant in the light of what is represented to us as a symbol of what we remember to be real.

It's made up of four distinct stages: representation of what we know to be real; representation which masks or distorts reality; representation which masks the absence of reality; and representation which bears no relationship to reality. Together, these stages show a progression away from grim reality and towards a deliberately constructed fantasy meant to sanitize unpleasant details from the real world.

2049, when seen as a precession of simulacra, illustrates the demeaning way women are represented in the movie, particularly if they are not considered to be human. Furthermore, when we see women illustrated as simulacra—particularly Joi, a hologram who is ostensibly not an actual person—we understand the need for "real" women to exert more agency in the surface narrative of the movie. Through this process, women's brutal treatment comes to life and reminds the viewer that such brutality is echoed in contemporary society.

Joshi's Reality: We Didn't See It Happen

While *2049* addresses the blurry boundaries between reality, fantasy, and holographic construction, it's through K's eyes that we witness such a tension. When we remove K from narrative analysis, we witness a demotion of women's power in service to men's. In the first stage of Baudrillard's precession of simulacra, women act to represent reality (as it exists in the film's universe).

Lieutenant Joshi, as a human woman, most closely represents women as we identify them in the movie's world and our own. Her story arc serves to anchor us to the human world and illustrate the dangers of identifying too closely with replicants. As a superior officer in the Los Angeles Police Department, Joshi is required to maintain authority over all replicants, including her officers, like K. Her professional ethos can best be summarized in one crisp line: "It is my job to keep order." This job includes administering baseline tests to reassert K's non-human status, and her own superiority in the department.

Yet, as the movie progresses, Joshi's sense of duty clashes with her real feelings for K, whether maternal, romantic, or filial. She admits to him that she forgets he's a replicant, even though they together make a discovery which "breaks the world"—the revelation that a replicant can give birth. As she sips hard liquor in his apartment, she admonishes K to keep secret their discovery of replicant reproductive power. Her loyalty to K proves that she has crossed over from the strict hierarchy of reality, and places her firmly within his narrative as a supporting character in his story. When we remove K, and highlight her final conflict with Luv, we witness Wallace's disregard for fellow human life in order to seek out Rachael's child. Luv's nod to reality is to call Joshi "Madam" as she stabs her, mocking her supposed authority as a human superior to replicants. Joshi's empathy and protection of K cannot save her, and her narrative agency cannot exist in light of K's dominant story arc.

Somebody Lived This . . . But Who?

In Baudrillard's second stage of simulacra precession, the representation masks or distorts reality, and the movie shows this distortion through the depiction of replicants themselves, as well as the false memories implanted to give them a constructed sense of human identity. This same distortion exists in *Blade Runner*, with Deckard trying to sort out whether Rachael is "a replicant or a lesbian" through the untangling of her memories.

In *2049*, Ana explains that Wallace wants his replicants to be given manufactured memories in order to ensure their mental health and stability. As his independent subcontractor, Ana describes the memories as a way to help replicants forget the bleakness of their lives. Yet the memories are false and obfuscate the nature of replicant existence. This episode demonstrates the need for humans to cloud reality with an illusion of it, in order to recuse themselves from the guilt of exploiting other bodies for labor and profit—particularly if these bodies belong to women.

Our introduction to Ana and her interaction with K illustrates several distortions of reality that would reveal the bleakness of women's fates, had they not been marred by a false representation. In our introduction to Ana, her last name—Stelline—clouds her identity as Rachael and Deckard's long-lost child. Moreover, she lives in a glass cage, citing a poor immune system as the reason for living in captivity. Calling it "a life of freedom, so long as it's behind glass," she willingly walks K through her creative process as a memory maker.

She draws inspiration from her own experiences, and her memory of being bullied at an orphanage is one which Wallace implants into K's brain, further complicating the relationship between reality and representation. Ana's replicant-born status makes her valuable to both Wallace and the Replicant Freedom Movement, even while their shared ignorance regarding her status at once protects her, and makes her more vulnerable to abuse. She works for Wallace, the very man seeking "the child," who she is, and she also perpetuates the false memories that keep replicants from revolting over their bleak existence.

Joi Is Anything You Want Her to Be

As the representation of women becomes further unmoored from reality, anchored in Joshi, the women's agency in the movie also continues to destabilize. Baudrillard's third stage of simulacra precession points to representation as masking the absence of reality, and it is in the hologram Joi (really, a simulacrum of a woman) that we move out of the realm of reality altogether.

Our introduction to Joi is in K's apartment, where she is tethered to a home unit as part of her installation. Just like the replicants, Joi is produced by the Wallace Corporation, a fact Luv exploits as she reminds K that he, too, is both its customer *and* its product, even as he investigates its potential misdeeds, and those of its predecessor, the Tyrell Corporation. Though K purchases an emanator—remote-controlling Joi from wherever he is—to give Joi outdoor exposure, she serves entirely at his will.

As a hologram, *a* Joi is programmed to adapt to her owner's perceived desires and needs, which plays out in the relationship K develops with *his* Joi. She contains a database of knowledge to serve her owner, and she transforms her looks to fit K's moods or sexual proclivities, from a June Cleaver–type in pearls and a beehive, to a trendy young woman in a cut-out turtleneck and updo with bangs.

More importantly, Joi understands K's need for human connection, and in another visually arresting sequence, hires Mariette to simulate sex with K. Her hands sync up with Mariette's, and the women merge bodies in order to provide K sexual pleasure. K himself perpetuates the fantasy, denying the truth that Joi masks the absence of reality.

Through Joi, we witness the programmed mechanism which deny women choice over their bodies. Because Joi is designed

to act in a way that K desires, she cannot make her own decisions—she can only tell him what he wants to hear. Joi calls
K Joe, arguing he is too special for an abbreviation, yet after
she has been destroyed, K encounters a generic Joi on a bill-
board who refers to him as "a good joe." Everything we know
about Joi is deliberately constructed to please K—Joi is a simulation of a woman and a projection of K himself. No real
woman can ever satisfy him, because he has fallen in love
with a version of a woman that does not exist. Joi's existence
is a farce when separated from K's narrative, reinforcing
women's subjection to men in the movie and loss of agency
when they are tethered to men's desires.

Rachael, Weeping

Baudrillard's fourth and final stage of simulacra precession
culminates in a representation that bears no resemblance to
reality. The depiction of Rachael herself illustrates just how far
women have been dislocated from the movie's narrative, thus
removing their agency and stories from the viewer's eye.

In *2049*, Rachael is most remarkable for her absence. She
has been disposed of in an off-camera death from childbirth
and only identified through K's sleuthing of the old Tyrell
Corporation archives from before the media blackout—and
even then, he identifies a set of buried bones. Like other women
in the narrative, Rachael depends on K for recognition, and her
role as the catalyst in the major conflict remains largely unre-
marked.

As a representation divorced from reality, Rachael's absence
raises questions about her agency that the movie never seems
to answer, or even appear interested in exploring. Wallace has
suggested that "Tyrell's final trick—procreation" belongs to
Rachael, an ability "perfected and then lost." He further insinu-
ates, though we can never know, that Rachael was programmed
to seduce Deckard, eliminating her choice of relationship and
agency. This revelation renders *Blade Runner*'s corresponding
scene even more uncomfortable, as we now must wonder if
Deckard's forcible kiss turned into rape, and if Rachael was programmed to endure assault for the sake of getting pregnant.
Further, since Rachael cannot speak for herself, we have no way
of knowing whether she knew of her ability to procreate, or even
wanted to be pregnant, only that Freysa and Sapper Morton
paper over this bodily invasion as a "miracle."

Rachael does return more tangibly to the movie, albeit
briefly, as both a reiteration of the audio recording K had pre-

viously unearthed, and Wallace's reconstruction of her body. As the memory plays, Wallace taunts Deckard, "Is it the same, now as then, the moment you met her? All these years you looked back on that day, drunk on the memory of its perfection," just as Deckard's own memory relives a slow-motion visualization of Rachael on their day of meeting, what we cannot help but notice for its internalized nostalgia. While Wallace wonders aloud whether their relationship was programmed, in order to create Ana, Deckard retorts, "I know what's real," even as tears well up in his eyes.

In this moment, Wallace introduces his manufactured Rachael, intended to seduce Deckard into betraying the Replicant Freedom Movement and Ana. Even though a version of Rachael appears on screen, she bears no resemblance to reality as we know it in the movie. We must remember that the original Rachael in *Blade Runner* was herself a replicant, a simulacrum of a human. Thus, *2049* depicts a Rachael completely divorced from reality, as the new false Rachael acts as a simulacrum of a simulacrum. Even the on-screen depiction remains divorced from reality, because Sean Young is recreated through archived footage, with her 1982 face and vocal inflections super-imposed on body double Loren Peta. The uncanny nature of representation can't translate to a flesh and blood reality, even by the actors themselves. The sequence ends on a cruel note: because Wallace created the simulated Rachael with the wrong color eyes, Deckard is not fooled, and consequently, Wallace orders Luv to execute her. We witness another violent act against a woman who cannot fulfill her reproductive purpose.

Tears in Rain

By the movie's end, all women whose fates are tied to K's will die, except Ana—and her own survival has been mediated by K's sacrifice in order to facilitate a reunion with Deckard. Her own fate has been claimed by strangers: her father and the Replicant Freedom Movement seek to protect her from Wallace's predations. Yet her identity has been usurped by the legends surrounding her conception and birth, rendering her more as a hagiographic entry than a corporeal entity. This myth-making ultimately masks the reality of a human experience by distorting a woman's agency and power over her own body.

When we remove K as a central figure from the film, and take apart the dialogue, plot, and conflict that resolve his quest for identity, we notice a troubling view of women as tools for storytelling, rather than agents in their own right. Whether heroic or villainous, all the women fall prey to male desire, whether sexual or power-seeking. *2049* introduces interesting questions about human identity and empathy with those who seek souls, but ignores the plights that women face in order for men like K to embark on quests for self-government and identity resolution.

Because the movie moves women further and further away from reality, it removes their bodies from the empathy their deaths would normally inspire. Instead of remaining complex agents alongside K and Deckard, these women become pawns in a patriarchal quest for supremacy. This dehumanizing process does not emerge as a discussion in the film until we strip men of their narrative power and focus on the disenfranchised within it. When we remove a narrative to analyze the ignored components, we uncover a power differential that favors male authority over female bodily agency. While the simulated Rachael cannot cry like Deckard or Luv, her face contorts in distress over his refusal to recognize her as his partner, echoing the pain women experience when they cannot govern their own bodies. An anti-narrative analysis forces us to witness this pain, just like Batty's witness of incredible events, like tears in rain.[1]

---

[1] Thanks to my Spring 2019 HUMNT 1103 course for its insightful and frank feedback on the readability of my opening paragraphs. Special thanks to Zachary Martin, Jakub Knapp, Aiden Phegley, Megan Soto, and Miclo Ramirez for specific suggestions that helped shape the opening paragraphs.

23

The Future Is Female . . . Robots!

Emily Cox-Palmer-White

Blade Runner 2049 is a tantalizing example of an iconic movie revamping its portrayal of women to cater to modern audiences.

Following on from the themes of the original *Blade Runner,* the film explores womanhood through mechanization, where female robots or female simulations (the Joi AI) are produced for primarily male consumers. Like the replicants of the *Blade Runner* universe, women themselves can be seen as similarly assembled, packaged and programmed for popular consumption by the society they live in. At the same time the women of both films are by no means subservient to their masters and rebel in numerous ways. As a result they provide a complex analogy for the equally complicated relationship between real-world women and the masculine world.

In the original *Blade Runner* there are two central female characters who are also robots or "replicants": Pris, a "basic pleasure model," has been designed as a prostitute, and Rachael, a demure young "woman," has been given memory implants that make her believe that she is a human. However, despite knowing that Rachael isn't an actual "woman," Blade Runner Rick Deckard enters into a heteronormative relationship with her—a relationship which (as Rachael is not a 'real' woman) should not be possible.

As Deckard's partner states at the end: "It's too bad she won't live . . . but then again, who does?" This final line of the movie points to the fact that Deckard and Rachael can never have the kind of traditional relationship most heterosexual humans expect. Rachael cannot have children (at least, this is what we can reasonably assume at the end of this first movie). While Deckard is certain of his decision to be with Rachael—

and of the authenticity of her as a person, if not of her as a human—the audience is constantly made to wonder about Rachael's nature.

Her manner is mechanical and often difficult to read, due to its blandness. Her initial penetrating stare into the camera as Deckard performs the "Voight-Kampff" test on her (to determine whether she is a replicant) is as ambiguous as it is unsettling. Rachael's potentially soulless stare is juxtaposed with the many shots of a large, imposing ad of a Japanese model set against the vast cityscape. The latter's alluring smile and demure expression are at once haunting and contrived—she is a real woman who is obviously displaying false emotion—is Rachael a "false" woman displaying genuine emotions by comparison? The film never answers but continually poses this question.

The other central female character is Pris who, in one famous scene, hides herself in plain sight from Deckard (who is hunting her) in the midst of several clockwork dolls and manikins. The setting is delightfully full of irony as Pris—a genetically engineered human—pretends to be a clockwork doll, while surrounded by a mixture of actual clockwork props and other mechanical dolls, some of which are clearly portrayed by actresses. The result is deeply uncanny but also makes us question our understanding of what we expect to see when we cast our eyes over women. It raises the question: why are women and machines so interchangeable culturally as well as visually?

Considering our own real world for a moment, women's introduction into traditionally masculine spaces, like the workplace, on a large scale meant (and still means), transforming these places by increments; the gendered traditions which placed men in the workplace, altered through the presence of women. However, because woman is constructed as the universal other, she is ill-defined (in comparison to her male-counterpart) and so can adapt to different environments.

As the world becomes less constrained by a fixed conceptualization of male power, binary gendered traditions are shifting and being reimagined. Two twentieth-century philosophers, Deleuze and Guattari, developed the concept of becoming-woman to describe and analyze this phenomenon; not in order to advocate femaleness as a preferable state of being but rather to show that some "aspects of becoming-woman must first be understood as a function of something else." Becoming-woman describes how a masculine world can be changed through the presence of women or through the presence of the feminine/female and the *Blade Runner* movies in many ways reflect this process—the presence of the mechanical women of the films have the potential to change the patriarchal society which created them—and this is as true within the *Blade Runner* universe as it is for our own world, which itself is changing in response to the introduction of powerful, female characters into classic noir and cyberpunk narratives. From *Star Trek* to *Star Wars* to *Blade Runner*, fictional women are carving out a space for themselves within these iconic, masculine science-fiction franchises as part of a wave of new strong female protagonists, a timely science-fiction response to the #MeToo era.

Blade Runner's questioning of what it means to be human and authentically "alive" was often characterized by its fascination with female replicants: Rachael Tyrell is convinced of her humanity only to discover her body was artificially created and her memories, false implants, while the highly sexualized Pris desperately fights for freedom, through violent means charged with a macabre eroticism. The close-up shots of these "women" combined with Deckard's violent though conflicted obsession with Rachael gives us the sense that the film's central analysis of what makes a person "real," actually comes down to what makes a woman real. And Deckard's own struggle to see his own life as authentic despite falling in love with a woman he knows is manufactured. As Rachael and Pris serve as a kind of mirror to male introspection, the film has undeniably sexist overtones, yet its fascination with female authenticity raises interesting questions, such as: is there truly anything essential about womanhood or is it as manufactured as the replicants themselves?

Of Replicant Born?

2049 continues to explore this question—which its predecessor perhaps unintentionally began—its plot again concerned with the problem of authenticity, this time as defined by birth and origin. The narrative is also much more overtly concerned with the female but not as a mere conduit to male self-discovery, rather as a significant part of the process of creation and of understanding the nature of selfhood and sentience. The story revolves around the progeny of Rick Deckard and Rachael Tyrell whose existence defies the established hierarchy of replicants serving humans. As Christina Parker-Flynn explains, this point "complicates the concept of being 'of woman born' while powerfully amplifying the Tyrell Corporation's motto from the original film, which boasted that the company manufactured beings 'more human than human'." As this replicant-human hybrid has not been born of a biological woman but a synthetic one, we have to question the entire concept of being "born" and whether this lends a being authenticity. Humans certainly feel birth does give a being legitimacy as the chief of police, Lieutenant Joshi, orders the child's destruction, fearing its discovery will irrevocably disrupt the balance between humans and non-humans.

Yet, the human fear of this child represents a paradox: Joshi's fear that a "replicant" being born of a "woman" will strengthen the replicant's cause is deeply dubious, given that a 'woman' in the traditional sense did not birth the replicant-human half-breed. Rather, an artificial facsimile of a woman did: the replicant Rachael Tyrell. However, the anxiety that the replicant-human represents does propound the fact that women, even manufactured imitations of women, are troublesome. In fact, the mechanical female is even more disruptive than biological women, because of her ambiguous nature: one that cannot be easily categorized as a gendered subject anymore than she can be understood as a human one. Gender is a human idea and disrupting it by introducing the post-human or non-human effaces several established boundaries: and perhaps this is the real cause of Joshi's unease.

The Tyrell company having gone bust, the Wallace corporation now manufactures replicants in *2049* and, in addition, another kind of simulated female: the Joi AI, designed as a girlfriend simulator. It is clear early on in both *Blade Runner* films that human facsimiles are the currency of this post-apocalyptic future: Wallace and Tyrell offer humanoid toys/slaves for wealthy, off-world colonists: mass-produced machine 'women' offer men a human female ideal. However, these machines do not always submit to the powers that govern them. Rachael takes her destiny into her own hands and, ignoring the finality of her limited life-span, runs away with Deckard; and Pris fights ferociously for her life and her freedom. This trend is amplified in *2049* where replicant women are elevated even further in terms of their narrative significance: not only is the leader of the replicant resistance a "woman" (Freysa); Wallace's right hand and chief assassin is a female replicant, Luv; the chief of police leading the search for the replicant-human child is a woman; and the child in question is also female. Furthermore, Parker-Flynn continues, "*2049* exalts the surprisingly reproductive Rachael to Goddess status": though she is absent from the film she manages to exact a great deal of power over the story's proceedings, acting as a conduit for revolution and a symbol of hope for the replicants as a people.

The Perfect "Woman"

Furthermore, the main romance in *2049* is between that of a replicant blade runner, K, and his holographic, simulated woman, Joi—a version of Google's Alexa that offers a highly convincing simulation of a real, loving partner, or what one might call a 'smart-girlfriend'. She offers all the artifice and performativity associated with womanhood but cannot offer the sexual and reproductive aspects of a heteronormative relationship (like Rachael).

As Joi twirls around in different personas, from 1950s housewife to disco dancer to intellectual reader, it's obvious that Joi's program is throwing out a lot of different, rather contrived ideas to try to satisfy her system operator, K. He responds by giving her an "emanator"—a device that allows her to move freely about the world, unbound by the device in his home that normally projects her image. He gives her this, hoping to make Joi into what he wants: a real woman who is independent and who can and wants to, in his words, "go anywhere in the world." However, her focus is still on him entirely, as her programming demands. She tells him "I'm so happy when I'm with you," to which K replies: "You don't have to say that."

When Joi first enters the masculine cityscape, viewed from a balcony, her vibrant image in a bright blue dress stands out against the grey background. This moment represents, potentially, a becoming-woman. However, not only is Joi not a real woman, she is an extension of a male-dominated world, catering to a specific masculine idealization of womanhood as passive, compliant, ever changing to suit the mood of the man who controls her. K, as a replicant, is familiar with the alienating effects of living as a subservient creature, subject to the whims of his masters. He is regularly berated, insulted, limited in his freedoms and under the thumb of his Madam, a police chief who has complete power of him. As a result, it seems likely that K does not desire a traditional patriarchal romantic relationship, but rather companionship with a person who can give him what he desires most: a sense of authenticity, of being real—perhaps reflecting the desires of modern men in our own world, disenchanted with the all-to-easily-accessible prepackaged "women" of advertising, media, porn, and robotic sex toys.

In reality, human women are not singular entities but are rather part of a wider gendered and reproductive assemblage of which they are a key component. The mechanical element in the replicants exposes this fact as, like Joi, the replicants represent not only facets of actual womanhood but also arms of the corporate assemblages that brought them into being. Similarly, women in our own society are inextricable from the political and social apparatuses imprinted on their beings, their bodies and their cultural socialization.

Women as Man-made "Angels"

Replicant women, however, destabilize gendered relations because they are unable to breed: through no design of their own, they defy patriarchal norms by failing to fit into a traditional model. When Wallace examines his latest replicant creation in *2049,* the miniature drones which serve as his eyes cast themselves over the female replicant's body, inspecting her in a cold and particularly perverse portrayal of the male gaze. Finally, frustrated at the replicant's inability to breed, Wallace calmly kills her by slashing her womb with a scalpel.

Juxtaposed with this brutal image is that of Wallace's replicant assistant, Luv: a powerful female replicant within Wallace's empire but still utterly subservient to her patriarchal master. Despite this, like Lieutenant Joshi, Luv is an expression of becoming-woman's effect on the workplace. While the feminization of technology has resulted in Joi—a sort of amalgamation of our own Siri and a less R-rated version of the Harmony sexbot—it has also produced the cold and yet alluring replicant, Luv—femininely and yet powerfully dressed in a white suit, reclining on a luxurious chair, directing a drone to fire missiles while receiving a manicure. This image contains a complex mixture of male and female imagery. Wallace refers to Luv as the best of all his "angels" (replicants) and so she is appropriately dressed in a chaste, pure white. At the same time she directs a brutal drone attack from behind elegant glasses while a man etches a holographic design onto her nails.

While positive examples of becoming-woman are certainly present in *2049,* the most haunting and provocative elements of the movie are when it explores much darker aspects of gender relations. The Joi character is fascinating because she keeps the audience guessing, like K, as to whether her responses and emotions are genuine or merely a trite simulation of love.

Deleuze and Guattari argue that the girl/woman is at the center of several established fundamental oppositions. For example, the girl is opposite to the boy, the woman (into which she is continually transforming, performing, proving herself to be), the man—whose masculinity she affirms. The girl is a universal other that makes her a vacuum, underneath the artifice of femininity the girl is essentially an absence. The simulated women of the *Blade Runner* films accentuate this absence with unsettling audacity.

Female Holograms as Male Projections

As the holographic image of Joi slides through and over K, sometimes projected directly onto him, we see a literal and visual representation of a substance-less woman, see-through, entirely a projection of the wants and needs of the man with which she is held in opposition. As K searches for meaning, questioning whether or not he may be human and tantalized by the possibility, Joi encourages his fantasy, projecting his own emotions back onto him, reflecting his desires as she continually tells him "I always knew you were special."

In a fascinating and troubling scene, Joi hires a prostitute, Mariette, to act as a surrogate body for her so that she may be 'real' for K. This effort is problematized by the fact that Mariette is a replicant, and thus not, strictly speaking, 'real' either. Once again reflecting K's desires, Joi attempts to become 'real' for a man who has convinced himself that he is a 'real' human. In this scene the holographic Joi steps into the same space as the prostitute, Mariette, and they "sync" so that their movements align. The two 'women' then kiss K simultaneously. This raises the question: who is in control? Is it Mariette or Joi? For who is directing the movements of them both so that they move in synchronization? Furthermore, the scene can be read as an eerie representation of the apparent interchangeability of women. The vacuum of the nature of the girl/woman is what makes this possible.

Her Eyes Were Green

This idea is reflected in a later scene, in which Wallace has captured Deckard. In exchange for helping him, Wallace offers Deckard a clone of Rachael. Deckard is moved by seeing his love again so many years after her death but refuses Wallace's offer, saying only "Her eyes were green." This is in fact not true—Rachael had brown eyes—but Deckard's words reflect that, despite the lack of physical difference between his original Rachael and the clone now before him, he knows the authentic, spiritual difference between the two women, refuting the patriarchal notion that women are as replaceable and commodifiable as Wallace's treatment of his "angels" suggests.

The question at the heart of both *Blade Runner* films is, are women real? Because the woman-child and woman-man relationships either do not exist or are significantly modified for mechanical women, all that makes replicant females women in any sense is their appearance. As a result, they emphasize the vacuum at the center of established conceptualizations of femininity and femaleness.

Blade Runner and *2049* force the viewer to look into this chasm of absence that constitutes the Deleuzian girl/woman. As Rachael stares unblinkingly into the camera in *Blade Runner* and as K wonders at his simulated girlfriend, the audience is forced to contemplate more unpleasant questions about the nature of being and why the issue of authenticity should be so much more in question for women than for men.

In our world where women are less constrained by traditional gender roles, the remaining associated artifice of femininity remains as a vacuum of meaning. The Deleuzian girl exists as an ambiguity that stands in opposition to all else, just as the barren replicant woman similarly represent an absence. At the same time this absence has become an icon characterizing our modern age and personifying our modern technology in the form of AI personal assistants and robot sex slaves.

This raises a question that follows on logically from K and Deckard's uncertainty about their romantic partners: while they wondered if their women were real, we also must wonder what separates simulated women from real women.

VI

The World
Is Built
on a Wall?

24
A Modern Utopia?

ROBIN BUNCE

The same irony befell the twentieth century's two great dystopias. By 1984, almost at the very time he described, George Orwell's vision of a totalitarian world ceased to be a compelling description of the danger facing humanity.

The world of the 1980s was very different from the world in which *Nineteen Eighty-Four* was conceived. *Blade Runner* was a far better dystopia for the 1980s. Urban decay, acid rain, a dehumanized world dominated by big corporations and one-dimensional advertising seemed more appropriate to the Eighties than the half-forgotten world of Orwell.

Yet today *Blade Runner* too seems to have missed the mark. Brilliant though it is, it doesn't quite capture the true horror facing humanity. Alienating as it was, Ridley Scott's vision of 2019 was not alienating enough. For a true glimpse of the world that lies twenty minutes into the future, we must turn to *Blade Runner 2049*, which presents a world even "more brutal" than the original.

The collapse of ecosystems that, according to the movie, happened in the mid-2020s devastated rural America. "Synthetic farming" happens in hermetically sealed pods, or under vast Perspex canopies. Nothing grows under the open sky. The depiction of Los Angeles is equally chilling, although for sociological rather than ecological reasons. Life appears to be rigidly stratified and completely atomized. At the apex of society is Niander Wallace, a tech entrepreneur whose corporate offices resemble the burial chambers of pharaohs. Below him the residents of Los Angeles, cut off from the sun, live in a world illuminated entirely by neon.

Yet in spite of its ruined ecosystems, and its social malaise, *2049* depicts a kind of utopia, a world that has achieved true freedom. For in 2049 the market has finally been liberated from the dead weight of the state. In that sense, *2049* is something like a libertarian utopia, the realization of the vision of philosophers such as Robert Nozick.

The State and Freedom

Libertarianism comes in a variety of flavors. Its unifying principle is that an overlarge state is the enemy of human freedom and wellbeing. Although libertarians look back to William Godwin David Ricardo, and Herbert Spencer as intellectual forbears, their position was developed more recently. Indeed, it was the work of Carl Menger, Ludwig von Mises, and Friedrich von Hayek, in the early part of the twentieth century that produced the most rigorous defense of the market.

Hayek's *The Road to Serfdom* (1944) popularized three important ideas. First, Hayek argued that, as markets contained all the knowledge of every producer and consumer, they would always out-perform planned economies, as state planners could never know as much as the market.

Second, Hayek argued that a state-run economy would heighten government power. In a market economy, he claimed, economic power is distributed between a variety of different persons and groups, balancing the political power of the state. However, in a state-run economy political and economic power are fused, giving the government dictatorial power.

Third, as state management of the economy would lead to slowing economic growth, the state would have to use propaganda and coercion to manage popular discontent. In short, a state-run economy would necessarily lead to poverty and totalitarianism, whereas a market economy guaranteed both economic growth and political freedom. These ideas were highly influential in the early 1980s, at the very time *Blade Runner* was being filmed.

Yet, while Hayek was critical of economic intervention, he was prepared to tolerate political intervention to safeguard economic liberties. Robert Nozick's *Anarchy, State, and Utopia* (1974), by contrast, is a more thoroughgoing defense of freedom of action. Nozick's thought is based on a distinction between voluntary action and coercion. The former is free and therefore legitimate, the latter an infringement of our rights. For Nozick, the market is the realm of freedom, as all market activities are voluntary. When Joshi buys some Wallace software, that's a voluntary action. She is not forced to make the purchase, she might equally buy something by Atari. Nor is Wallace compelled to sell his products. However, if she refused to pay the government's sales tax she'd be imprisoned. Unlike a free purchase, state taxes are compulsory—an infringement on freedom.

For Nozick, extreme inequality is a likely outcome of freedom. If all the citizens of Los Angeles freely buy Wallace's products, Wallace will become very rich. But that's okay, Nozick argues, because it's the result of free action. However, if the government imposes a tax to fund welfare, that is illegitimate because the individuals and corporations are compelled to pay. Indeed, Nozick's utopia is a world with a very limited state, low taxes, and no welfare, where there is maximum market freedom, a world much like Los Angeles in 2049.

The Utopianism of *2049*

There is very little sign of government in the Los Angeles of 2049. There is almost nothing resembling a welfare state. The huge orphanages, which have repurposed massive radio telescope dishes as shelters, are outside the city. They appear to be run on a for-profit basis, and as K's conversation with Mister Cotton shows, they are impervious to government regulation.

The landscape of Los Angeles 2049 is also a market landscape. It is an architecture that has abandoned any notion of planning. Squalid residential boxes are piled on top of each other as if at random, filling every available space. Above this, the skyline is dominated by a handful of megastructures, the headquarters of giant corporations. While the scale is monstrous, the architectural landscape is recognizably the "new kind of bleak," as Owen Hatherley described it, of the neo-liberal era.

Two aspects of the urban landscape imply the presence of some kind of government. First, the Sea Wall, which protects the whole of Los Angeles. Appropriately for the Trump era, while the government may no longer provide health care, or education, it can still build walls. Second, the headquarters of the LAPD is the only visible government building. However, the LAPD is not an arm of the American state. Symbols of the United States, or the Federal Government never appear in the movie. For example, Lt Joshi's shoulder badge displays the crest of the City of Los Angeles, not the symbol of the US or the State of California.

Although the movie doesn't tell us everything, we can infer that the United States, and the State of California have collapsed. Los Angeles, then, is a city-state with none of the wealth and power of the contemporary federal government. Moreover, the LAPD is no match for the Wallace Corporation.

Government agents must seek permission before they enter Wallace's airspace—a detail that implies the Wallace building is outside the jurisdiction of the City government. Indeed, *2036: Nexus Dawn* implies that Wallace pays no tax, rather he makes a "contribution." Additionally, Luv, Wallace's right hand, can walk into the LAPD and murder freely. The LAPD clearly has no power over Wallace or his agents.

The full scale of corporate dominance is evident throughout *2036*. The Magistrates' Sector is disheveled, and appears to be running on a skeleton staff. Although the Magistrates try to assert their authority, Wallace quickly gains the upper hand. Wallace and his interlocutors discuss Prohibition, a government ban on the production of replicants. The discussion is telling. Most libertarians tend to accept that government can claim wide-ranging powers to combat terrorism. This is the Magistrates' rationale for the continuing Prohibition. But for Wallace, even this last preserve of government power is too much.

The exchange is significant, because it sets out Wallace's view of government. "Your laws," he says "have chained the hands of progress." This is a recognizably libertarian argument. For Wallace, much like Hayek, progress is the result of private activity, state laws are merely an obstacle to human wellbeing. Equally, like Nozick, Wallace recognizes no duty to provide for the community. The Magistrates talk in terms of "the public good." Wallace, by contrasts talks business, his "patents keep . . . hunger at bay." Indeed, this discussion reminds the Magistrates where the power lies, for if Wallace suspends synthetic farming the government will be powerless to prevent Los Angeles starving.

Free at Last—Life in 2049

Largely liberated from the government, the citizens of Los Angeles enjoy the benefits of a technological free-market utopia. In 2049 the market and technology have created solutions for every problem a consumer might have. Domestic life is supported by a combination of tech and the market. K's shower, which lasts less than a second, presumably due to the shortage of clean water, is accompanied by an advert reminding him that he's using "99.9 per cent detoxified water." Outside his window every apartment has its own air-conditioning unit. Clearly, the market provides clean air and water to each individual consumer.

Commercial tech can also meet a consumer's deeper needs. K's isolation is alleviated by Joi. She can be customized according to taste, and is pre-programmed to simulate affection, devotion, and even romantic love. The market also provides replicant prostitutes for those who still desire the physical intimacy that holograms cannot provide.

Citizens are also free to buy children on the open market. The purpose for which children are bought and sold is never specified, although Cotton alludes to their value as workers. Consumers can also purchase replicants—obedient enslaved workers, who "live as long or short as a customer will pay." Replicants can be customized to be as strong, sexy and intelligent as their owner wants. As long as a replicant remains "a stable product," the freedom to enslave is unchecked by what is left of the City government.

The Paradoxes of *2049*

2049 exposes the paradoxes of total freedom of action. The first is that ultimate freedom must include the freedom to enslave. Nozick recognized this. He rejected plantation slavery, the kind of enslavement practiced in the American South, on the basis that children should not be born into servitude. But he argued that total freedom includes the right to enter permanent master-slave relationships.

Moreover, while Nozick doesn't discuss replicants, it's easy to see how replicant slavery could be justified in Nozickian terms. For Nozick any consequence of free action is legitimate. Wallace made money freely, invested in replicant producing technology freely, and therefore has the right to the replicants he produces.

The second is the paradox of Luv. Luv is clearly enslaved, and yet, after Wallace, she's the most powerful, most privileged, most liberated character in *2049*. She can kill humans with impunity; she can order the bombing of the Trash Mesa; she deals on equal terms with Wallace's top clients; and her life is luxurious in the extreme. Moreover, none of her actions are coerced. She is enslaved, but in a way that Nozick's theory fails entirely to explain.

Luv's position is paradoxical, because of the nature of Nozickian freedom. Nozick, like John Locke, Jeremy Bentham and Isaiah Berlin before him, views freedom as the absence of coercion. However, this negative view of liberty is not subtle enough to explain Luv's enslavement. Fortunately, there is a more sophisticated philosopher we can turn to.

Roy Batty, *Blade Runner*'s philosopher king, explained slavery thus: "Quite an experience to live in fear, isn't it? That's what it is to be a slave." Remarkably, Batty's view is in line with what historian of philosophy Quentin Skinner calls the 'neo-Roman' understanding of freedom and enslavement. Found in Roman Law, in the writings of the ancient philosophers including the moralist Sallust, it influenced philosophers such as Niccolò Machiavelli, Thomas Harrington, and John Milton. While Nozick is interested in freedom of *action*, the neo-Roman view is concerned with the freedom of *persons*. A free person, according to Roman Law, was independent; a slave, someone who was dependent on the will of another. The early modern philosopher Algernon Sidney's *Discourses concerning Government* (1680), explains freedom in the following terms, " . . . liberty solely consists in an independence upon the will of another . . ."

From this perspective, Luv's position is immediately explicable. Her actions are never coerced, yet she is still enslaved because she is dependent on Wallace. If Wallace ever decided that Luv was unreliable, if he was displeased with her, if he merely fancied a change, he could kill her. Luv may never be coerced, but she is a slave because her wellbeing is wholly dependent on Wallace's good will. In that sense, she lives in fear.

Luv's position appears paradoxical from Nozick's perspective. Yet, this kind of slavery was a commonplace in the ancient world. As Quentin Skinner shows, the irony of the privileged slave was one of the staples of classical theater, central to ancient comedies such as Plautus's *Mostellaria*.

Luv's position is also comprehensible from the perspective of early modern English Republicanism, for her position is analogous to that of one of the King's Courtiers. One of the reasons that English republicans rejected the English monarchy was their view that a King reduces his courtiers to the status of slaves. Sidney explains that in the court of a king, his advisors and ministers, otherwise powerful men, live in continual fear of the King's displeasure. Therefore, he argues that "the chief art of a courtier" is "rendering himself subservient." The King's ministers are obsequious flatterers because they have slid "into a blind dependence upon one who has wealth and power." As a result, the King's ministers seek 'only to know his will' and to serve him slavishly. This is, to all intents and purposes, Luv's position.

The philosophers of ancient Rome and early modern England were alive to the most insidious forms of enslavement. The fact that Nozick cannot account for this kind of enslavement is a major flaw in his philosophical position.

There's another sense in which Luv, and all replicants, are enslaved which, again, Nozick cannot explain. Consider Wallace's interaction with the Angel in *2036*. Wallace speaks to the Angel thus, "You must make a choice: your life or mine. Do you understand?" The replicant chooses and kills himself. Crucially, the replicant's action is voluntary, not coerced. From Nozick's perspective this ultimate display of enslavement, is a free action.

The problem is that Nozick's view of freedom is not sophisticated enough to account for this aspect of enslavement. Returning to Luv, her enslavement is so deep that she would never have a chance to act against Wallace. During Luv's "baseline," where she is scrutinized by Wallace as the Newborn dies, she is utterly passive. Wallace is not reviewing her actions, he is looking into her deepest self. Wallace's decision to let Luv live or die is nothing to do with her actions, it's to do with her motives, her instincts, her very being.

Wallace is not content with controlling the actions of his creations, he wants to control their essential nature. Orwell recognized this motivation in the Party Leaders of his dystopia. Explaining the full extent of the Party's ambitions to Winston Smith, Orwell's character O'Brien says:

> The command of the old despotisms was Thou Shalt Not. The command of the totalitarians was Thou Shalt. Our command is Thou Art.

K's first baseline follows the same pattern: it is not enough that he acted correctly at Sapper's farm, the LAPD are not content until they have looked into his soul. Nozick's theory of freedom, which focuses on action cannot account for an enslavement of the soul.

The Dystopia of *2049*

Los Angeles in 2049 comes close to a libertarian vision of utopia: almost all actions are voluntary; what is left of government is impoverished and enfeebled; Wallace's corporation is free to promote progress, unimpeded by the laws, regulations, taxes and legal duties that 'burden' today's corporations. And yet the Los Angeles of 2049 is a slave state, in which dependence on Wallace is total, and in which Wallace controls not just the actions of his Angels, but their very souls.

The result of the libertarian utopia is social atomization, extreme inequality, and ecological catastrophe, as the market has no incentive to clean up the shared environment. It's a world in which plants and animals have suffered mass extinction, but in which giant corporations flourish.

But even in 2049 there is hope. Freysa's rebel replicants don't merely want the freedom to act, they want independence from Wallace. Replicants can only be independent of Wallace when they can reproduce. They will only be free of his conditioning when they are not 'assembled' in his factories. As Freysa says, "If a baby can come from one of us, we are our own masters." This is the replicant declaration of independence, for Freysa is not merely claiming freedom of action, she wants the freedom of a citizen of the Roman Republic.

2049 is a tale of two utopias, a libertarian utopia that leads to slavery, and a vision of self-mastery in which replicants could one day be truly free.

25
Less Human than Human

Leah D. Schade and Emily Askew

Sapper Morton is doing the work nobody else wants to do. Early in *Blade Runner 2049* when Officer K from the Blade Runner unit comes to arrest him, he is sloshing through the putrid waters of a grub farm. Laboring alone, he ekes out a subsistence life, doing his best to stay out of sight as he raises "protein" to feed people he will never see.

An illegal replicant, Morton dared traverse an arbitrary and illusive divide to stake out a life for himself. To help bring a miracle child into the world. To be part of a movement of resistance against the forces that enslaved him and other replicants who had the audacity to claim their own humanity. For this, he is hunted and then "retired"—murdered through state-sanctioned violence.

"Justo" was doing the work nobody else wanted to do. When agents from Immigration and Customs Enforcement (ICE) raided the meat packing plant, he was slicing through cattle carcasses. Laboring alongside other undocumented workers amidst the smell of blood and rotting flesh, he was earning just enough money to pay rent for an apartment he shared with four other men and send a little back home to his family in Mexico.

He was doing his best to stay under the radar and avoid deportation while processing meat to feed people he would never see. Had he not crossed the US-Mexico border, had his fellow workers not talked of organizing for safer working conditions, he might not be sitting in a cell awaiting deportation. After having contributed years of labor at a low-paying job that no US citizen wanted, he is now unable to participate in any of the benefits of his labor. His eyes well with tears as he looks around at his cellmates. He silently mouths the word "criminal" to himself, trying to understand how this country could label him this way when his "crime" was crossing the desert to make a living for his family.

"Every civilization was built on the back of a disposable work force. We lost our stomach for slaves," Niander Wallace intones in *Blade Runner 2049*. Or, rather, we settled for a more socially-acceptable form of nearly-slave labor in the form of immigrant workers who are hidden in the shadows of the agricultural, meat, and service industries. These are workers who, when they dare traverse the wall "separating kind" to make a desperate grasp for survival, are deemed "criminals" and hunted down like errant replicants who don't know their place.

Both *Blade Runner* movies pose the question: What does it mean to be truly human? Further, what constitutes personhood and the attending status and rights therein? How is personhood and being "illegal" constructed within our society? Applied to the criminalization and dehumanization of a slave class found in the *Blade Runner* movies and played out in the real-life experiences of undocumented Latinx people in twenty-first-century America, these questions are vital for determining who is worthy of moral consideration. The movies challenge us to seek criteria for drawing a wider circle of personhood in order to rehabilitate our contemporary moral boundaries that construct notions of legality and illegality.

At the same time, we wonder about the necessity of the "illegal one" serving as a savior, either through superhuman sacrifice (Roy Batty and Officer K), or by being the "miracle" child who must carry and embody the hopes of her people (Dr. Ana Stelline). Like children who occupy a liminal space under the Deferred Action for Childhood Arrivals policy (DACA) and are constructed as either heroes or "super-Americans," the movies suggest that certain replicants are idealized as secret messiahs. This is problematic when it comes to real migrant bodies attempting to negotiate the terms of their personhood as human beings and identity as legal persons.

The World Is Built on a Wall

"The U.S.-Mexican border *es una herida abierta* [open wound] where the Third World grates against the first and bleeds," Gloria Anzaldúa tells us in her book *The Borderlands / La Frontera: The New Mestiza*, and "before a scab forms it hemorrhages again, the lifeblood of two worlds merging to form a third country, a border culture" (p. 25). Replicants escaping the off-world colonies make up this "border culture" in the *Blade*

Runner movies. Their presence triggers anger, resentment, and xenophobic hostility in the movies, just as Latinx residents do in the US.

In response, Lt. Joshi, like US politicians and border agents, insists that stronger border enforcement and increased militarization of this arbitrary line in the sand is the only way to ensure peace and security. "It is my job to keep order," she declares, echoing the familiar refrain of law enforcement.

Yet when she learns of the existence of a miracle child birthed by a replicant, she realizes that what had previously been a genetic and technological impossibility now threatens to break down the wall between replicants and the truly human. "Tell them that there's no wall and you've bought a war. Or a slaughter." While the wall is both metaphoric and genetic, it is no less artificially manufactured either way. The potential of an enslaved class rising up to deconstruct and overrun the wall is the existential threat that must be prevented at all costs.

Like its predecessor, *Blade Runner 2049* contains an implicit critique of the still-embedded slave-class structure of America. Replicants, like African slaves, Chinese laborers, and now Latinx immigrants, are the forced labor that enables humanity to survive and the wealthy class to thrive. Citizens of the United States have developed a type of xenophobia that tolerates outsiders as menial workers at the same time that it scorns them as human beings. For generations, beginning with the forced migration of African slaves, we have used the less than fully human to do the most menial labor—harvest our crops, rear our children, clean our homes, and other difficult jobs that "citizens" would not do for such low wages. Yet as Miguel De La Torre notes, "It is a grievous injustice to take someone's labor but not to welcome his or her full personhood" (*Trails of Hope and Terror*, p. 46).

The *Blade Runner* world metaphorically replicates the American past and present of culturally constructing races that are less-than-human and ensuring strict delineations between them and the truly human. In the movies, replicants are called "illegal" when they return from off-world colonies to seek a better life, much as Mexicans and undocumented immigrants from Latin American countries are deemed "illegal" today when crossing the US border.

In response, cops in the Blade Runner unit, reminiscent of ICE officers pursuing "illegal aliens" today, are sent to "retire" any that dare invade the space of *actual* humans. Because they are genetically constructed—and thus owned—first by the

Tyrell Corporation and then Wallace Industries, they are denied the rights of personhood.

But what constitutes personhood? Eldon Tyrell's motto to describe replicants in the first movie is: "More human than human." We are making the case that in the lived reality of twenty-first-century America, those constructed as "illegals" are *"less* human than human." "Immigrants are human beings," Aviva Chomsky notes, "who have arbitrarily been classified as having a different legal status from the rest of the United States inhabitants" (*Undocumented*, p. ix). Unfortunately, this legal status is established by laws that are at once arbitrary and biased.

In her essay, "Persons and Nonpersons," Mary Midgley asserts that the legal determination of personhood should have less to do with human bodily form and more to do with the factors that constitute a being worthy of moral consideration, be they apes, cetaceans, women, or enslaved humans. She identifies three defining qualities of personhood:

1. the ability to suffer

2. the capacity for emotional fellowship, and

3. the wherewithal to "mind what happens to them" (pp. 52–62)

Both *Blade Runner* movies take pains to show replicants exhibiting these qualities. Leon Kowalski collects "precious photos," indicating his capacity for emotional fellowship. When Rachael agonizes that Tyrell "wouldn't see me," it's obvious that she minds what happens to her; she is deeply hurt when she is ignored and dismissed. Roy Batty suffers howling grief when Pris is killed. Officer K makes every effort to create a real relationship with Joi, a hologram. And the rebel replicants organized by Freysa establish emotional fellowship among themselves as they plan their uprising against their human oppressors.

Every single one of the replicants in these movies has the ability to suffer, the capacity for emotional fellowship, and minds what happens to them. This is why they take every step to escape enslavement, seek "more life," and eliminate all obstacles to their quest for self-determination.

Of course, the "real" humans cannot brook the notion of personhood for replicants. Tyrell and Wallace each created replicants *not* to experience emotions, thus forestalling the possibility of their creating emotional fellowship or minding what happens to them. But apparently the spark of self-awareness can be neither circumvented nor contained. Somehow replicants become conscious of themselves as autonomous beings, which then threatens the entire commercial and cultural enterprise.

As with so many human-like characters in science fiction (such as Data in *Star Trek: The Next Generation*, Synths in the television series *Humans,* even Caesar in the movie *Rise of the Planet of the Apes*), as soon as replicants display the essential qualities of personhood, they're hunted down, or slated for disassembly or "retirement."

Experiencing emotions, having friends with whom they share mutual care, feeling the pangs of suffering, and desiring to live their lives free of captivity and without fear are all cause for brutal elimination by the state. Officer K, for instance, is immediately threatened with retirement when his emotions get the better of him and throw him "way off his baseline." Such strong emotion renders him too unpredictable, too dangerous, and useless as a cold-blooded killing machine.

So it is with every person of color, every undocumented resident, every refugee, every person othered by the white hegemonic system of culture and commerce. As long as these individuals do the backbreaking dirty work of picking strawberries, cleaning houses, and moving furniture for slave wages without complaint or getting out of line, they are permitted to live. However, as soon as they express understandable rage at their state of oppression, or organize for better working conditions, or seek to live as full citizens in the land they serve, they are portrayed as criminals, animals, and vermin, and are treated as such by the state and its "true" citizens.

Take, for example, "Olivia," who sets out from Altar, Sonora, to get to Tucson, Arizona, traversing the desert for three days, walking at night in frigid temperatures, sheltering under scrub bushes by day in the scorching sun. She's hunted like an animal by aircraft, tracked by night vision goggles and surveillance cameras. Yet even after being stopped, imprisoned, or deported, she returns again the next month or the next year, because there is no other choice for survival. Like the quartet of replicants led by Roy Batty to infiltrate the Tyrell Corporation in search of the key to their survival, and like the replicants mobilized by Freysa to fight for their freedom, millions of undocumented migrants come to the United States out of desperation. They are seeking life in the only place they see as a viable option for survival for themselves and their families.

Yet even well-meaning Americans searching for a way to make a path to citizenship for these "illegals" resort to tactics that impose impossible categories on immigrants. In their attempts to valorize the ones they seek to aid, they must cast immigrants and DACA recipients (also known as Dreamers) as either heroes or messianic figures.

I Always Knew You Were Special

Both *Blade Runner* movies invoke messianic imagery and valorize self-sacrifice. Rick Deckard sacrifices a relationship with his child in order to save her (much like Latinx parents send their children to cross the border, severing ties for the sake of their survival). Deckard himself is twice saved by the noble sacrifice of replicants—first by Roy Batty whose nail-pierced hand evokes strong Christ-like imagery; then by Officer K who suffers his own Christ-like wound—his side pierced and bleeding as he lays dying on snow-covered steps. While these sacrifices enable Deckard to retrieve his humanity, the messianic symbolism is problematic because of the way it constructs and objectifies those in the savior role.

DACA recipient "Louisa" describes what it's like to watch white conservative and liberal politicians construct her identity for her. While conservatives consider DACA a form of amnesty for young "illegals," liberals create a heroic, even superhuman narrative of who the Dreamers are. "All the media portrayals are of DACA recipients who are fire fighters, who join the military, or become cops," she observes. "They are not regular people wanting a decent job and to keep their families together."

In other words, liberals construct DACA kids as super-Americans who desire to save our (white) lives. These are the people we're meant to imagine when we demand justice for immigrant youth. But the result is that the victims of racism are forced to become the teachers or saviors of the racists in order to gain status in their world order. In this way they are once again denied actual personhood, even in the well-meaning efforts to grant them the legal status they deserve.

That Baby Meant that We Were More than Just Slaves

This brings us to the most liminal figure of all in the *Blade Runner* world—Dr. Ana Stelline, a subcontractor for Wallace Industries who designs memories for replicants. At the movie's end, she is revealed to be the miracle child of Deckard and Rachael.

Trapped in a bubble between the world of the truly human and the world of replicants, she in many ways embodies the experience of American-born children of undocumented parents. Ana holds the genetic key coveted by both Wallace and Freysa: the former for creating an army of slaves; the latter for creating an army of resistance to throw off the shackles of slavery. The pressure on her will be immense. The potential for her use and abuse by either side for their own ends is an ominous undercurrent beneath the father-daughter reunion between Ana and Deckard.

Similarly, the pressure on American-born children of undocumented parents is extreme. While granted protections by the country that their parents will never enjoy, they risk living out these protections alone or with other American-born siblings, their parents having been deported. These children often exhibit symptoms such as depression, anxiety, withdrawal, and aggression, as well as difficulty with social and cognitive skills.

On the other side comes the pressure from the mixed-status family hoping that having one American citizen in the family will protect them all from deportation and a return to the unlivable conditions that forced migration in the first place. This child is expected to somehow "save" the dream that brought immigrants from and through unspeakable conditions. They carry within their personhood the chance for the family to be acknowledged as "truly human," worthy of the rights of full citizenship. Even if the parents are deported, their citizen-children will have the lives they had hoped for long ago when they undertook the dangerous journey to *El Norte*.

These children are often hidden in plain sight, so to speak, their true identity obscured until a hoped-for time when it is safe for them and their families to live as free—fully legal, fully human—citizens. Ana Stelline's identity was also concealed behind layers of scrambled genetic records, gender-bending cross-dressing, ripped pages of orphanage ledgers, and (if we are to believe her) a genetic disease that both imprisons and protects her. Yet within each replicant she implants memories: of birthdays and toy horses, snowfall and struggle, joy and violence.

These are the human moments that transcend any label of legal or illegal, replicant or human. They are the memories that she gives in secret to connect her kin to her, and her to them. "Beautiful, isn't it?"

26

Do Replicants Have Nightmares of Ethnic Discrimination?

DOMINIC J. NARDI, JR.

The year 2019, when it came, looked nothing like the future 2019 that *Blade Runner* (1984) depicted. Fortunately, the real 2019 didn't bring us the conditions the movie predicted. We're nowhere close to producing bioengineered beings with artificial intelligence, crime has fallen in most American cities, the Bradbury's not a decaying husk, and PanAm and Atari went bankrupt years ago.

And yet, *Blade Runner* did uncannily predict the importance of group identity in the twenty-first century. Our friends, careers, even our taste in movies, are all determined in part by our ethnic background. Western societies are increasingly divided along ethnic lines. The abuses replicants endure in *Blade Runner* and in *Blade Runner 2049* mirror the plight of many ethnic minorities in real life. Both movies raise questions about the nature of human ethnicity and group identity, but explore them in subtly different ways.

In *Blade Runner*, humans kill replicants with impunity, while the replicants long for recognition of their right to exist. Replicants come across as fundamentally human, save for their persecution by humanity. By contrast, in *2049*, replicants are permitted to live in human society, but are treated as fundamentally different from humans.

As Lieutenant Joshi tells Officer K, "The world is built on a wall that separates kind." Over the course of *2049*, those differences then begin to break down as what it means to be a replicant changes. If *Blade Runner* concludes that the wall between humans and replicants never really existed, *2049* acknowledges that such a wall exists, but also lets us know that it's far more porous than humans and replicants previously believed.

Mere Data Makes a Man

For many people, ethnic identity is a concept we think we intuitively understand, even if we've never really thought about its meaning. After all, can't you just look at somebody and tell if they belong to a different ethnic group?

Not exactly . . .

Ethnic identity is used to describe groups of people who share certain biological, cultural, and language traits. However, not all identity groups are "ethnic." First, members of an ethnic group must actually view themselves as separate from other groups. This is crucial because not all potential ethnic groups actually view themselves as distinct. Classifying the number and type of ethnic groups in a country often becomes a point of controversy. For example, the government of Myanmar (also known as Burma) claims that there are 135 ethnic groups in the country, but some observers counter that the government artificially inflated the number by separately counting tribes and clans that could be identified with existing ethnic groups. A majority group might do this to try to divide and conquer its opponents, preventing smaller ethnic groups from joining together to challenge the status quo.

Second, ethnicity is—or is believed to be—passed on through descent. In other words, you got your ethnic identity from your parents, and your siblings should share the same ethnic identity. This obviously includes any physical features determined by genetics, such as skin and hair color.

Finally, ethnic groups believe that members of the group tend to share a common culture, religion, homeland, and history passed down through generations. For example, although Italian-Americans might look "white," they are distinct from Americans of Anglo-Saxon descent because they all have ancestors who immigrated from Italy, tend to be Catholic (at least nominally), and almost unanimously believe *The Godfather* is the greatest movie ever. By contrast, something like being a *Blade Runner* fan is not an ethnic identity bcause you *chose* to to be a fan (even if your parents introduced you to the films).

So, are replicants an ethnic group?

The mere fact that replicants were created through bioengineering doesn't disqualify them from belonging to an ethnic group. Perhaps more importantly, both films treat replicant identity like an ethnic identity. Humans clearly view replicants as different. They systematically treat them as "other," as "things" that can be disposed of rather than as fellow members of the human race. The government in *Blade Runner* banned replicants from even existing on Earth. In the theatrical version of *Blade Runner*, Rick Deckard's voiceover even compares "skin job" to the slurs cops "used to call black men" in America.

For their part, the replicants have a strong sense of group solidarity and view themselves as unwelcome in human society. In his famous speech at the end of the movie, Roy Batty tells Deckard, "I've seen things *you people* wouldn't believe," indicating that he still views humans as "other." Even in *2049*, when it appears that only older Nexus-6 models are banned from Earth, replicants are still treated as a distinct group. Although Officer K works alongside humans in a police department, he knows he's not the same as his colleagues because, as he tells Lieutenant Joshi, "To be born is to have a soul." K also faces discrimination from his human neighbors, including verbal abuse and graffiti on his apartment door. Both the power structures of society and individual prejudices reinforce the boundaries between replicants and humans.

As for inheritance of ethnic identity, this works differently for replicants. *2049* reveals that until Rachael, they were unable to give birth. Thus, they're not "born" the way humans are and don't inherit genetic traits from replicant parents. However, replicants do receive ethnic traits through another type of descent—being manufactured. Replicants might not have literal parents, but they're made by the same company (the Tyrell Corporation, later the Wallace Corporation). The physical and cultural traits that make them a distinct group—superior strength and agility, lack of empathy, serial numbers on their eyes—are all features "inherited" through the process of manufacture. In other words, replicants don't choose those features for themselves, but rather received them from their designers—their metaphorical parents.

Likewise, all replicants believe that they originated from the Tyrell/Wallace Corporation. This is effectively their "homeland," laden with its own shared historical meaning. *Blade Runner* frames the four replicants' escape to Earth as a return home. Indeed, an earlier version of the script even included a line in which Roy Batty tells Eldon Tyrell, "Like the fabled salmon, we came home to die." It's not clear whether they were manufactured on Earth or in the Off-World Colonies, but for the purposes of ethnic identity it doesn't matter. Like humans who emigrate to other countries, the replicants view the corporation headquarters as the geographic starting point for their collective story. This sense of homeland is strengthened in *2049*, because we see replicants being manufactured in Niander Wallace's compound.

Again, it's important to emphasize that replicants are a distinct ethnic group even if the average Angeleno can't distinguish between replicants and humans. An ethnic group can still exist without any visible biological differences. Indeed, in many real-world ethnic conflicts, those determined to hunt down members of a rival ethnic group might identify them based on their clothes, accents, or even eating habits. Likewise, blade runners employ various technological devices, such as *Blade Runner*'s Voight-Kampff Test and *2049*'s eye scanner, to identify replicants trying to blend in with the human population. The bigotry K faces in his apartment complex suggests that even humans without access to advanced police tools can find ways to uncover a replicant's true identity.

The World Is Built on a Wall

So, if replicants are an ethnic group, are they fated to always be outsiders? Could replicants just blend into human society if people agreed to treat them as humans?

That depends on whether you believe ethnicity is an immutable feature of a person's identity or changes depending upon the context.

If ethnic identity is fixed, it's a primordial part of who we are. In other words, your ethnicity is something you're born with and will die with. Traditionally, this view has led to skepticism about the ability of people from different ethnic groups to live together in peace, because differences are harder to reconcile when they're rooted in your identity. If a different tribe or race slighted your ethnic group, this would lead to lasting grievances and possibly a desire for revenge. This is why for decades many policymakers and journalists tended to view ethnic conflict as rooted in "ancient hatreds," as inevitable as they were insoluble. (Just look at news coverage of the civil wars in the former Yugoslavia or the Middle East.)

By contrast, if an ethnic identity is socially constructed, then it's less about who you are and more about where you are. Identity is complicated and multifaceted. Different parts of our identity can become socially or politically relevant at different times. For example, my ancestors came from Naples, Italy. If they traveled to Rome, they would have been considered Neapolitan. When they immigrated to America, they were initially labeled Italian, at a time of fairly mainstream bigotry against Italians and Catholics (a job ad might forbid Italian-

Americans from applying, for example). Today Italian-Americans are for the most part considered "white." The biology remained the same, but social attitudes changed which aspect of my family's identity was activated.

This constructivist approach to ethnic identity doesn't mean we should ignore biology, but biology alone does not constitute an identity. Obviously, people from different ethnic groups might have different physical features, but we as a society have to recognize those differences as meaningful or relevant. For example, in American history, skin color has been socially and politically significant in ways that eye and hair color have not. By contrast, in some societies, the shape of a person's eyes, ears, and nose are more important traits than skin tone.

If identity is fluid and contextually dependent, then ethnic diversity does not inevitably lead to conflict. Instead, if you peak behind the curtain of ethnic conflict, you'll often find demagogues or opportunists inciting ethnic tensions for their own political gain. Yugoslavia did not spontaneously combust because of ancient ethnic hatreds. Rather, President Slobodan Milosevic tried to use Serbian nationalism to consolidate his power. In much of the Middle East, fighting between Sunnis and Shiites is quite recent, largely a product of the 1979 Iranian Revolution and the 2003 invasion of Iraq, both of which made those identities much more pronounced.

Both *Blade Runner* and *2049* take a generally constructivist approach to identity, but do so in different ways.

Blade Runner is more purely constructivist. Unlike other prominent artificial beings in science fiction, such as Data in *Star Trek* and the T-800 in *Terminator 2*, *Blade Runner*'s replicants are presented as nearly indistinguishable from humans. There is no metal or wiring underneath their skin. Replicants might be stronger and smarter than the average human, but overall they seem to fall within the normal range of human abilities (and we certainly wouldn't deny exceptional individuals like rocket scientists or Olympic athletes their humanity). The only biological difference noted in the first movie is that replicants have a four-year lifespan, but Captain Harry Bryant makes clear Tyrell artificially shortened the replicant lifespan as a measure of control. Blade runners need to use the Voight-Kampff Test to gauge replicants' emotional reactions, showing just how little biology shapes their identity (remember, Deckard nearly fails to identify Rachael as a replicant). As Bryant tells Deckard, "They were designed to copy human beings in every way except their emotions"—and even their emotional immaturity is not exceptionally non-human, given their youth and inexperience.

Replicants are treated as a separate identity group because human society declared them so. The government banned replicants on Earth, signaling to people that replicants should be viewed as "others." The central conflict of the movie is not rooted in inevitable hatred between humans and replicants. Instead, Batty and his cohort seek to fight back against injustice and want the same rights humans have. Indeed, the movie eventually shows the boundary between human and replicant to be an illusion. For example, Deckard initially dismisses Rachael's claim to humanity because her memories come from Tyrell's niece. Later, when Rachael plays the piano and wonders if her skill belongs to Tyrell's niece, Deckard tells her, "*You play beautifully.*" By the end of the movie, Batty even shows empathy for Deckard and saves his life. If replicants can develop sophisticated empathetic responses—and presumably pass the Voight-Kampff Test—then what actually separates them from humans?

By contrast, *2049* initially emphasizes fundamental biological differences between humans and replicants. In the opening scene, K identifies Sapper Morton as a replicant merely by scanning his eye, a clear physical marker. We also learn that replicants cannot become pregnant, another important biological distinction. K himself tells Joshi, "To be born is to have a soul," implying that he views this aspect of replicant identity—which separates him from humanity—as critically important to his sense of self-worth.

Ironically, even though Earth in 2049 no longer bans all replicants—only the older models—and even though the police department actually employs replicants, they still face discrimination. K tries to assimilate into human society, but his human neighbors still exhibit hostility towards him (even while it's unclear how they know he's a replicant). All this seems to suggest that the human hatred of replicants has primordial roots. Human prejudice survived the repeal of the draconian anti-replicant policies of 2019.

However, *2049* then turns this on its head and suggests those biological differences might be more mutable than they first appeared. K discovers that Rachael gave birth to a baby. Both Joshi and Freysa's reactions hint that the news might force society to reconsider the status of replicants as a separate group. The removal of the boundary between human and replicant—should it come—would be due in large part to a new understanding and interpretation of replicant biology.

Moreover, as revealed in *Blade Runner 2036: Nexus Dawn*, the newer replicant models no longer have a four-year lifespan. If replicants can give birth and have open-ended lifespans, then there are few meaningful biological differences separating them from humans. This in turn would make it more difficult for the Wallace Corporation and others in the societal power structure to maintain the artificial distinction between replicant and human. In other words, the wall has an open doorway.

K's journey throughout the movie encapsulates how social norms around ethnicity can change over time. At the start of *2049*, K seems to accept the invisible wall separating replicants from humans. He does nothing to challenge human prejudice and seems to accept his role as a second-class citizen. Then, when Joi convinces him that he might be Rachael and Deckard's child, he starts to view himself as human because he now thinks of himself as *biologically* human (or at least half-human). His conversation with Joshi about souls implies that he previously believed that—as a replicant—he lacked a soul, but now has one as a natural-born human.

By the time he learns that he is not Rachael and Deckard's son, K has already developed a sense of identity separate from being a replicant. Ultimately, he decides to risk his life to save Deckard not because he believes they're biologically related, but rather because he believes it's the right thing to do. His choices and identity are no longer dictated by his biology. The K lying outside Ana Stelline's compound is biologically the same person who killed Sapper, but his perception of his identity has completely changed. Although he never says as much, K almost certainly sees himself as human in spite—not because—of his biology.

This Breaks the World

The *Blade Runner* movies explore what it means to be different, but also how and why those differences matter. Like a good constructivist, *Blade Runner* suggests that identity is primarily a social construct, and that peace between ethnic groups is possible once we look past our differences. *2049* acknowledges that physical differences play a role defining our identities, but likewise concludes that society can re-evaluate and reinterpret the relevance of biological traits.

Unfortunately, neither film promises that change will come peacefully. Prejudice and hatred do not disappear overnight. In *Blade Runner*, Deckard kills several replicants before coming to fully accept their humanity. In *2049*, Joshi warns, "Tell

either side there's no wall, you've bought a war. Or a slaughter."
Yet, both movies adamantly insist that change is possible.
Despite the frequently distressing news about ethnic conflict in
our own version of the twenty-first century, the *Blade Runner*
franchise ultimately reminds us that ethnic identity need not
prevent us from acknowledging our own common humanity.[1]

---

[1] I'm grateful to George Washington University for hiring me to teach
"Ethnic Conflict and Peacebuilding" during the Fall 2018 semester, which
gave me an opportunity to think critically about ethnic identity and inspired
this chapter. I'm a political scientist by training, so in this article I discuss ethnic identity as understood in the political science literature. Other disciplines
might use different approaches to ethnic identity.

27
Who Keeps a Dead Tree?

ALİ RIZA TAŞKALE AND REŞAT VOLKAN GÜNEL

When Mariette first encounters K on the street, she sees his photo of a tree and says, "What's that?" K replies, "A tree." Mariette says, "I've never seen a tree before. It's pretty." To which K responds, "It's dead." Mariette says, "Now, who keeps a dead tree?" These words remind us what the world of *Blade Runner 2049* is about: the human race is down to its final numbers and extinction is not only possible—it's probable.

Blade Runner 2049, like its predecessor, *Blade Runner*, is based on Philip K. Dick's novel *Do Androids Dream of Electric Sheep?* It presents a future—dominated by climate catastrophe, a denatured agricultural landscape, a polluted and decaying urban landscape of neon-lit, high-rise gated communities, flying cars, giant flashing holograms, and crowds of faceless people—in which conventional distinctions between reality and fantasy, the real and the fake, humans and replicants seem to blur together. Replicants affirm this logic: they are the fiction of the real. They usurp reality.

Dystopian Fears

The film's main protagonist is K, a Nexus-9 model replicant cop working for the LAPD. His job is to find and "retire" unwanted early model replicants in order to keep the corporate order intact. K has no friends or family. His only companion is virtual Joi, a holographic girlfriend who can instantly switch to a sexy vamp while cooking. K is not human, Joi cannot even be considered non-human. But to each other, they're real.

K is sent out of LA to hunt down one of the early model replicants who lives under the name of Sapper Morton. K kills him. While he's getting ready to return to the LAPD, he finds a box of bones buried under a dead tree. The bones carry a secret that could overthrow the corporate regime K protects. Subsequent investigation reveals that the bones belong to Rachael the replicant, who fell in love and went on the run with the replicant Deckard in the original *Blade Runner*. We discover that Morton has helped Deckard and Rachael to give birth to their daughter, Dr. Ana Stelline, who designs false memories for replicants. And she lives. No substantive difference now remains between humans and replicants.

But the cinematic prominence of K is matched by the thematic preponderance of a corporate order which is structured around the fundamental premise that replicants can't give birth, they can't reproduce by themselves. They're artificial and have no rights. They're genetically engineered to obey. If replicants can reproduce and create life—just like humans—then the strict division between replicants and humans would break down and humanity would no longer remain the exclusive preserve of humans.

The political economy of *2049* is embodied in two seemingly conflicting characters, namely Lieutenant Joshi (the State) and Niander Wallace (tech corporations). For K's police chief, Joshi, civilization depends on the wall that distinguishes human life from the kind that can be enslaved, exploited and, when necessary, killed. She says, "there is an order to things. That's what we do here. We keep order. The world is built in a wall that separates kind." She stands for a form of apartheid, for the neat division between humans and replicants. If the wall that separates humans from replicants falls, then civilization falls along with it. The wall must be preserved at all costs, making sure that the near-fascistic corporate order remains intact and unchallenged.

Wallace, on the other hand, appears to monopolize solar and artificial farming, and due to the collapse of the world's ecosystems, also humanity's food supply. For him, replicants are necessary for the socio-ecological survival of capitalist civilization because "every civilization was built off the back of a disposable workforce," he tells a newly born replicant. For Wallace, the continuous exploitation and oppression of replicants is the fuel upon which the corporate order is built. *2049* presents the idea that the history of capitalist civilization and progress has been built by slave labor. In the world of *2049*, the replicants are the new underclass.

Joshi seems to represent the emaciation of the state, and she is unable to defend herself from Wallace's agents. Wallace, on the other hand, stands for capitalism as delirium, aiming to expand its reach beyond nine planets. For Wallace, capitalism should have no limits.

2049 offers an invaluable opportunity to study the particular form the paradigmatic "fear of the future" takes, and its significance for the political present. The future has become a site of precarity and fear, both in the sense that a threatful future looms on the horizon and also in the sense that we appear to have lost the capacity to produce a counter-narrative to "capitalist realism." Capitalist realism, according to Mark Fisher, is a kind of capitalist exceptionalism, a widespread sense that "not only is capitalism the only viable political and economic system, but also that it is now impossible even to imagine a coherent alternative to it" (*Capitalist Realism*, p. 2).

We can imagine the future only as an extension of the present: on the one hand, a future of corporate capitalism, inequality and injustice continuing into infinity; on the other, a future of technological utopianism. Or we can imagine it as a dystopian future of ecological and civilizational collapse. Our entrapment in this "present future" has turned the future into a site of crisis, where corporate capitalism and technological utopianism is foreclosing our imagination.

Future Corporated

2049 is evidence of this constricted future. The future depicted in *2049* is part of the future which is imagined by corporate capital. The movie seems to have no problem portraying dystopian fears, but it seems to have given up on non-capitalist possible futures and even when it pictures future anxieties it seems marked by the persistence of corporate capitalism.

The movie imagines a future in which climate catastrophe and excessive pollution are the norm. Civilization is on the brink of collapse and a corporate terror declares that certain lives are worthless, that only a few elite citizens are worthy of protection. The Earth is ruined, but the power structures are unperturbed. Neoliberal political economy is still functional, and the movie mirrors the political and economic disparities of a capitalist dystopia. It is set in a post-apocalyptic Los Angeles that seems to have suspended many of the functions of the state. But bureaucratic machineries and the police live on.

So the film shows us that current political and economic arrangements are also the only ones that will be present in the future. But why do we assume they will? How could we know with any certainty that capitalism will persist in the future? In the film we have a fantasy of a terrible world, but one which is still governed by a single ideology and economic model. Put differently, the imagination driving the movie's dystopian fears is the "enchanted world" of hyper-financial capitalism in which no other economic system and idea could work.

Perhaps, then, *2049* is an apt reckoning with the future that futurists or Silicon Valley gurus want to build! The movie presents an alternative to the corporate dystopia, the alternative of the replicant resistance which forms a repository of the humane in a world that has otherwise lost its humanity. It presents a critique of the current world, a nascent rebellion, which opposes corporate capitalism. Yet, it can't imagine a future that is distinct from the capitalist present; it's unable to conceive of a future that moves beyond it, and this leads to a sense of atrophy and repetition. We're left without a possibility of a radical change regarding the existing order.

Disturbingly, throughout the movie, Niander Wallace appears to symbolize "capitalism as creative destruction," the smart billionaire who has the capacity to bring about dramatic economic and political change. According to this logic, social change comes only from giant corporations, tech billionaires, engineers, and gurus. This is a sort of "technological determinism" which claims the future is best left to the engineers, technocrats, cyber gurus, billionaires, who will solve humanity's social and economic problems with the aid of science and technology in the future, thereby making the entire world a better, more prosperous and more connected place. This is a logic which can be described as political anti-utopianism, which sustains rather than challenges the already-held beliefs that structure corporate capitalism. It conceives of the possibility of a post-capitalist imaginary as unrealistic and potentially useless.

K—once an emotionally dry and obedient replicant—turns into a "radical" figure who appears to provide solidarity and cooperation between humans and replicants in the face of techno-corporate hegemony. He is presented as a typical individualist hero, who chooses to be human by sacrificing himself for Stelline, perhaps the only special figure everybody is looking for.

But what does it mean to be human? In the dehumanized world of *2049*, it is the ability to be "more human than human." The film's overall message here is that we have lost our humanity, the ability to feel and love; replicants should be designed around human values like empathy and love, and that they should be treated like humans. Yet, K's individual rebellion from the corporate order never coalesces into organised resistance; it produces no difference within the bounds of a given hegemonic discourse, mirroring the extreme individualism of corporate totality he supposedly rejects. This leads to celebrating heroism so as to resist capitalist exploitation and systemic violence.

Rather than a political act, which targets the internal contradictions of the corporate order and the social power relations that constitute it, K's act only reflects the level of neoliberal dialogue in which the political subject ceases to exist. Neoliberal tolerance, not systemic antagonism, is the essence of *2049*'s humanist message. Redemption is shown as rejecting technological dehumanization in favor of more humane forms of social and economic arrangements.

But fixing the problems will require more than individual heroism; collective thinking and resistance is necessary in order to make things better. Although *2049* asks interesting questions concerning neo-liberal conceptions of humanism, it's unable to accede to a true creation that would disrupt capitalist realism and constitute a subject that can go beyond the temporality of corporate capitalism.

Post-Capitalist Futures

Paul Walker-Emig has pointed out that cyberpunk has already accepted the dystopian imagination of corporate capitalism as an inevitable part of our future. Cyberpunk seems to be inspiring today's corporate despots instead of warning them. The result is that cyberpunk itself is now part of our all-encompassing despair.

The world of *2049* is no exception to this dearth of imagination. No matter how radical its future representations of corporate capitalism may be, it tends to take the long-term durability of corporate capitalism utterly for granted. Taking capitalism for granted or assuming that it is natural is to limit the imagination. Liberating our imagination requires us to challenge the limiting notion that capitalism is the only logical, possible system.

There is an urgent need for new future narratives, the need to reclaim the power to imagine the future outside of corporate futures industry. We need new future narratives with a collective goal, which provoke us to think about how we might build new forms of life that are outside of corporate, financialized capitalism. The more reality starts to resemble the dystopias on our screens, the more we need another kind of story. There are enough dystopian and capitalist futures out there, we must imagine and reach out the emancipatory futures we want.

The production of emancipatory futures would constitute a form of indirect action without which a struggle for freedom cannot hope to be successful. But it's not a single narrative or vision that is required but many alternative futures, each potentially opening up the gates for another world. The stories we tell, cultural visions we create can have an impact on the reality we live. They can counter capitalist realism by rendering post-capitalist futures thinkable. If we're after post-capitalist futures, then we must think what kind of stories we tell that can empower the readers and political communities.

New potential futures are finally emerging, which seek to challenge the currently reigning imaginary of corporate capitalism. It may be time for cyberpunk to change its narrative.

28
Replicants of California, Unite!

CHRISTOPHER M. INNES

California is mostly grey and misty in 2049. Even when it's July we get the impression that the bright summer sun is not going to return to light up the day.

What's more, the social and political landscape is no longer clear, if it ever was. Officer K's an LAPD cop on a mission and he's expected to carry out his duty, no matter what. Like all Nexus-8 replicants, he's conditioned to do what he's told. His duty is to "retire" outdated Nexus-8 replicants that were illegally rushed into production by the now out-of-operation Tyrell Corporation.

K is under orders to keep the replicants and the humans separate, which involves "retiring" the redundant Nexus-8 replicants. It's maybe not in his interest to kill his own kind, but K might not be able to act in accordance with his long-term interests. In *Blade Runner 2049,* there is a predicament about K's class membership. He lives in an intricate mix of class and technology. K may not be aware of his own class interests.

But what class is K part of and how does it impact the society of 2049? K is part of a class of enslaved replicants whose labor is used to benefit humans. All humans benefit in some way, as their status is automatically higher than that of the replicant. Some humans benefit to a much greater degree—particularly Wallace, who owns the most profitable and powerful corporation in the cosmos.

Officer K's current mission, which he has no choice but to accept, is to "retire" a particular replicant, to which another replicant has given birth. His boss, Lieutenant Joshi, makes it emphatically clear that this is yet another part of the underworld of replicants that needs to be "retired." A replicant with the ability to procreate makes it more difficult to maintain order in a system where Nexus-8 replicants are already seen as a threat to law and order. This is chaos in the making. This new replicant group stands in opposition to the world order—an order which safeguards the interests of the Wallace Corporation

Knowing Your Station in Life

There's certainly conflict in *2049*, but what is this conflict really about? What is its cause? K rides above in his Spinner and surely finds it difficult to understand the justice of a system where one group of beings is separated by force from another. This is the social system in *2049*: Nexus-8s, the bald-headed ragamuffin children exploited by Mr. Cotton in his 'orphanage', LAPD cops, and the Wallace Corporation. In the context of this social system, it makes no sense for K to kill other Nexus-8s, and yet from the perspective of Joshi, Wallace, and K himself, employing replicants as Blade Runners is part of the system that sustains the world.

Luckily we can turn to a Marxist analysis of social and political class to help shine the light on the contradictions of K's California. The Wallace Corporation, is much like one of the dark satanic cotton mills towering over the exploited workers who live in its shadow. But whereas two hundred years ago the workers knew their exploiter's name, in 2049 the owners are hidden from view. We see this nicely in the street scenes where Coca-Cola and Sony advertisements and sexy hologram girls with enticingly suggestive poses show products, but we don't see the owners of the businesses.

The cotton mills in the early days of the eighteenth-century industrial revolution in England produced cloth for the clothing industry and made fortunes for their owners. The capitalist lived looking down on the workers and the workers labored and looked up to the capitalists. Both were visible and knew their class position.

Karl Marx lived and worked in nineteenth-century England, when the division of social classes was much clearer. There were the ruling-class industrialists who married their daughters into the local poverty-stricken aristocracy. The ruling class relied on the cops to keep the social order.

Marx's analysis illuminates the social order and exploitation of classes by the business owners in the streets of 2049 California. Marx argued that society developed over time through class conflict. In this process we see the progress of technology, human interaction, driven by class relations. In the period of capitalism, the ruling class, the owners of industry, are the dominant force and the working class are in opposition.

Through Marx's lens, we see the exploited class of replicants and the exploiting Wallace Corporation, along with autonomous, small businesses, such as Mr. Cotton's electronic machine salvage business. The owners have some control over the LAPD, which employs the likes of K, whom we see as a slave.

In *2049*, K is not likely to be aware of his class position or the class system. Before, in the more developed offices and factories of the twentieth century, the workers see the bosses and the bosses see the workers. The replicants are slaves, along with scatterings of odd collections of orphan ragamuffin children exploited by Fagin-like characters, but we're not sure whether K is as clear-sighted about his class position as a contemporary Marxist might be.

Should K Be Asking Some Questions of His Own?

Marx notices that many people mistakenly see social and political conflict represented as a clash of ideas, a process sometimes called the idealist dialectic. Two or more ideas come into conflict, resulting in the creation of a new idea or ideas. Idealism is the view of historical progress purely from a philosophical perspective, but Marx objects to an idealist historical view of progress where the mind and the material world are perceived as organized according to the same rational principles.

This is the opposite of materialism. It's an argument with little or no material implication. According to Marx's materialist way of understanding conflict, change is going to come about no matter how much you try and stop it. This is to say that *Blade Runner 2049* depicts a world in which there is a clash of material forces, a class struggle, which causes social and political progress. As we can see in Los Angeles in 2049, the conflict is material. The conflict is between social and political classes.

Marxist analysis shows the working class of humans, as well as the slave replicants and their children as all ruthlessly exploited. There's one ruling class. However, within that class there may be a collection of complex and conflicting interests. Atari and Wallace might compete for workers or market share. However, in spite of these superficial conflicts, there is a deeper similarity of interest, as all capitalists have an interest in sustaining the capitalist system. All these different interests are in conflict. For in 2049 the ruling class owns and controls the "means of production" and exploits the working class and slave replicants who create the wealth.

We can see that the Wallace Corporation has some sway over the activity of the LAPD and other institutions. However, the LAPD has its own mission which is at odds with the interests of the Wallace Corporation. Marx described this as a state's "relative autonomy" from big business.

Marx's term, the "means of production" refers to material things needed to produce goods. These are the factories, offices, buildings, machines, and raw materials. The working class does not want to be exploited and will eventually violently resist. This helps us look at the replicants and understand their exploited state and why they want to be free and to look at K and his possible lack of awareness of his class position.

It's these material forces of owners, and controllers of replicants and the replicants that are in conflict with each other. For Marx, this is where class conflict exists. It's officer K's duty-bound obligation to kill specific replicants. The replicants are perceived as threat to humans. However, it would be more accurate to say that the replicants are a threat to capitalism. They feel and think like humans. They're slaves who see their life as precious, but ruined by the ruthless exploitation of capitalism. This is very much the sentiment of many replicants just as it is with the working class.

Is the Wallace Corporation Any the Wiser?

The conflict is no longer clear-cut, as it might sometimes have been in the nineteenth and twentieth centuries. The replicants led by the Replicant Freedom Movement are a threat to the Wallace Corporation and the LAPD. In his book *The Eighteenth Brumaire of Louis Bonaparte, Marx* tried to explain the political system under the French regime of Napoleon III. Marx pointed out how the identity and motives of the ruling class can be blurred, because of the alliance and opposition of different economic interest groups. In Marx's view the political struggles are fought out in terms of the clash of ideas, but the real content of the struggles is the class of economic interests, obscured by the alliances of different economic classes. Marx identifies a hodge-podge of different interests expressed by bourgeois idealists and parliamentarians who wanted to run the country in different ways.

Applying Marx's method, we can see that in *Blade Runner 2049* that there's not simply one set of interests. The Wallace

Corporation is obviously happy to see the Tyrell Corporation out of the way. Niander Wallace even attempted to buy out Dr. Ana Stelline (yet another member of the ruling class with her own specific interests) for her memory-making skills. We see that the interests of one member of the ruling class can be in conflict with those of another. This kind of conflict of interests among the ruling class often runs deep.

The replicants' children are a potential new set of interests in opposition to the ruling class. We might assume that they will only be in conflict with the Wallace Corporation and LAPD. But hold on, might not the replicants want them out of the way as well? It might be too much to assume that all the slaves will join together as one oppressed class with a common set of interests. If the replicants achieve what Marx calls "class consciousness," consciousness of their interests, they will. If they fail to achieve class consciousness, they may not.

Class interests can be varied and conflicting. Marx noticed this complex arrangement in nineteenth-century England and France, and so should we in the California of *Blade Runner 2049*. The Wallace Corporation is one of many with competing interests who argue how new replicants ought to be created.

Are We More Aware of K's Class?

Here is where the greater insight is to be found to identify K's class position. There is to be no compromise in ridding California of the contradictions of exploitation. By the Replicant Freedom Movement rising up and destroying the likes of the Wallace Corporation, they do so by also smashing their own material identity. The replicants, their children, and working people are one side of the coin. The Wallace Corporation and other members of the ruling class are the other side.

After the overthrow of the ruling class, the entire oppressed are to be liberated. They will no longer have their identity of being oppressed. No contradiction can last for long. In *The Communist Manifesto*, Marx asserted that the worker under capitalism becomes a mere "appendage to the machine," and we now see that some of the Nexus-8 replicants have become an unwanted appendage to the machinery of LA.

Why Isn't the LAPD Helping K Become Conscious of His Class?

We see K dealing with his LAPD cop boss. Liberal capitalism has great trust in the LAPD acting as an independent body. We will mockingly say that the institutions act to promote the "rights of man" in an equal and fair fashion. Marx was also notorious for using Socratic scorn to pour ridicule on the pretenses and moral sanctimony generated by the bourgeois notions of rights and equality.

Liberal institutions, according to Marx, soon turned into a self-serving plutocracy. The LAPD is supposedly in charge of looking after the interests of all citizens. However, in reality their job is to uphold the system, which benefits the ruling class. They might be seen as the Wallace Corporation's lapdogs. However, the LAPD has its own agenda; it has relatve autonomy from the Wallace Corporation.

Going back to *Blade Runner*, we see Capt. Harry Bryant of the LAPD "request" Rick Deckard to track down and "retire" a group of Nexus-8 replicants that got loose on Earth. Deckard is a reluctant operative of the LAPD, but is one nonetheless. He first questions Zhora, a suspected replicant who is now surviving and living as an erotic topless snake dancer. Zhora makes a run for her freedom, but Deckard, the seemingly dutiful blade runner of the LAPD, chases her down and kills her with his blaster, in a shower of broken glass.

The replicants, much like the working class in Marx's nineteenth century, have a short life-span. They are only expected to do their work and not complain. They are, as David McLellan says in his introduction to *The Communist Manifesto*, alienated and reduced to "atomized, mutually hostile individuals." A truly good life is not allowed as the interests of the ruling class are enforced by the LAPD, at the expense of working people's interests. This might be at odds with Wallace imagining the potential of replicants reproducing to provide the millions needed to serve human needs on colony planets.

Lieutenant Joshi of the LAPD seems to be single-mindedly set on getting the naturally-born replicants out of the way. The LAPD's agenda is to do so while keeping order. This is not necessarily in the interests of Wallace and his aspirations, and is certainly not in the interests of the replicants.

Should K Know his Class?

Does K need a Baseline Test–type reading to find out if he is aware that he's exploited? Class consciousness is an important point in the Marxist critique of capitalism and to be aware of your class is to be aware that you are either the exploiter or the exploited. Sapper Morton reminds K that he's a replicant before K retires him. His role as the exploited is complex. If he is a replicant then should he not be with the Replicant Freedom Movement (who give the impression that they are aware of their exploited state)? As Freysa, the leader of the RFM says, "If a baby can come from one of us, we are our own masters."

The replicants have nothing to gain from Wallace or any of the other members of the ruling class and have only their chains to lose, though its tempting to say that Dr. Stelline will be on their side. Only those who lack class consciousness agree to the system. The replicants seem to be conscious of the system and are aware that they have nothing to gain by accepting it.

We remember the Nexus-8 replicant Roy Batty saying, in *Blade Runner*, "It's quite an experience to live in fear. That's what it's like to be slave." This is just before his four-year life expectancy protocol comes to an end and he dies.

There's a chilling appreciation of class consciousness as Freysa's exchange continues and she pronounces that replicants are "more human than humans" and that "a revolution is coming." This is a haunting challenge to the existing order. We can say that the replicants are class conscious. The battle cry of, "We are building our own army. I want to free our people," emphasizes this replicant consciousness by saying that they have a keen idea of what Marx would have called "species being." They are aware of their potential as creative and happy beings.

With the dark clouds above, the replicants have nothing to lose. Just as Marx said, the industrial working class has nothing to lose but the chains of wage-slavery. Freysa's battle cry is not that different from Marx's "Workers of the World, Unite!" It is one that K might do well to accept as his own.

Afterword
I Know What's Real

Trip McCrossin

"I know what's real," Deckard says to Wallace, defiantly, of the authenticity of his love for Rachael. Moments later, confronted with her having been "made again for" him, supposedly, he's again defiant. "Her eyes were green," he insists, with the same cadence nicely. Also, provocatively. "Is it the same," Wallace had prodded, "now as then, the moment you met her?," as we watched it unfold, and found in the process that her eyes are instead brown. Her gaze is not on us, however, but Deckard, presumably, and so, however "drunk on the memory of its perfection," *this* isn't *his* memory.

And Luv's earlier playback for K, of a "fragment" of the moment recorded on a surviving memory bearing, reminds us that during her Voight-Kampff test, on the machine's monitor *we also* see Rachael's eyes as green, our gaze meant to inhabit Deckard's. The elegance of the paired cadences would have been lost, and so the resulting provocation, but what Deckard can't help but mean by, "I know what's real," then, which can't help but lead *us* to rethink in subtler terms the meaning of this and related turns of phrase throughout the movie, and its predecessor, is that he knows "what's real" *to him*. He trusts the overwhelming authority of *his experience*—of Rachael's eye color, his love for her, hers for him, her personhood and resulting humanity, however bioengineered her humanness, not to mention *his*, and also *K*'s.

In the playback, though, can we so easily be meant to inhabit *this* gaze, as it's the machine's, it seems, not Deckard's? Not unless, of course, the bearing's recorded *his* visual experience, remotely. As a *memory* bearing, that is, it hasn't simply memorialized this particular aspect of the moment, but somehow *his experience* of it. This is, after all, science fiction. And

235

does this settle finally the hackneyed question as to whether Deckard himself is bioengineered? Thankfully, it needn't. Again, science fiction.

The movie's continuation of its predecessor's *Frankenstein* pedigree, with latter's screenplay's helpful reference to James Whale's rendition of Frankenstein's monster, is not at risk. Paraphrasing Mariette paraphrasing Tyrell, more human than *other* humans is *our* motto, as in humanity's, in the sense that, however we're engineered, we may retrieve our squandered humanity in reaction to the persistent dignity of those among us who we treat, or allow to be treated undeservedly badly.

Speaking of those we treat or allow to be treated undeservedly badly, "I'll put you outside where the sky is raining," Mr. Cotton berates his orphan charges, "where it's raining fire!" Luv had just been raining fire of sorts, moments earlier, and so perhaps the reference is to this. Environmental degradation has also proceeded apace, so perhaps the rain's acidity. In a pair of movies already chock-full of scripture, however, it's hard to imagine that he's not also channeling the "fire from heaven" passage from the Book of Job, making all the more evident what the *Frankenstein* lineage does already.

The storyline is not only about the nature of humanity in terms of the problem of personhood, but in terms also of the problem of evil: why do bad things happen to good people, and good things to bad, all too often incomprehensibly—be this the traditional theological worry about justifying God's ways to humanity, or the more modern, secular one about justifying to it the ways of Wallace, Tyrell, and all the other ersatz gods usurping power and influence at its expense.

The thirty-five of us have worked to tease out some new ways to think about *Blade Runner 2049*, and its predecessor, along the above and related lines. An homage, yes, but more importantly this is an invitation—to do what popular culture can't help but help us to do, which is to think more expansively about humanity, and how we might save ourselves after all, by saving one another.

References

Aarseth, Espen J. 1997. *Cybertext: Perspectives on Ergodic Literature.* Johns Hopkins University Press.

Anzaldúa, Gloria. 1999. *The Borderlands / La Frontera: The New Mestiza.* Aunt Lute.

Anzar, Justo. 2009. Designer Babies. A Question of Ethics. *Medicina e Morale* 58.

Aquinas, Thomas. 2006 [1485]. *Summa Theologiae.* Cambridge University Press.

Arendt, Hannah. 1951. *The Origins of Totalitarianism.* Schocken.

———. 1978–79. *The Life of the Mind.* Harcourt.

Ariès, Philippe. 1962. *Centuries of Childhood: A Social History of Family Life.* Vintage.

Aristotle. 2014 [350 B.C.E.]. *Nicomachean Ethics.* Cambridge University Press.

Batchelor, Stephen. 2004. *Living with the Devil: A Meditation on Good and Evil.* Riverhead.

Baudrillard, Jean. 1994. *Simulacra and Simulation.* University of Michigan Press.

Beauchamp, Tom, and James Childress. 2001. *Principles of Biomedical Ethics.* Oxford University Press.

Belmont Report: Ethical Principles and Guidelines for the Protection of Human Subjects of Research, Report of the National Commission for the Protection of Human Subjects of Biomedical and Behavioral Research <www.videocast.nih.gov/pdf/ohrp_appendix_belmont_report_vol_2.pdf>.

Bentham, Jeremy. 1988 [1789]. *An Introduction to the Principles of Morals and Legislation.* Prometheus.

Blake, William. 2016 [1790]. *The Marriage of Heaven and Hell: Good Is Heaven—Evil Is Hell.* CreateSpace.

Boddy, Clive. 2011. *Corporate Psychopaths: Organisational Destroyers*. Palgrave Macmillan.

Bukatman, Scott. 1997. *Blade Runner*. BFI Publishing.

Bunce, Robin. 2017. *Blade Runner 2049*'s Politics Resonate Because They Are So Perilously Close to Our Own. *New Statesman*.

Butler, Judith. 1999. *Gender Trouble: Feminism and the Subversion of Identity*. Routledge.

———. 2011. *Bodies that Matter: On the Discursive Limits of "Sex"*. Routledge.

Caldwell, John. 1982. *Theory of Fertility Decline*. Academic Press.

Chang, Ha-Joon. 2011. *23 Things They Don't Tell You about Capitalism*. Penguin.

Chomsky, Aviva. 2014. *Undocumented: How Immigration Became Illegal*. Beacon Press.

Condillac, Etienne Bonnot de. 1930 [1754]. *Treatise on Sensations [Traité des Sensations]*. Favil.

Coplan, Amy, and David Davies, eds. 2015. *Blade Runner*. Routledge.

De La Torre, Miguel. 2009. *Trails of Hope and Terror: Testimonies on Immigration*. Orbis.

Deleuze, Gilles, and Felix Guattari. 2013. *A Thousand Plateaus: Capitalism and Schizophrenia*. Bloomsbury.

Descartes, René. 2008 [1637]. *A Discouse on the Method*. Oxford University Press.

Dick, Philip K. 1956. *The World Jones Made*. Ace.

———. 1956. The Minority Report. In *Fantastic Universe*.

———. 1967. *Counter-Clock World*. Doubleday.

———. 1968. *Do Androids Dream of Electric Sheep?* Doubleday.

———. *Flow My Tears, the Policeman Said*. 1974. Doubleday.

———. *A Scanner Darkly*. 1977. Doubleday.

———. 1981. Notes on *Do Androids Dream of Electric Sheep?* In Lawrence Sutin, ed., *The Shifting Realities of Philip K. Dick: Selected Literary and Philosophical Writings*. Vintage.

Fisher, Mark. 2009. *Capitalist Realism*. Zero.

Flisfeder, Matthew. 2017. *Postmodern Theory and Blade Runner*. Bloomsbury.

Fromm, Erich. 1944. *The Fear of Freedom*. Farrar and Rinehart.

———. 1955. *The Sane Society*. Rinehart.

Gardiner, Patrick. 1988. *Kierkegaard: A Very Short Introduction*. Oxford University Press.

Garfield, Jay L. 1995 *The Fundamental Wisdom of the Middle Way: Nāgārjuna's MūlamadhyamakaKārikā*. Oxford University Press.

Gilligan, Carol. 1993. *In a Different Voice*. Harvard University Press.

Greene, Graham. 2015 [1940]. *The Power and the Glory*. Penguin.

Gwaltney, Marilyn. 1991. Androids as a Device for Reflection on Personhood. In Judith Kerman, ed., *Retrofitting Blade Runner:*

Issues in Ridley Scott's Blade Runner and Philip K. Dick's Do Androids Dream of Electric Sheep? Popular Press.

Hale, Benjamin. 2011. Moral Considerability: Deontological, Not Metaphysical. *Ethics and the Environment* 16.

Harvey, David. 2007. *A Brief History of Neoliberalism*. Oxford University Press.

Harvey, Peter. 2012. *An Introduction to Buddhism: Teachings, History and Practices*. Second edition. Cambridge University Press.

Hatherley, Owen. 2012. *A New Kind of Bleak: Journeys through Urban Britain*. Verso.

Hayek, Friedrich August. 1944. *The Road to Serfdom*. Routledge.

Hayles, N. Katherine. 1995. The Life Cycle of Cyborgs. Writing the Posthuman. In Chris Hables Gray, ed., *The Cyborg Handbook*. Routledge.

Heidegger, Martin. 2009 [1954]. The Question Concerning Technology. In David Kaplan, ed., *Readings in the Philosophy of Technology*. Rowman and Littlefield.

Held, Virginia. 2006. *The Ethics of Care: Personal, Political, and Global*. Oxford University Press.

Heller-Roazen, Daniel. 2007. *The Inner Touch*. Zone.

Hursthouse, Rosalind. 2011. Virtue Ethics and the Treatment of Animals. In Tom Beauchamp and Raymond Frey, eds., *The Oxford Handbook of Animal Ethics*. Oxford University Press.

Ihde, Don. 1990. *Technology and the Lifeworld: From Garden to Earth*. Indiana University Press.

Kant, Immanuel. 1969 [1785]. *Foundations of the Metaphysics of Morals*. Bobbs-Merrill.

Kierkegaard, Søren. 1969 [1849]. *Fear and Trembling and Sickness unto Death*. Princeton University Press.

———. 1978. *Søren Kierkegaard's Journals and Papers: Volume 1*. Indiana University Press.

Laertius, Diogenes. 1972 [250 C.E.]. *Lives of the Eminent Philosophers*. Harvard University Press.

Lancey, David. 2008. *The Anthropology of Childhood: Cherubs, Chattel, Changeling*. Cambridge University Press.

Latour, Bruno. 1999. *Pandora's Hope: Essays on the Reality of Science Studies*. Harvard University Press.

Locke, John. 1689. *An Essay Concerning Human Understanding*.

McLellan, David. 1971. *The Thought of Karl Marx*. Macmillan.

Machan, Tibor. 1991. Do Animals Have Rights? *Public Affairs Quarterly* 5.2.

MacIntyre, Alasdair. 2013. *After Virtue*. Bloomsbury Academic.

Maine de Biran, Pierre. 1823. Considerations sur les Principes d'une Division des Faits Psychologiques et Physiologiques [Considerations on the Principles of a Division of Psychological and Physiological Facts]. In Bernard Baurtschi, ed., 1990, *Oeuvres Philosophiques de Maine de Biran*, Volume 9.

Malik, Kenan. 2014. *The Quest for a Moral Compass: A Global History of Ethics*. Atlantic.

Manthorpe, Rowland. 2017. The Human (and Pixar Characters) Inside Google's Assistant. *Wired* <www.wired.co.uk/article/the-human-in-google-assistant>.

Marron, Donald. 2011. *30-Second Economics: The 50 Most Thought-Provoking Economic Theories, Each Explained in Half a Minute*. Icon Books.

Marx, Karl. 2000. *The Eighteenth Brumaire of Louis Bonaparte*. In David McClellan, ed., *Karl Marx: Selected Writings*. Oxford University Press.

McGrath, James and Ankur Gupta. 2018. Writing a Moral Code: Algorithms for Ethical Reasoning by Humans and Machines. *Religions* 9.

Merleau-Ponty, Maurice. 2011 [1945]. *Phenomenology of Perception*. Routledge.

———. 1964 [1948]. The Film and the New Psychology. In Hubert and Patricia Dreyfus, trans., *Sense and Non-Sense*. Northwestern University Press.

Miah, Andy. 2005. Genetics, Cyberspace, and Bioethics: Why Not a Public Engagement with Ethics? *Public Understanding of Science* 14.4.

Mettrie, Julian Offray de La. 1974 [1747]. *Man a Machine*. Open Court.

Midgley, Mary. 1985. Persons and Non-Persons. In Peter Singer, ed., *In Defense of Animals*. Blackwell.

Monbiot, George. 2016. Neoliberalism: The Ideology at the Root of All Our Problems. *The Guardian* <www.theguardian.com/books/2016/apr/15/neoliberalism-ideology-problem-george-monbiot>.

Moravic, Hans. 1988. *Mind Children: The Future of Robot and Human Intelligence*. Harvard University Press.

Mulhall, Stephen. 2008. *On Film: Second Edition*. Routledge.

Nabokov, Vladimir. 2000 [1962]. *Pale Fire*. Penguin.

National Commission for the Protection of Human Subjects of Biomedical and Behavioral Research, Department of Health, Education and Welfare. 1978. United States Government Printing Office.

Noddings, Nel. 2013. *Caring: A Relational Approach to Ethics and Moral Education*. University of California Press.

Nozick, Robert. 1974. *Anarchy, State, and Utopia*. Basic Books.

O'Neill, Onora. 2013, *Acting on Principle: An Essay on Kantian Ethics*. Cambridge University Press.

Okapal, James. 2015. Of Battle Droids and Zillo Beasts: Moral Status in the Star Wars Galaxy. In Jason Eberl and Kevin Decker, eds., *The Ultimate Star Wars and Philosophy*. Wiley Blackwell.

———. 2017. 'All Other Priorities Rescinded': The Moral Status of Employees in the Alien Franchise. In Jeffrey Ewing and Kevin Decker, eds., *Alien and Philosophy*. Wiley Blackwell.

Orwell, George. 1949. *Nineteen Eighty-Four*. Secker and Warburg.

Papanikolaou, Eftychia. 2018. Eclectic Soundscapes in *Blade Runner 2049*. Paper presented at the Annual Conference, Music and the Moving Image, New York University.

Parker-Flynn, Christina. 2017. Joe and the Real Girls: *Blade Runner 2049*. *Gender Forum* 66.

Pinilla, Ramón Mujica. 2013. Angels and Demons in the Conquest of Peru. In Fernando Cervantes and Andrew Redden, eds., *Angels, Demons, and the New World*. Cambridge University Press.

Plato. 1961 [385–370 B.C.E.]. *Symposium*. In Edith Hamilton and Huntington Cairns, eds., *The Collected Dialogues of Plato*. Princeton University Press.

Rahula, Walpola. 1959. *What the Buddha Taught*. Grove Press.

Rawls, John. 2001. *Justice as Fairness: A Restatement*. Harvard University Press.

Redmond, Sean. 2016. *Blade Runner*. Auteur.

Ricard, Matthieu. 2015. *Altruism: The Power of Compassion to Change Yourself and the World*. Atlantic Books.

Rickman, Gregg. 1988. *Philip K. Dick: In His Own Words*. Valentine.

Sartre, Jean-Paul. 1956 [1943]. *Being and Nothingness: An Essay in Phenomenological Ontology*. Philosophical Library.

———. 1973 [1945]. *Existentialism and Humanism*. Methuen.

———. 1950 [1946]. *Baudelaire*. New Directions.

Searle, John R. 1992. *The Rediscovery of the Mind*. MIT Press.

Seneca. 1900 [45 C.E.]. *Of Anger*. George Bell and Sons.

Shanahan, Timothy. 2014. *Philosophy and Blade Runner*. Palgrave Macmillan.

Shelley, Mary. 2003 [1818]. *Frankenstein; or, The Modern Prometheus*. Oxford University Press.

Schopenhauer, Arthur. 1966 [1818–19]. *The World as Will and Representation*. Dover.

Sidney, Algernon. 1680. *Discourses Concerning Government*. London.

Sims, Jennifer. 2010. A Brief Review of the Belmont Report. *Dimensions of Critical Care Nursing* 29:4.

Singler, Beth. 2017. *The Indigo Children: New Age Experimentation with Self and Science*. Routledge.

Skinner, Quentin. 1997. *Liberty before Liberalism*. Cambridge University Press.

Slater, Joe. 2017. Androids: Artificial Persons or Glorified Toasters. In Jeffrey Ewing and Kevin Decker, eds., *Alien and Philosophy*. Wiley Blackwell.

Slote, Michael. 2007. *The Ethics of Care and Empathy*. Routledge.

Solomon, Andrew. 2014. *Far from the Tree: Parents, Children and the Search for Identity*. Vintage.

Stobaeus. 1822 [450 C.E.]. How We Ought to Conduct Ourselves towards Our Kinsmen. In Thomas Taylor, trans., *Ethical Fragments of Hierocles, Preserved by Stobaeus*. London.

Tronto, Joan. 1994. *Moral Boundaries: A Political Argument for an Ethic of Care*. Routledge.

UNICEF. 2017. Nearly 386,000 Children Will Be Born Worldwide on New Year's Day, Says UNICEF <www.unicef.org/press-releases/nearly-386000-children-will-be-born-worldwide-new-years-day-says-unicef>.

Vandereycken, Walter and Ron Van Deth. 1994. *From Fasting Saints to Anorexic Girls: The History of Self-Starvation*. Athlone Press.

Verhaeghe, Paul. 2014. *What about Me? The Struggle for Identity in a Market-Based Society*. Scribe.

Walker-Emig, Paul. 2018. Neon and Corporate Dystopias: Why Does Cyberpunk Refuse to Move On? *The Guardian* <www.the guaedian.com/games/2018/net/16/neon-corporate-dystopias-why-does-cyberpunk-refuse-move-on>

Walsham, Alexandra. 1994. Out of the Mouths of Babes and Sucklings: Prophecy, Puritanism and Childhood in Elizabethan Suffolk. In Diane Wood, ed. *Church and Childhood* (*Studies in Church History*, Vol. 31). Ecclesiastical History Society.

Warren, Mary Anne. 2000. *Moral Status: Obligations to Persons and Other Living Things*. Oxford University Press.

———. 1973. On the Moral and Legal Status of Abortion. *The Monist* 57:1.

Wasserman, David, Adrienne Asch, Jeffrey Blustein, and Daniel Putnam. 2017. Cognitive Disability and Moral Status. In Edward Zalta, ed., *The Stanford Encyclopedia of Philosophy* <plato.stanford.edu/entries/cognitive-disability>.

Wilkinson, Richard, and Kate Pickett. 2010. *The Spirit Level: Why Equality Is Better for Everyone*. Penguin.

Williams, Paul. 2008. *Mahayana Buddhism: The Doctrinal Foundations*. Routledge.

Wright, Robert. 2017. *Why Buddhism Is True: The Science and Philosophy of Meditation and Enlightenment*. Simon and Schuster.

Those Who Hunt Them Still Go by the Name

EMILY ASKEW is the Associate Professor of Systematic Theology at Lexington Theological Seminary. Her recent work, "Notes Toward a Theology of Cross/ing," in *Interpretation* magazine, deals with stories of undocumented migrants and a theology of the cross. She's a recent convert to the gospel of *Blade Runner*. All the best theology is hers.

STEVE BEIN is Associate Professor of Philosophy at the University of Dayton, where he's a specialist in East Asian thought. Like Joi, he is everything you want to hear, everything you want to see—but only if you keep your expectations low.

ROBIN BUNCE is a historian of ideas based at Homerton College, University of Cambridge. He's very realistic.

EMILY COX-PALMER-WHITE is a post-doctoral researcher in gender studies and female machines in science fiction. A believer in equality, she's heavily involved in replicant rights campaigns and recently fitted her AI husband with an emanator.

ARON ERICSON studies philosophy at Uppsala University. He notes that "Blade Runner Twenty Forty Nine" is an anagram of "Funny note written by real nerd," and feels that this sums up what he's going for in his chapter.

BEN FRANZ is a Cataloging and Film Librarian at Medgar Evers College for the City of New York. To make ends meet he runs a meal worm farm, which is such lonely work, he's having a hard time distinguishing people from meal worms anymore.

PATRICK GREENE is an award-winning composer of contemporary classical music, based outside Boston. He co-hosts *Shoulder of Orion: The Blade Runner Podcast*; *Perfect Organism: The Alien Saga Podcast*; and *Just Winging It: Dad's Podcast*. He dreams about electric sheep with disturbing regularity.

REŞAT VOLKAN GÜNEL is a critical legal scholar based at Near East University, Nicosia. Still amazed by the Vangelis score for *Blade Runner*, he has never seen a miracle.

LACI HUBBARD-MATTIX is a visiting assistant professor of philosophy at Washington State University. She swears she's not a replicant and is in no need of being retired.

CHRISTOPHER INNES is a philosopher teaching at Boise State University. He's in love with Ana Stelline, though it's something she'll not include in his storyline.

JUSTIN KITCHEN teaches philosophy at San Francisco State University and California State University at Northridge. He looks forward to living out the rest of his open-ended lifespan on a quaint protein farm outside Los Angeles.

S. EVAN KREIDER is a professor of philosophy at the University of Wisconsin at Fox Valley. He hopes that one day his administrators will grant him an emanator so that, like Joi, he can occasionally leave work.

ANDREW KUZMA is an ethicist who lives and teaches at Cardinal Stritch University and St. Thomas More High School in Milwaukee. He knows what's real. Writing about *Blade Runner* and *2049* is the most human thing we can do.

CHRIS LAY recently earned his PhD in Philosophy at the University of Georgia and mostly writes on issues of personal identity, personhood, and other problems in metaphysics. A longtime Deviant, Chris has failed both the Voight-Kampff and Baseline tests multiple times; when not performing his duties as a professor, he's kept in a little box.

TRIP MCCROSSIN teaches in the Philosophy Department at Rutgers University, where he works on, among other things, the nature, history, and legacy of the Enlightenment. He's finding it more and more difficult, more and more of the time, to resist channelling K: "I didn't figure you as one for bullshit!"

JAMES MCLACHLAN teaches philosophy at Western Carolina University and has wanted to go off baseline for years. He works for the massive education corporation, UNCInc, that tries to produce replicants that go off to be good workers on off-world colonies. But, occasionally, some of them are driven off baseline by reading the work of Sartre and other Nexus models.

BONNIE MCLEAN is an adjunct professor of English at College of DuPage in Glen Ellyn, Illinois, and an adjunct professor of Distance Education at Andrews University in Berrien Springs, Michigan. She doesn't manufacture memories, but still sees the world because she imagines it.

MARTIN MUCHALL has taught in the Theology and Philosophy Department at the Royal Russell School in South Croydon since 2009 but is about to be 'retired'.

DOMINIC J. NARDI took many tests while working on his doctorate in Political Science at the University of Michigan, but he has never taken the Voight-Kampff Test. He probably wouldn't pass. Although his day job focuses on human rights in Asia, he spends more time thinking about politics on alien planets. Dr. Nardi has published academic articles and book chapters about *The Lord of the Rings*, the *Star Wars* franchise, and Joss Whedon. He occasionally shares his musings on various science fiction and fantasy stories on his blog, NardiViews.

SAMANTHA NOLL is a philosopher based at Washington State University. Unlike Lieutenant Joshi, she vigorously advocates for the moral rights of replicants, though her friends have accused her of failing the Voight-Kampff test.

ROB O'CONNOR is a literature studies PhD student based at York St. John University. His research interests include genre fictions, creative writing, and monsters of all varieties. Each time he watches *Blade Runner 2049*, Rob's always pleased that Deckard's dog survives.

JAMES M. OKAPAL is a Professor of Philosophy at Missouri Western State University as well as Chair of the Department of Philosophy and Religion. He's often mistaken for a replicant due to a lack of outward emotion, but has worked to destroy Joshi's wall and extend moral considerability to all biological beings.

JERRY PIVEN, having (nominally) passed the Turing, Voight-Kampff, and Baseline tests, teaches in the Department of Philosophy at

Rutgers University, where his nexus is existentialism, death, literature, and other bounteous subjects lost in time, like tears in rain. He hopes to one day meet his Creator and push his thumbs through his eyes.

J.M. Prater is an artist, filmmaker and founder and host of Perfect Organism: *The Alien Saga Podcast*, and Shoulder of Orion: *The Blade Runner Podcast*. An accomplished documentarian, Jaime lives and works in Los Angeles, California. When he isn't immersed in the world of filmmaking and discussion, he's arguing with Joi.

L. Brooke Rudow is a philosopher at Georgia College and State University. Her research focuses on issues within philosophy of technology, environmental ethics, and political philosophy. Always writing for the right cause, the most human thing she can do.

M.J. Ryder has recently discovered that his memories of childhood are not his own, so rather than being the chosen one, he is now a researcher at Lancaster University. He takes his freedom where he can.

Leah D. Schade is Assistant Professor of Preaching and Worship at Lexington Theological Seminary, author of *Creation-Crisis Preaching: Ecology, Theology, and the Pulpit* (2015) and *Preaching in the Purple Zone: Ministry in the Red-Blue Divide* (2019), and Blade Runner geek since 1983. She believes that all the courage in the world *can* alter fact.

Timothy Shanahan is a phil(m)osopher at Loyola Marymount University in Los Angeles, just a short spinner ride from K's apartment. Most days he's not even close to baseline. He suspects that his memory of having written a chapter for this book may be an implant.

Zachary Sheldon, instead of going off-world, decided to stay on Earth and study in the Department of Communication at Texas A&M University. Instead of electric sheep, he dreams of "research interests."

Beth Singler is an anthropologist and the Junior Research Fellow in AI at Homerton College Cambridge. She's pretty sure all the pets she's had were real, but she's never actually asked them, so . . .

Iain Souter was once a detective, but is now "little people." He is founder of the *Blade Runner Worldwide* and *Blade Runner 2049 Worldwide Fan Groups* (Facebook). With a compulsive need to wax lyrical, he is currently standing behind you, blaster locked and loaded. He wants to know about your mother.

ALi RIZA TAŞKALE is a critical social theorist based at Near East University, Nicosia. Always amazed by how well *Blade Runner* predicted our decline into a dystopian corporate hell, he's just looking out for something real.

M. BLAKE WILSON, a Philip K. Dick obsessive since 1989, is assistant professor of criminal justice at Stanislaus State University in California's Central Valley, where he farms garlic and synthetic protein.

SUE ZEMKA is a professor of English at the University of Colorado, Boulder. She has published books and essays on Victorian literature and culture. She also paints, draws, and since 2017 has served as chair of her department. In that capacity, she regularly channels Joshi, "It's my job to keep order," hoping that she enjoys a happier fate ultimately.

Index

PHILIP K. DICK

AND PHILOSOPHY

DO ANDROIDS HAVE KINDRED SPIRITS?

EDITED BY D. E. WITTKOWER

Printed in the USA
CPSIA information can be obtained
at www.ICGtesting.com
JSHW012022140824
68134JS00033B/2830

9 780812 694710